ART OF THE SOVIET UNION
STILL LIFES

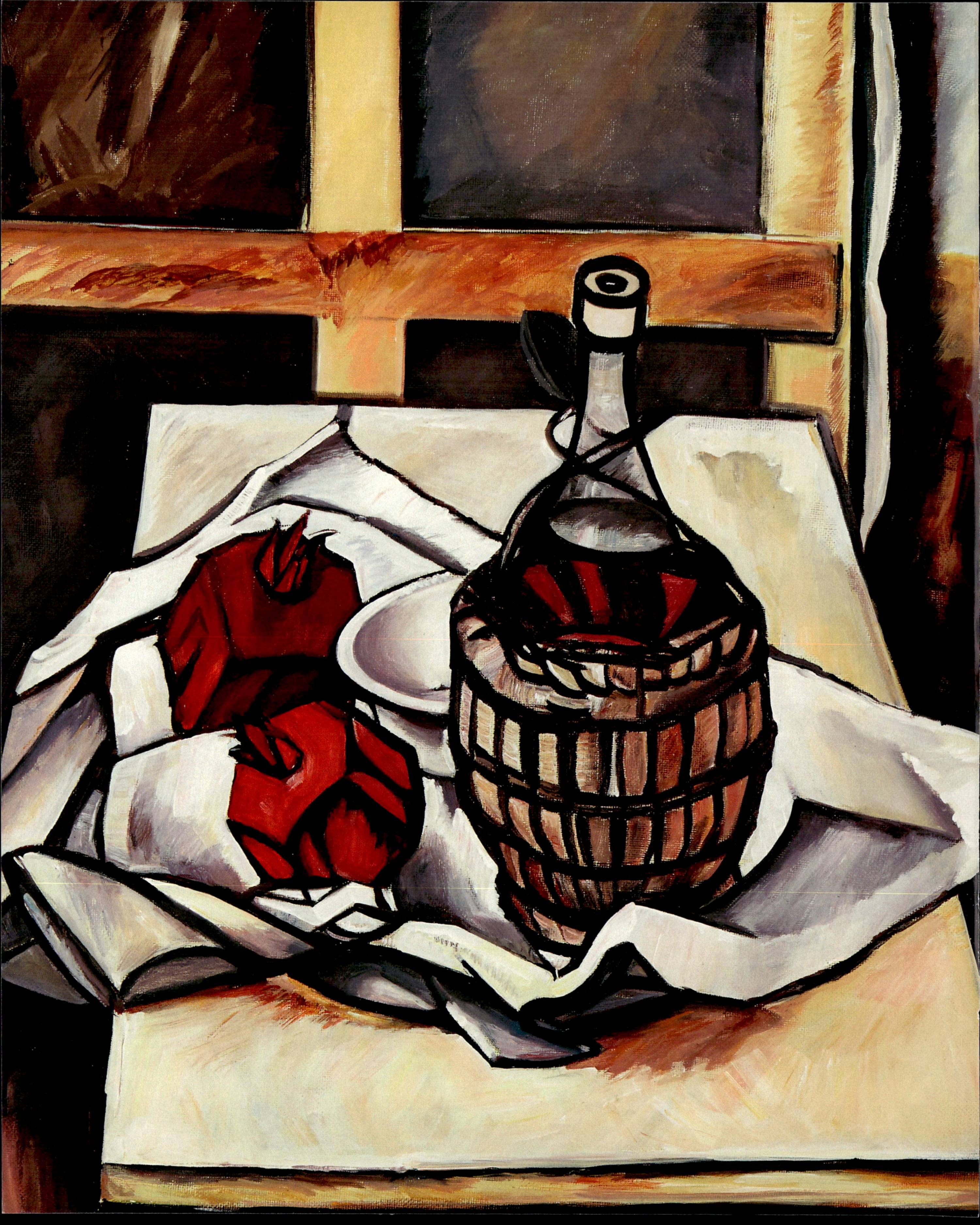

ART OF THE SOVIET UNION

STILL LIFES

Rena Lavery & Ivan Lindsay

Series Editor: Katia Kapushesky

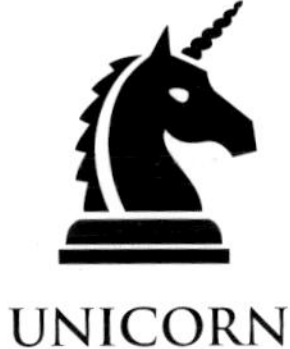

UNICORN

Published in 2018 by
Unicorn, an imprint of Unicorn Publishing Group LLP
101 Wardour Street
London W1F 0UG
www.unicornpublishing.org

The author asserts the moral right to be identified as the author of this work
A catalogue record for this book is available from the British Library

ISBN 978 1 910787 88 5

Typeset in Galliard and Milliard

Design by Nick Newton Design

Printed and bound in China for Latitude Press

FRONT COVER: Detail of *Bird Cherry Blossom in a Glass* by Kuzma Petrov-Vodkin (see page 64)
BACK COVER: Detail of *Still Life with Melon* by Alexander Osmerkin (see page 97)
FRONTISPIECE: Detail of *Still Life from a Series with Pomegranates* by Tair Salahov (see page 127)

ACKNOWLEDGEMENTS

Thanks to:

Mountain Art Foundation, Taiwan

Nikolay and Tatiana Plastov

Dr Aljona Grigorasch

A. Lyubimova

Irkutsk Regional Art Museum named after V. P. Sukachov

Ryazan State Regional Art Museum named after I. P. Pojalostin

The State Russian Museum, St Petersburg

The State Tretyakov Gallery, Moscow

Kursk State Picture Gallery named after A. A. Deineka

Tver Regional Picture Gallery

Perm State Art Gallery

Samara Regional Art Museum

Krasnoyarsk Art Museum named after V. I. Surikov

Yaroslavl Art Museum

Kiev National Picture Gallery

The State Museum of Fine Arts of Tatarstan Republic, Kazan

Tula Regional Art Museum

Various private collectors

Rena Lavery is an art dealer, specialising in European art of the nineteenth and twentieth centuries, and in Russian art of the late nineteenth and early twentieth centuries and art of the Soviet period from 1917 to 1990. Rena is Managing Director of the Art Russe collection which was founded in 2010 with the aim of developing a greater awareness and understanding of Soviet and Russian cultural contributions between 1917 and 1991 and the period of Socialist Realism. She has written a number of books, including *Masterpieces of Soviet Painting and Sculpture*, her first joint venture with Ivan Lindsay, as well as an extensive list of catalogues for the numerous exhibitions supported by Art Russe in London, Venice, Moscow and Abu Dhabi.

Ivan Lindsay is an art dealer specialising in European paintings and sculpture. After Eton College and the Royal Military Academy Sandhurst he became an Infantry Officer in the British Army. He then worked in the City of London before starting his art dealing business in 1990. He lectures on art and the art market, and has previously written *A History of Loot and Stolen Art*.

STILL LIFE AND SOVIET ART:
A BRIEF HISTORY

The painting or drawing of an object or a collection of objects, often artfully arranged on a table, has been on-going for thousands of years. Originally the objects would have been flowers or food, especially fruit, or dead animals (the French for still life is *nature morte*, meaning 'dead nature'), but nowadays it refers to any objects that can be arranged in front of the painter.

Paintings of objects are found in ancient Egyptian temples and tombs. Here the painters were principally concerned with recording the offerings left for the gods, so their intent was to identify the object clearly, and they were not concerned with showing perspective or making the objects look realistic. In contrast, the objects depicted in mosaics on the floors and walls of Greek and Roman villas are much more decorative. In these, the colouring is more accurate and shading is used to give a sense of perspective.

In Europe in the Middle Ages, art was supposed to serve Christianity and artists tended to illustrate scenes from the Bible, so still-life painting was not widely practised. However, even in the 1400s and 1500s, objects would sometimes be included in these scenes, as, for example, in the paintings of Jan van Eyck. However, it was not until the seventeenth century that still life became an art form in its own right, although it was still not as well regarded as religious art or portraiture. Even so, many skilful still-life works were created and it became a very popular art form, especially in the Netherlands.

So-called vanitas paintings also grew in popularity at this time. The term comes from the Bible's Revelations, 'vanity of vanities – all is vanity', and these paintings all depicted expensive objects, such as musical instruments or wine goblets. However, at the same time they always included an expression of the futility of all the worldly pleasures that wealth can buy, with reminders of our mortality in the form of an hourglass or a skull.

It was not until the nineteenth century that still life became a respected art form. With the invention of photography, artists no longer felt the need to make their paintings realistic, and so the Impressionists and Post-Impressionists were free to experiment. And experiment they did, not only with colour and shape but also with how they applied the paint to the canvas. Paul Cézanne was the greatest exponent of still lifes of this type, and he and Vincent van Gogh made the still life not only a respectable but a much admired art form. They used intense colours and bold obvious brush strokes to create paintings of great vibrancy and impact. One of Van Gogh's *Sunflowers* sold for US $40 million in 1987.

Cézanne also influenced two painters of the Cubism style, Georges Braque and Pablo Picasso. These artists took his technique of painting objects from more than one perspective to create still lifes that were verging on the abstract. However, all the great artists first learnt to draw and paint accurately and with proper perspective.

In pre-Revolution Russia, Ilya Yefimovich Repin (1844–1930) and Vasily Surikov (1848–1916) were best known among a number of artists who painted still lifes, along with landscapes and portraits. The work of this period often expressed moral and political messages, but between the fall of the Czar and the rise of the Bolsheviks there was a brief period in which painters were able to indulge in artistic exploration. The October Revolution in 1917 brought that to an end as the newly created Soviet state sought to control art for political ends, compelling artists to return to more traditional forms of art and painting.

This was reinforced when Anatoly Lunacharsky was appointed head of Narkompros, the People's Commissariat for Enlightenment. His belief that the depiction of the perfect human form would show citizens how to be perfect Soviets was the founding force behind the Socialist Realism that would dominate Soviet art for many decades. Now the aim was to produce the most realistic depictions possible, and this theme extended from portraits to include still lifes.

At this time, there were dozens of Soviet artists who were skilled at painting still lifes. One of these was Sergei Gerasimov (1885–1964), a student of Konstantin Korovin (1861–1939), himself a master of still life. Gerasimov went on to teach at the state art school Vkhutemas in the 1920s and '30s, where he designed posters and artwork in the Soviet Realist style. Although this work conformed to the requirements of the Communist government, he was also known for his liberal stance, and some of his early watercolours, now considered masterpieces, reflected a more modernist style, with Impressionist influences. In spite of this modernist tendency, he held several prominent positions throughout his career, including Chairman of the Moscow Union of Artists. Under Joseph Stalin, however, this brought him into direct conflict with Aleksandr Gerasimov (1881–1963, no relation), who replaced him as head of the Russian Artists' Union. Aleksandr Gerasimov favoured a style known as Heroic Realism, and is best known for his portraits of Stalin and Lenin, among other Soviet leaders.

After Stalin's death, Sergei Gerasimov was reinstated as leader of the Artists' Union and went on to become one of the most important Russian artists of the twentieth century, whose works are displayed in the Tretyakov Gallery in Moscow. As an early proponent of Socialist Realism, Gerasimov was an important force in the flourishing of the Russian Realists, not least because of the influence he had on the next generation of Soviet artists. Painters such as the Tkachev Brothers (Sergei b. 1922, Alexsei b. 1925), Yuri Kugach (1917–2013), Vladimir Stozharov (1926–73), Aleksei Gritsai (1914–98), Geli Korzhev (1925–2012) and Tair Salahov (b. 1928) all came under his tutelage, and produced some of the greatest paintings of the Soviet era – paintings whose quality has only recently been appreciated by the West.

During this period, the Realists were known for their technical mastery, their skills being handed down through a system of master–apprentice relationships, all under the auspices of the great Russian art institutes, the Surikov Institute in Moscow and the Repin Institute in St Petersburg. At a time when European artists were experimenting with more abstract styles of painting, Soviet artists remained dedicated to the techniques of the masters of the past, honouring and building on their traditions.

Throughout the political and social turmoil of the early twentieth century, these artists remained faithful to their art, producing works that remain popular to this day. We are therefore proud to present in this book some exceptional still-life works by some of the Soviet era's most remarkable artists.

Rena Lavery

STILL LIFES IN SOVIET ART

Still-life paintings first appear as tomb decorations in ancient Egypt. The Egyptians believed that items depicted on walls and left beside those buried could be used in the afterlife. The Greeks portrayed everyday objects on their mosaics and vases, and the Romans formulated the idea of carefully juxtaposing man-made and natural objects on wall frescoes at Pompeii and Herculaneum. On a fresco in the Villa Boscoreale there is a painting of fruit in a glass bowl.

Still-life painting was a popular subject all through the Soviet period, and Russian artists of the period were influenced primarily by Western traditions. From the Renaissance onwards, still lifes have been used to convey themes such as religious meaning, an examination of nature, a celebration of wealth or natural abundance, a demonstration of artistic skill through the traditions of trompe-l'oeil and *memento mori* (reflections on the fleeting transience of life).

Memento mori works do not appear in Soviet still lifes, as presumably this was too macabre a subject for a school of work that was supposed to be optimistic. However, still lifes were an acceptable subject within the Socialist Realism framework, and artists were taught composition, perspective and the ability to capture texture at art school. Virtually all the Soviet artists painted still lifes and these paintings were collected by the Russian museums.

Soviet artists created these works as contemplative studies examining everyday objects, a celebration of nature with seasonal fruits and flowers, and as exercises in working out solutions to compositional challenges. After art school, finding models to pose for portraits and nude studies was often difficult and, during the long winters when artists were confined to their studios, it was easy to arrange some objects and make a still-life painting.

In the early Soviet period there were three main schools of this type of painting. Konstantin Korovin (1861–1939) and Igor Grabar (1871–1960) focused on a fluid approach that drew inspiration from the French Impressionists. Avant-garde painters, including Ilya Mashkov (1881–1944) and Petr Konchalovsky (1876–1956), painted densely coloured and carefully arranged objects on tables in a style they had developed within the Jack of Diamonds group that combined Russian folk-art traditions with the advances of Matisse and Cézanne. The first generation of artists who came to prominence during the Soviet era, such as Aleksandr Deineka (1899–1969), Alexander Samokhvalov (1894–1971) and Yury Pimenov (1903–77), utilised a modest linear approach that emphasised simplicity and portrayed subjects like a single vase of flowers or a few items on a table.

In the 1930s, as the influence of the avant-garde faded with the emerging dominance of Socialist Realism, artists such as Mashkov and Konchalovksy continued to paint still lifes but in more matter-of-fact style. Soviet authorities seem to have given little direction on how still lifes should be painted, and most artists developed their own style. Aleksandr Laktionov (1910–72), for example, a leading portraitist of the 1940s and '50s, gave his still lifes a polished and neo-classical look that was fashionable for a brief period. Around the same date, Arkady Plastov (1893–1972), who mainly lived quietly in his village of Prislonikha so as to avoid having to navigate the fraught politics of the Moscow Union of Artists, developed a broadly applied and thickly painted technique that is credited with creating a second generation of Russian Impressionists.

Throughout the summer months Plastov gathered whichever flowers were in season and made numerous studies that he then incorporated into his famous pastoral paintings. He enjoyed depicting village life in the provinces, dependent on the changing seasons, in a timeless rhythm little changed for centuries.

The classical style of Laktionov lost ground to the fresh approach of Plastov, who influenced accomplished still-life painters such as Vladimir Gavrilov (1923–70) and Vladimir Stozharov (1926–73). Although these artists continued painting in this style in the 1960s, after the death of Stalin in 1953 and the period known as the Khrushchev thaw, another talented group of artists emerged who developed the movement known as the Severe Style.

The Severe Style artists, many of whom had either fought as teenagers in World War II or been evacuated to Samarkand, wanted to portray subject matter that they felt better reflected the harsh reality of a country shattered by war. The leading members of this group were Nikolai Andronov (1929–98), Geli Korzhev (1925–2012), Viktor Popkov (1932–74), Pavel Nikonov (b. 1930), Petr Ossovsky (1925–2015), Victor Ivanov (b. 1924) and Tair Salahov (b. 1928). All these artists started off using the broadly applied and rough technique of the 1950s, and their early works can be difficult to tell apart. However, when they branched off on their own individual paths, they developed very distinctive styles and all took pride in their still lifes. Andronov's works initially look rough, but through clever compositional devices, they slowly reveal themselves. His work tends to be coloured with limited earth tones as he made his own paint through necessity when he was periodically banished from Moscow to the area around Ferapontov monastery.

Salahov's still lifes show the influence of his Azerbaijani origins in his choice of subject matter and props. Nikonov departs into the metaphysical where he focuses on atmosphere and only hints at representation, while Ivanov uses blocks of carefully arranged colour underpinned by magnificent linear drawings. Korzhev, who is best known for his monumental over-life-size figures and gritty subject matter, said in a 2009 interview that he believed that, with the passage of time, his still lifes would come to define his work. His Moscow studio was full of props, including samovars, metal water flasks and plaster copies of antique sculpture, that he returned to again and again. Even when he had a major multi-figure work in production, there was always a still life in progress in a corner.

Apart from discouraging the avant-garde production of the 1920s, the Soviet authorities seem to have had little negative influence on the production of still-life painting during the Soviet era. Still lifes were popular with both museums and the state, who decorated countless offices, hotels, government buildings and sanatoriums with them. Soviet artists received a high level of training at art school, largely abandoned in the West by the mid-twentieth century, which they utilised to create an accomplished body of work within the still-life genre.

Ivan Lindsay

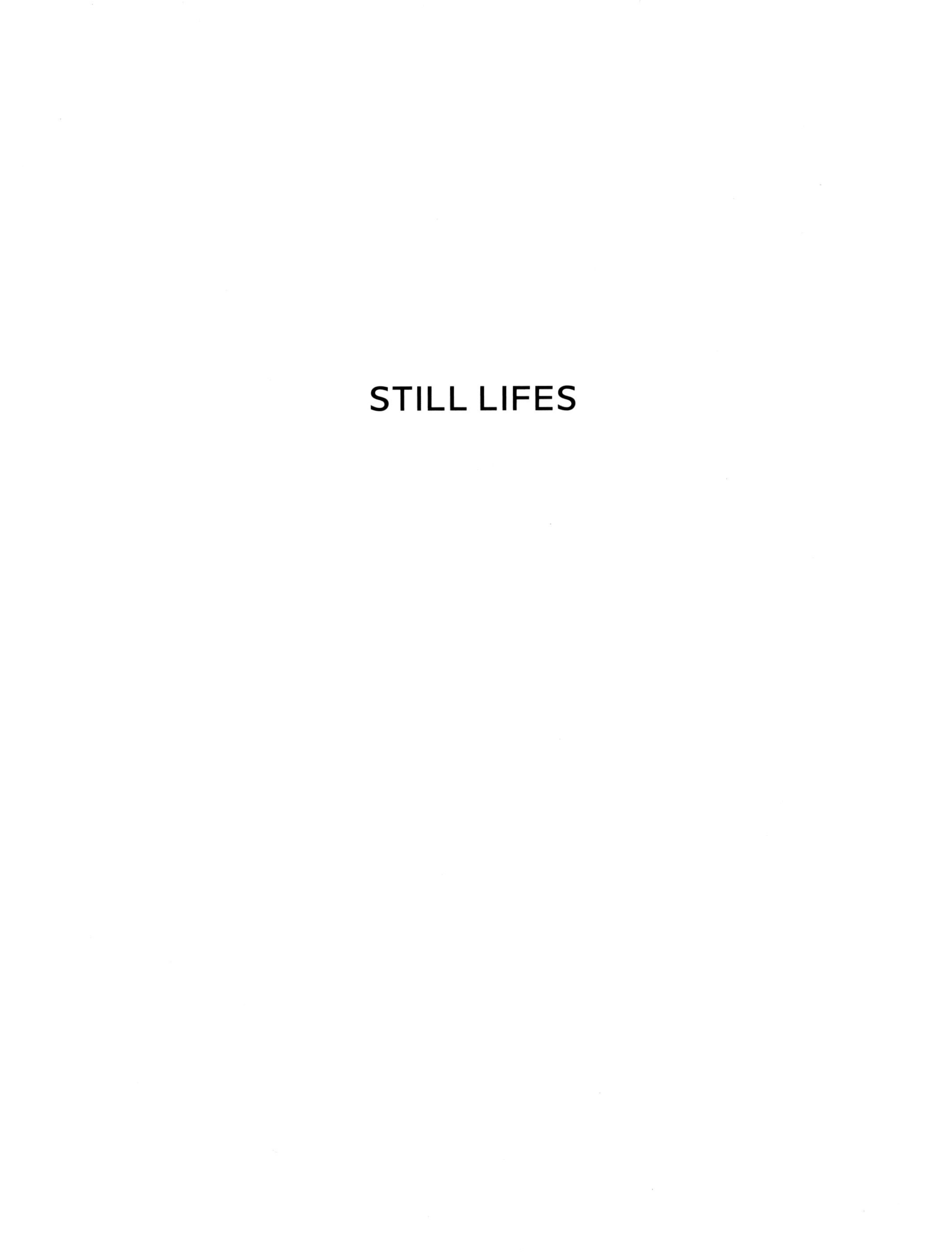

STILL LIFES

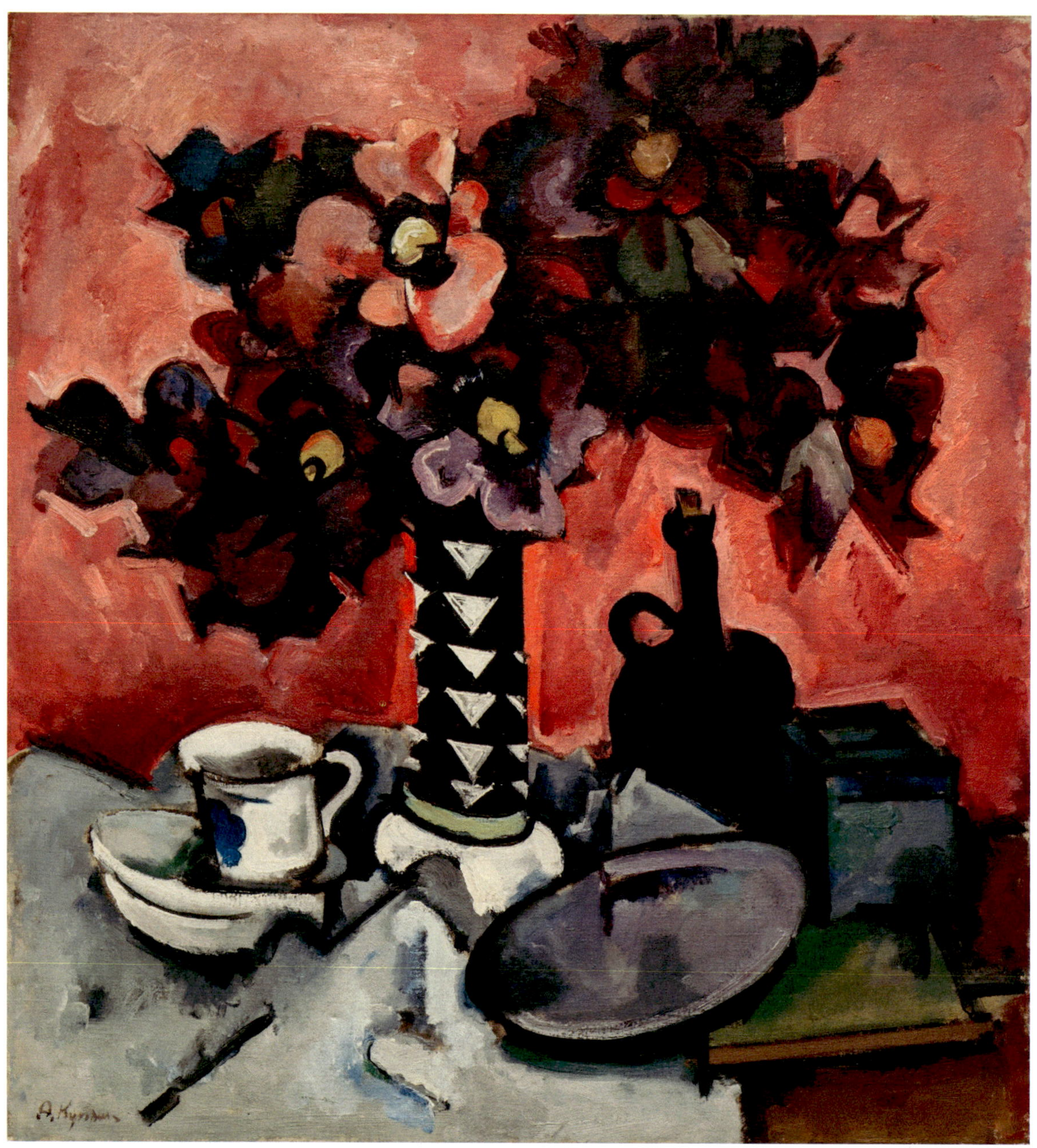

KUPRIN Aleksandr Vasilievich | *Bouquet of Flowers*
1917
Oil on canvas, 103.5 × 93 cm
The State Russian Museum, St Petersburg

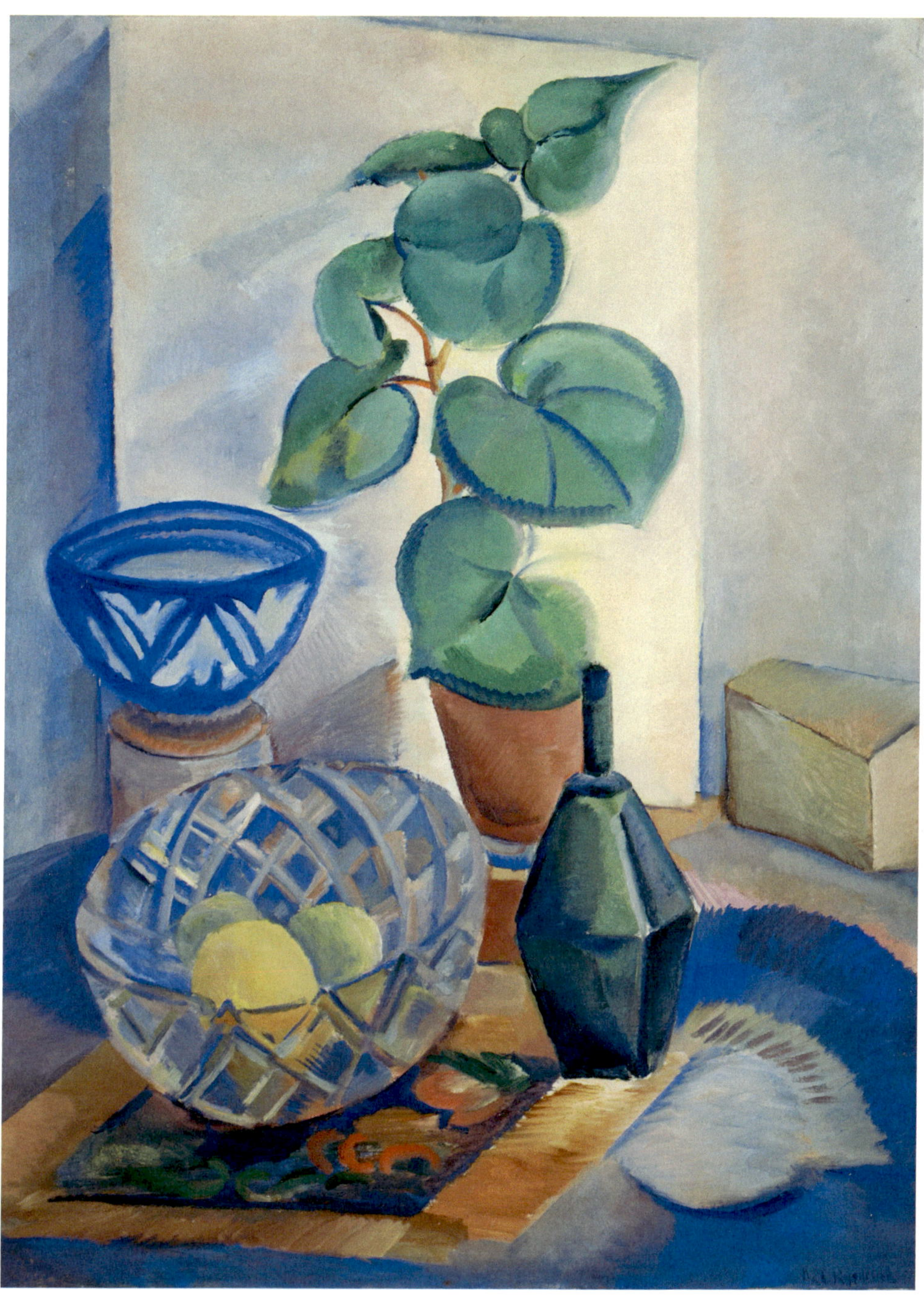

KUZNETZOV Pavel Varfolomevich | *Still Life with Crystal*
1917–20
Oil on canvas, 98 × 72 cm
The State Russian Museum, St Petersburg

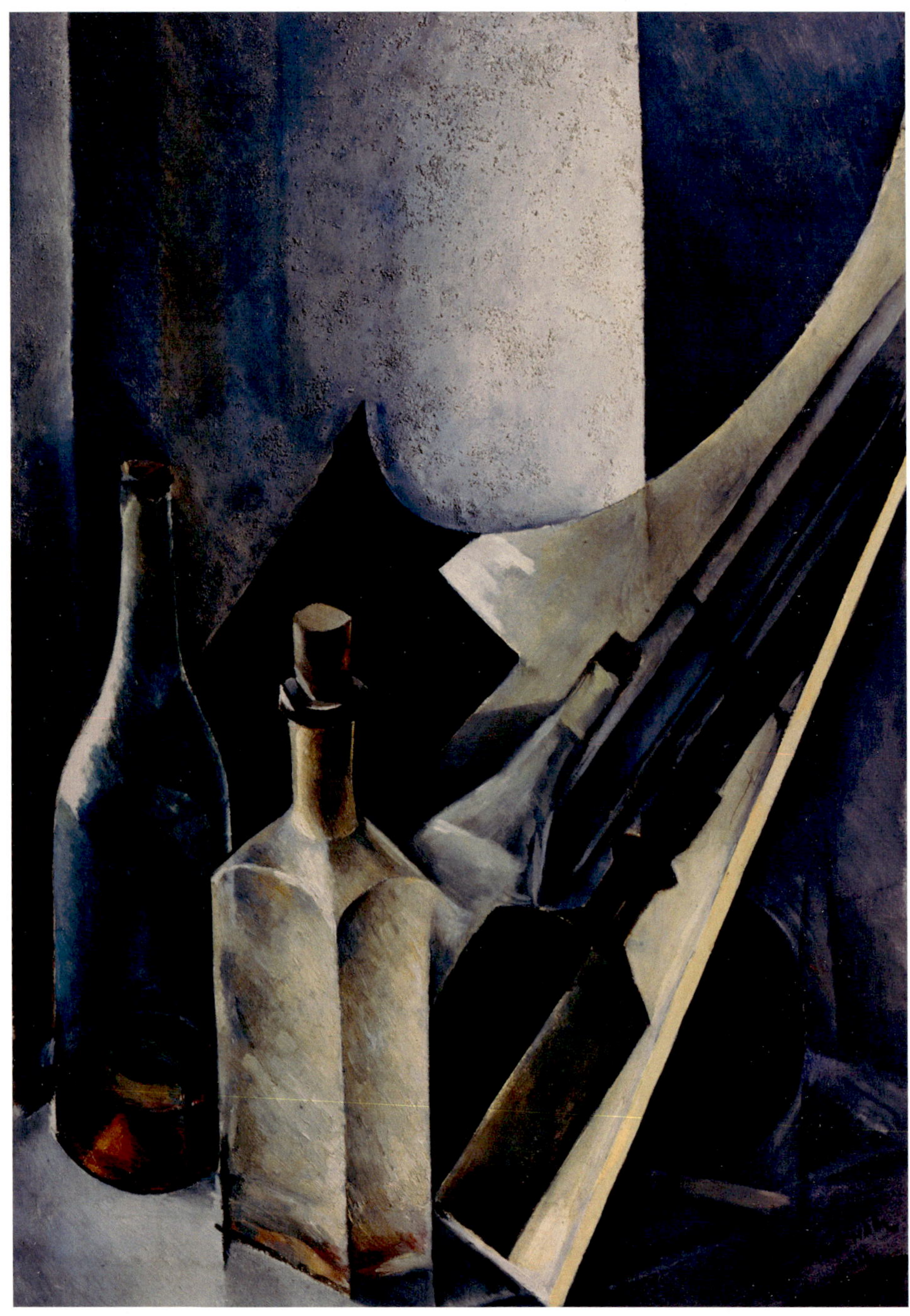

ALTMAN Nathan Isaevich | *Colour Volumes and Planes*
1918
Oil on canvas, gypsum particles, 59.5 × 43.5 cm
The State Russian Museum, St Petersburg

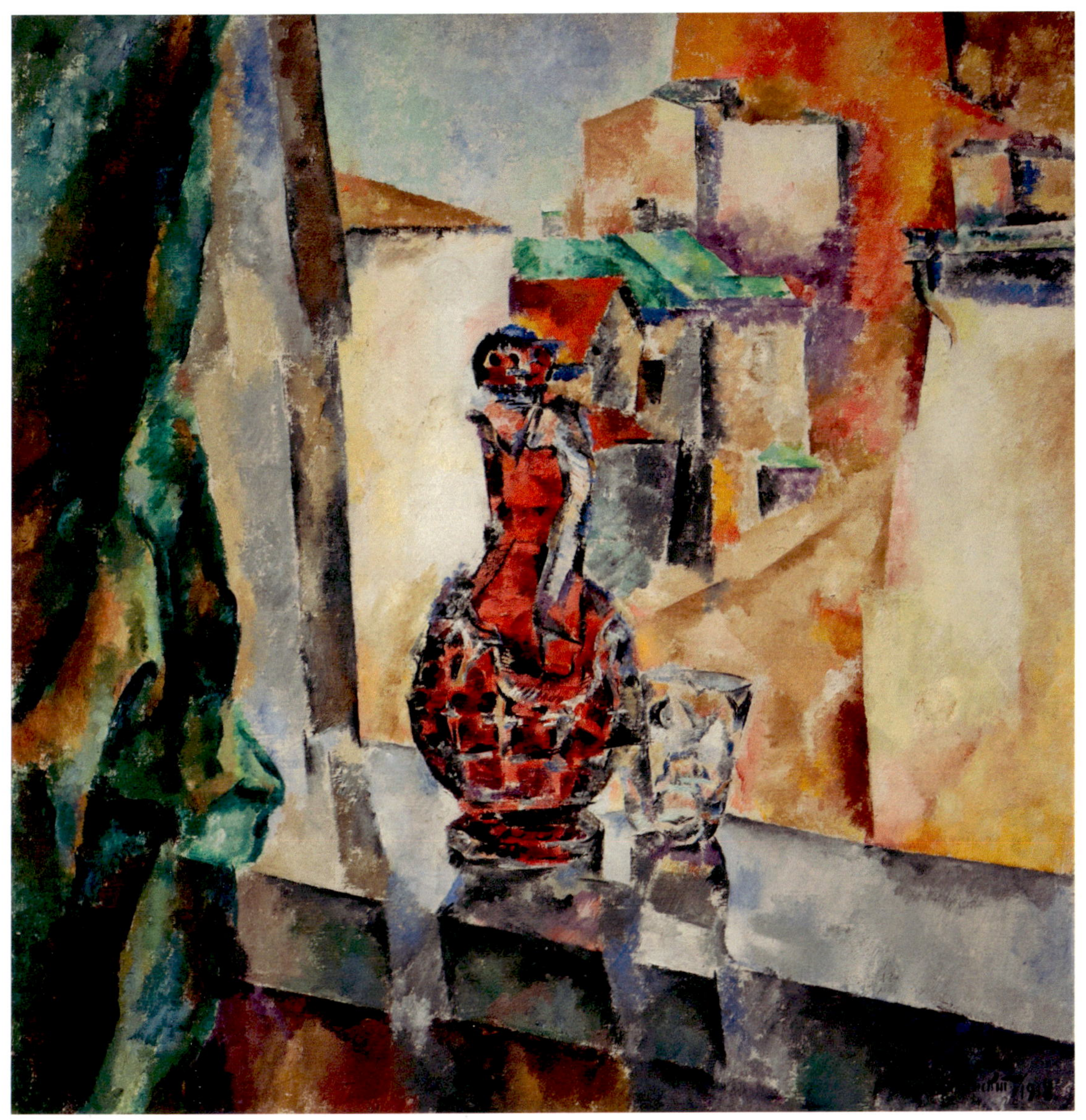

ROZHDESTVENSKY Alexander Illarionovich | *Still Life with Red Jug*
1918
Oil on canvas, 89 × 84 cm
The State Russian Museum, St Petersburg

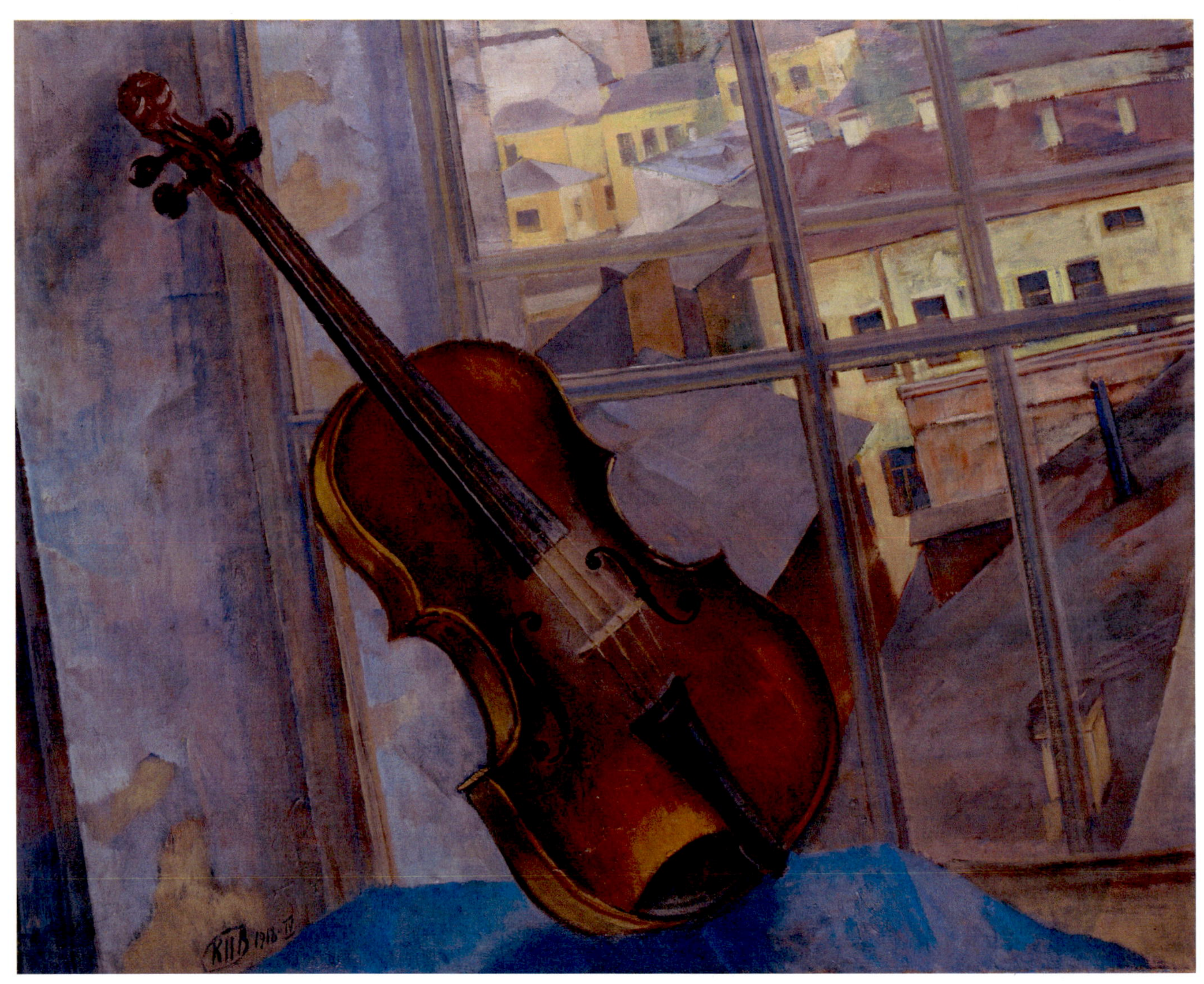

PETROV-VODKIN Kuzma Sergeevich | *Violin*
1918
Oil on canvas, 65 × 80 cm
The State Russian Museum, St Petersburg

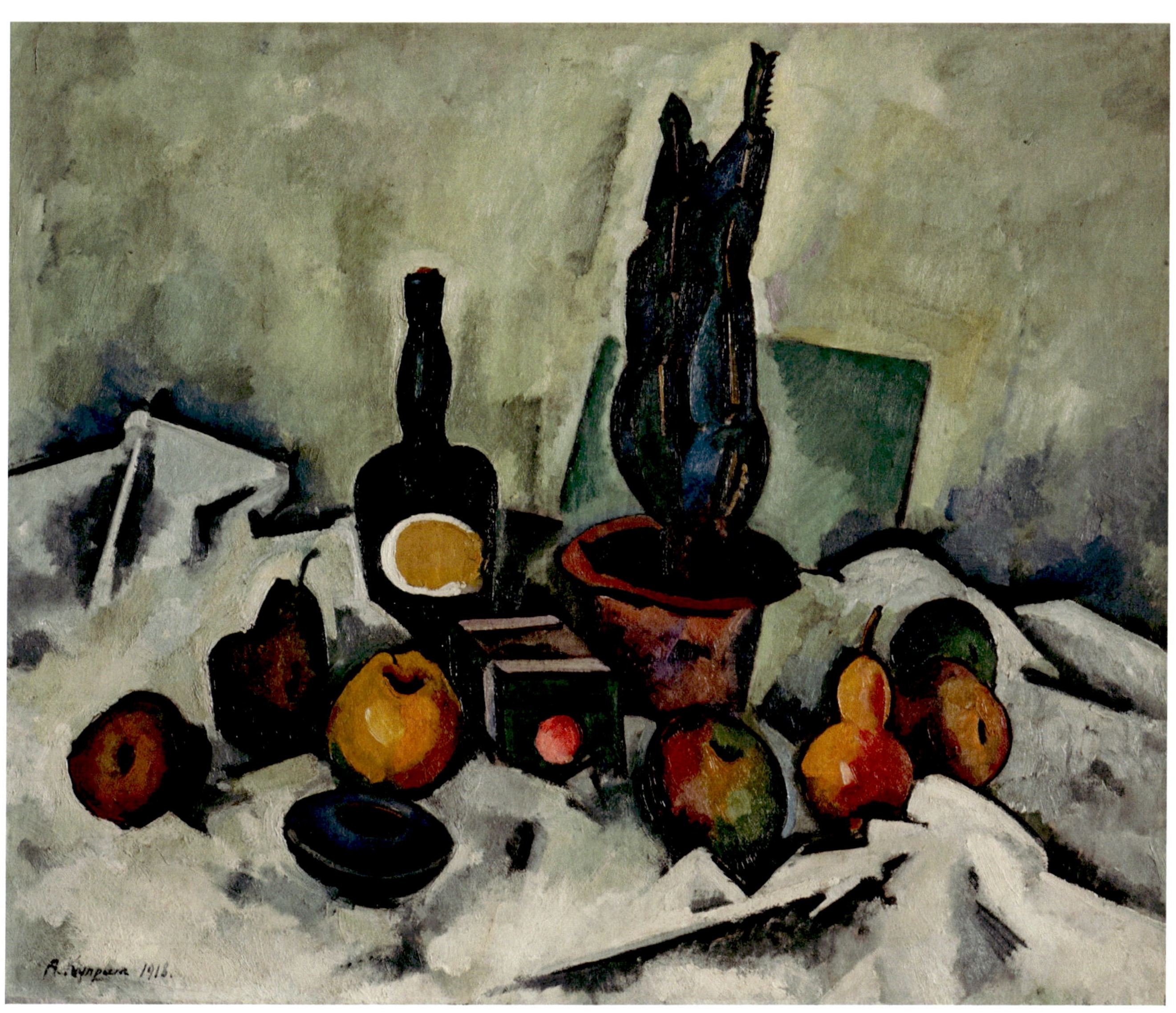

KUPRIN Aleksandr Vasilievich | *Cacti and Fruit*
1918
Oil on canvas, 97 × 113.5 cm
The State Russian Museum, St Petersburg

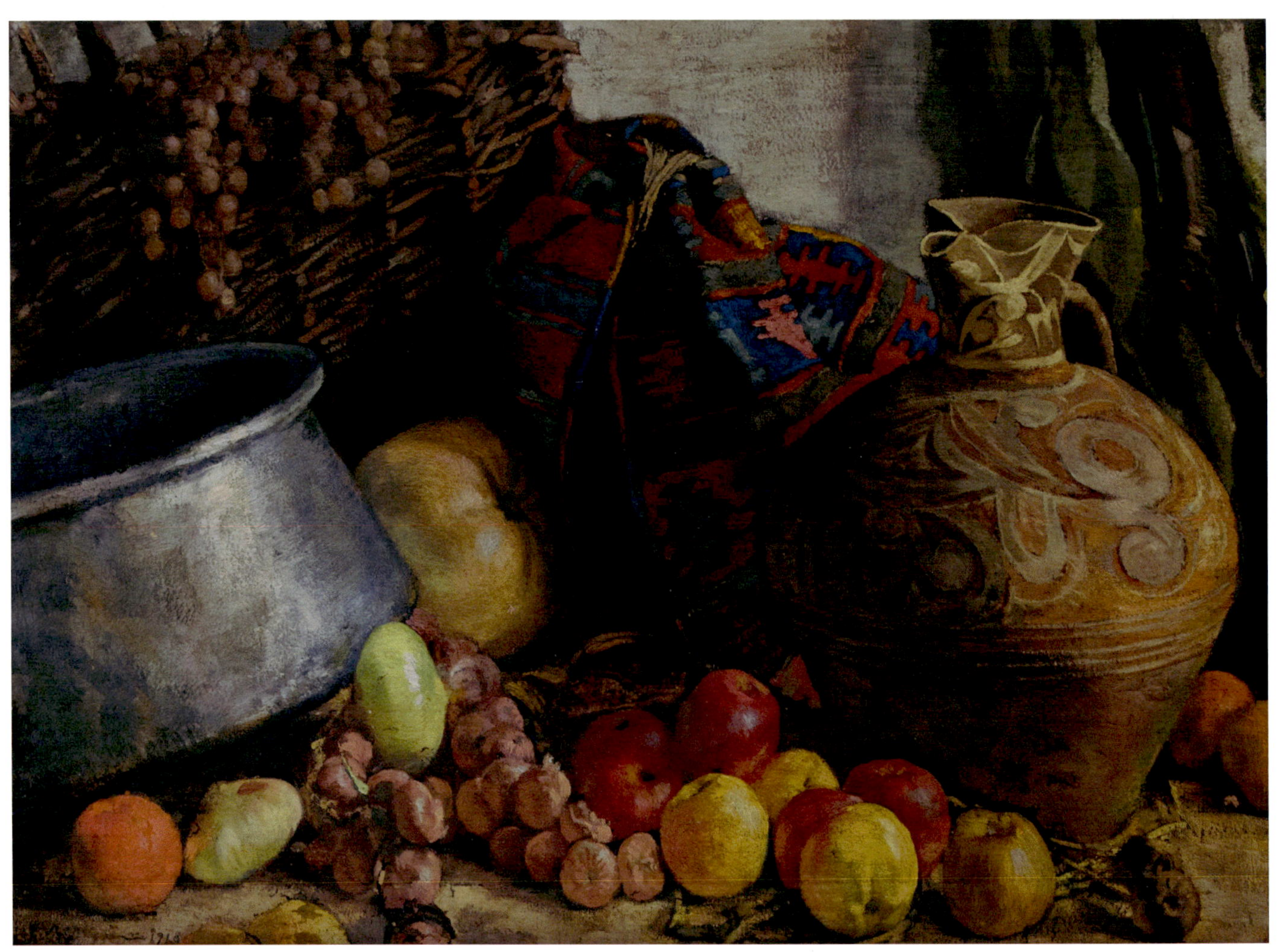

LANSERE Evgeny Evgenievich | *Still Life*
1918
Oil on canvas, 65 × 86 cm
The State Museum of Fine Arts of Tatarstan Republic,
Kazan

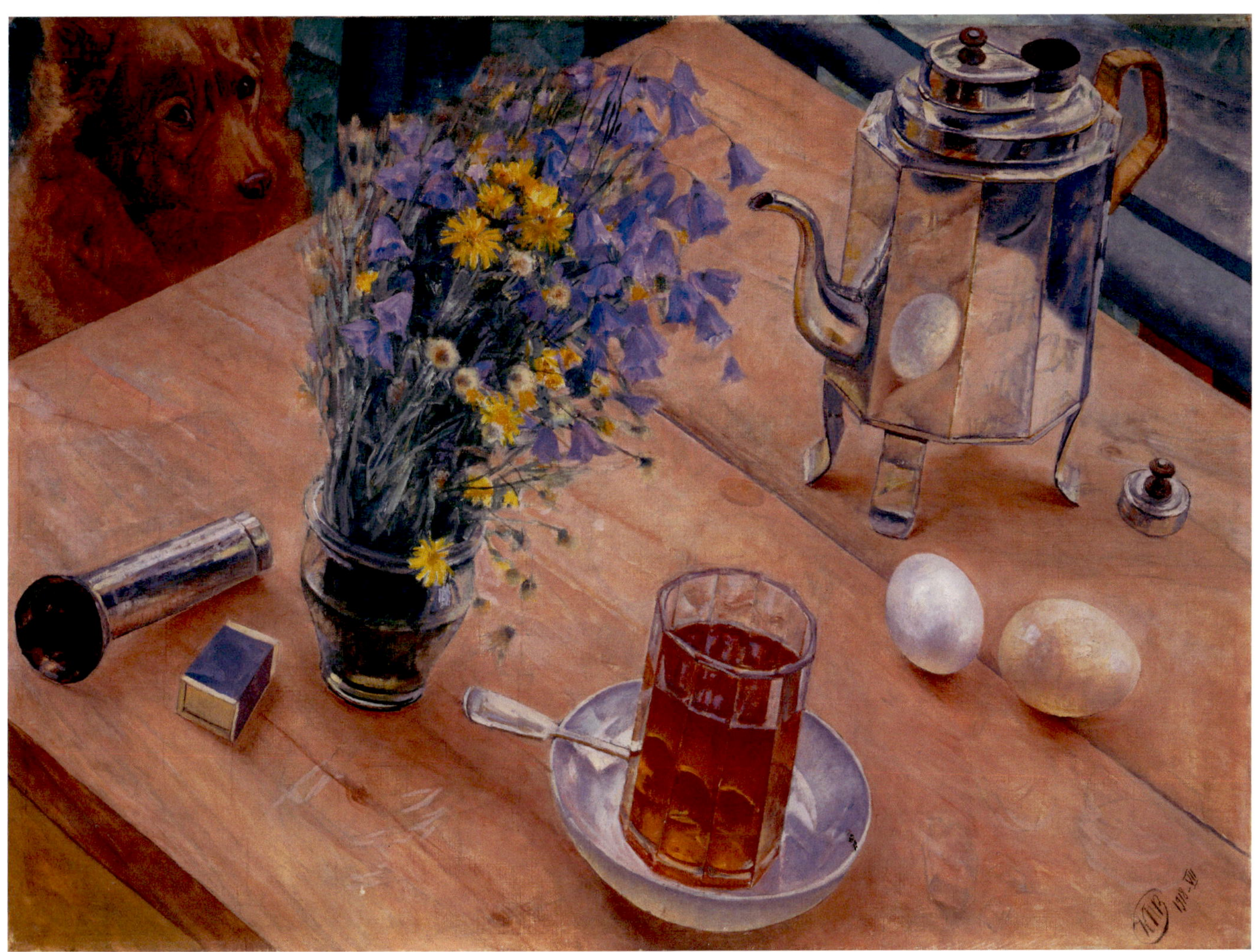

PETROV-VODKIN Kuzma Sergeevich | *Morning Still Life*
1918
Oil on canvas, 66 × 88 cm
The State Russian Museum, St Petersburg

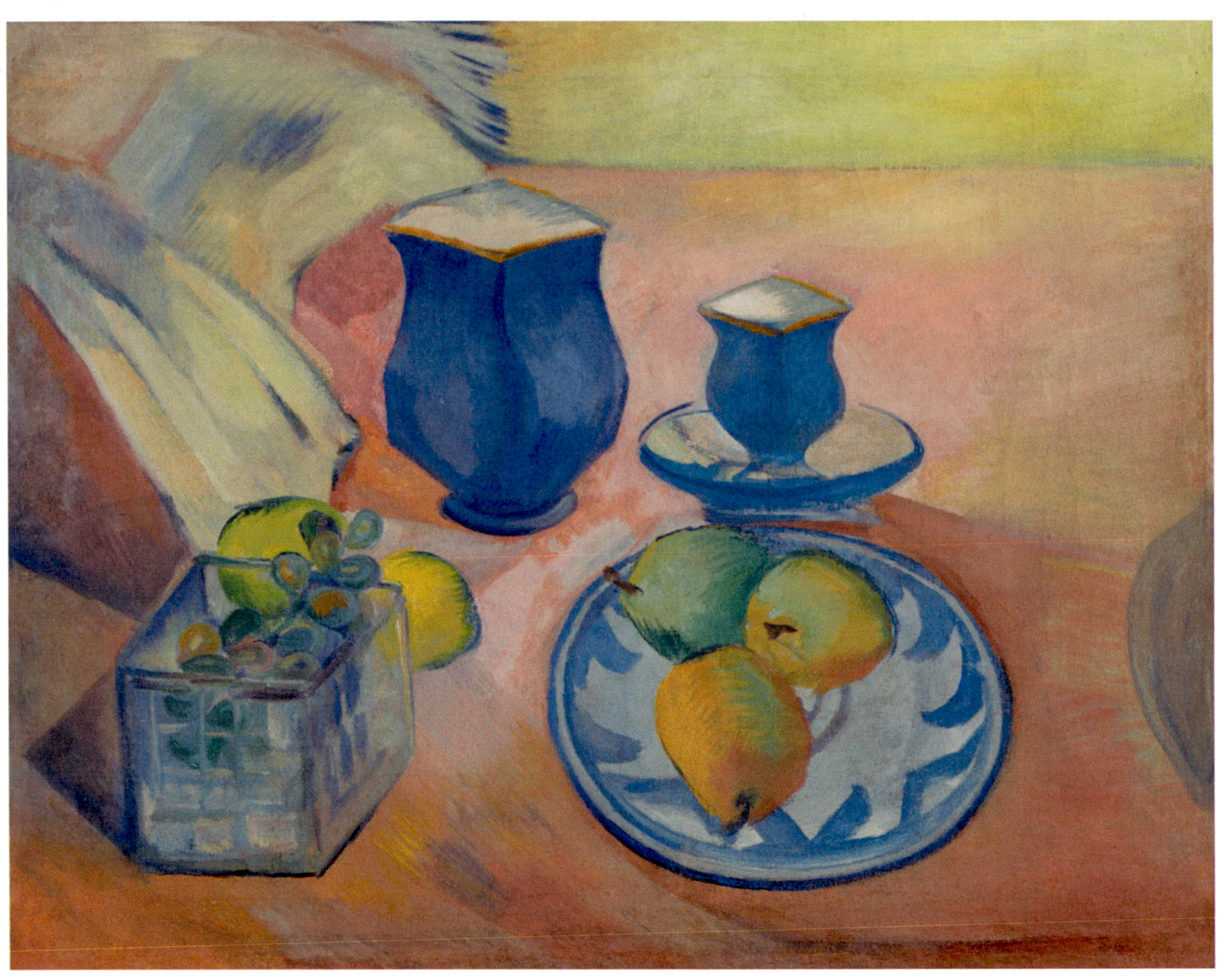

KUZNETSOV Mikhail Varfalofevich | *Still Life*
1918
Oil on canvas, 57 × 72.5 cm
Samara Regional Art Museum

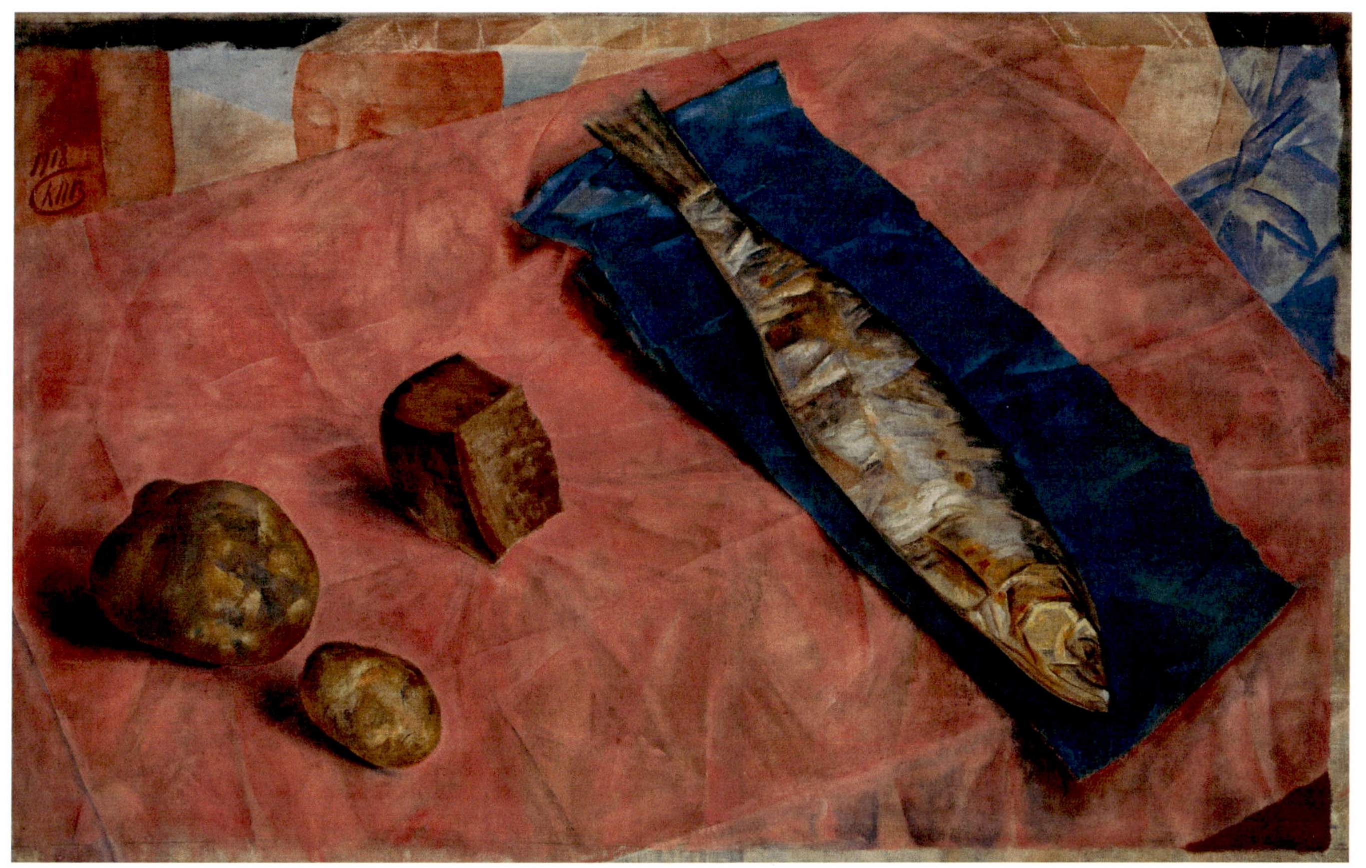

PETROV-VODKIN Kuzma Sergeevich | *Still Life with a Herring*
1918
Oil on canvas, 58 × 88.5 cm
The State Russian Museum, St Petersburg

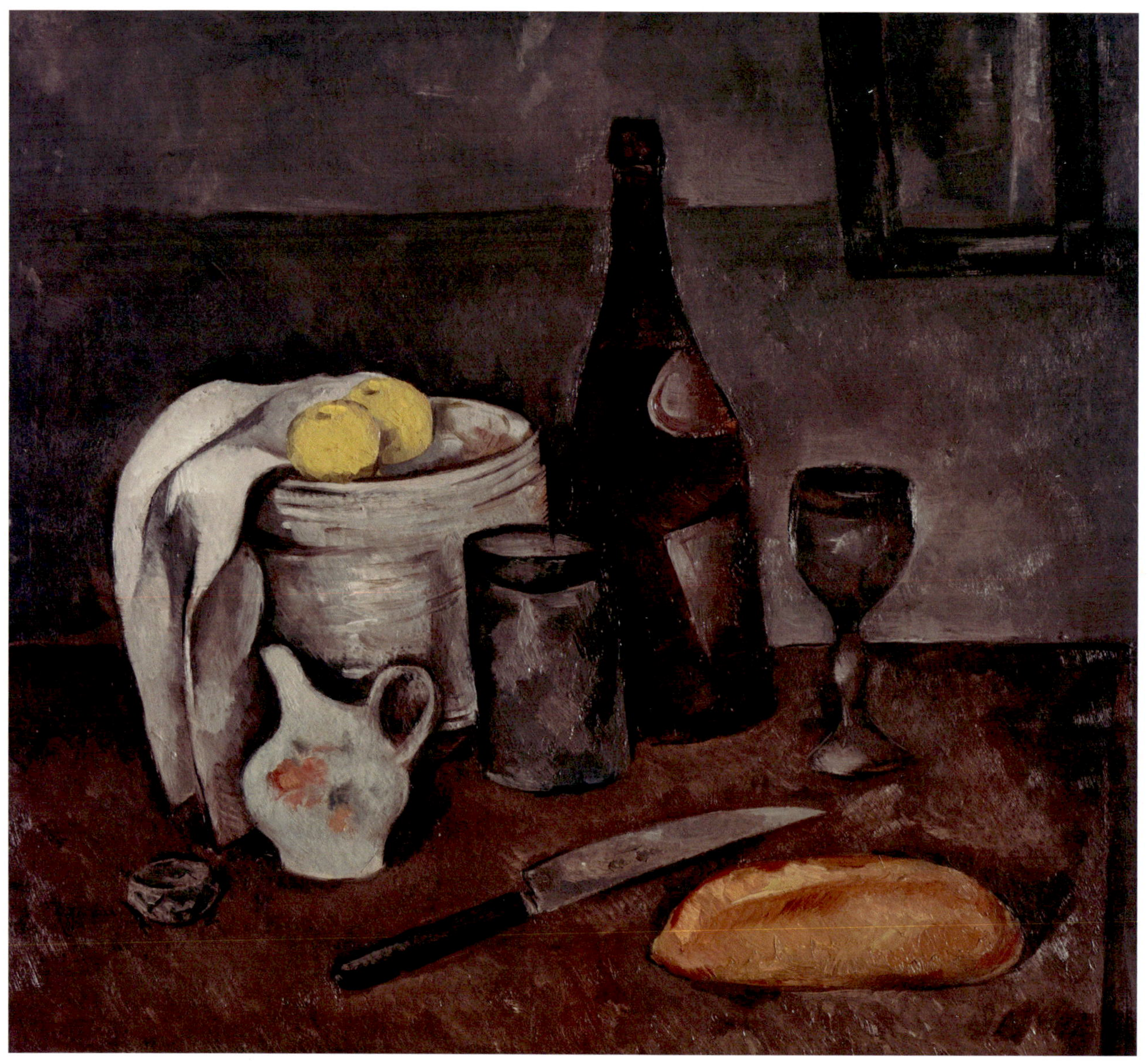

SHEVCHENKO Aleksandr Vasilievich | *Still Life with Plates*
1919
Oil on canvas, 69 × 74.5 cm
The State Russian Museum, St Petersburg

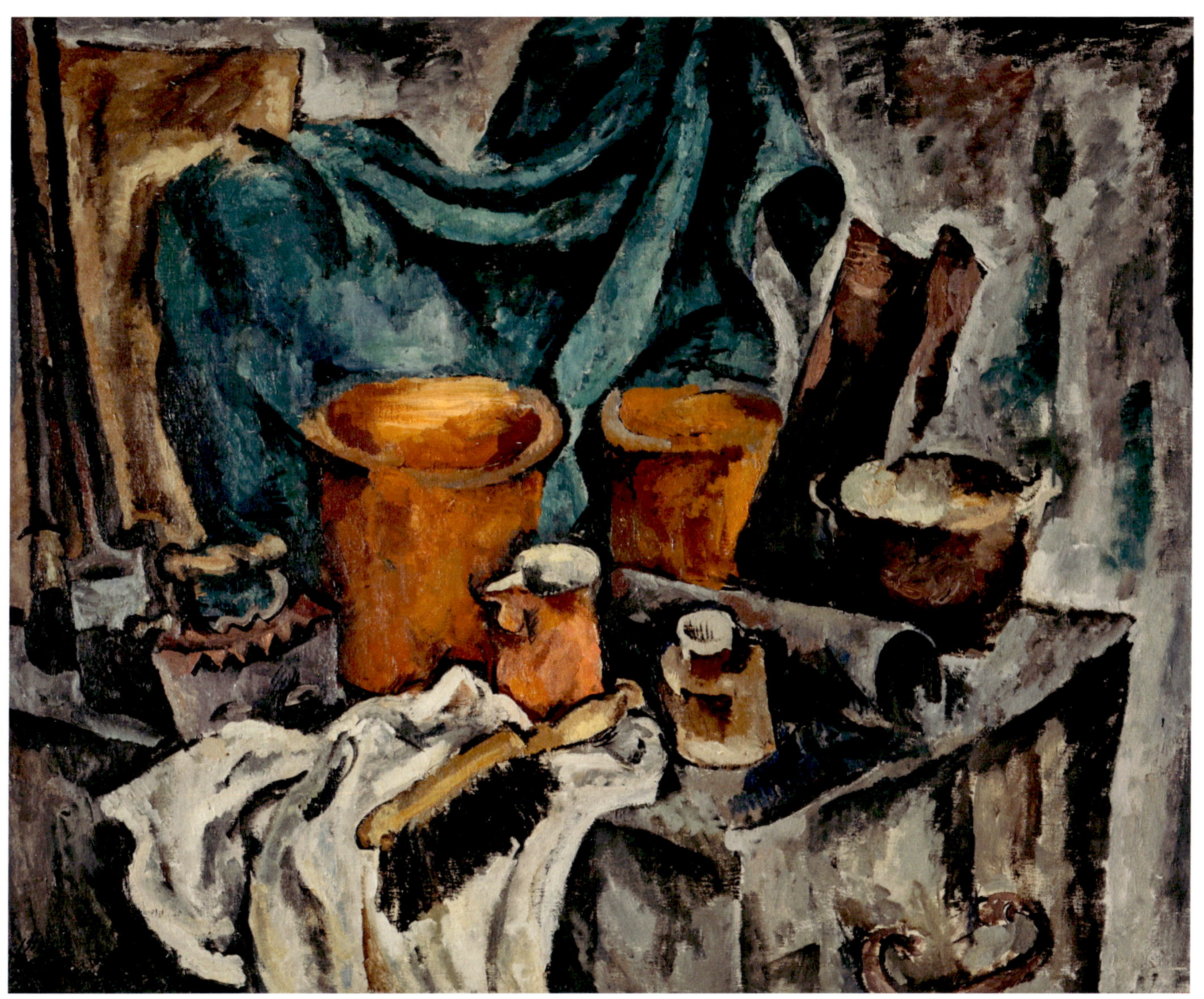

KONCHALOVSKY Petr Petrovich | *Dower Chest and Clay Pots*
1919
Oil on canvas, 143.5 × 174 cm
The State Russian Museum, St Petersburg

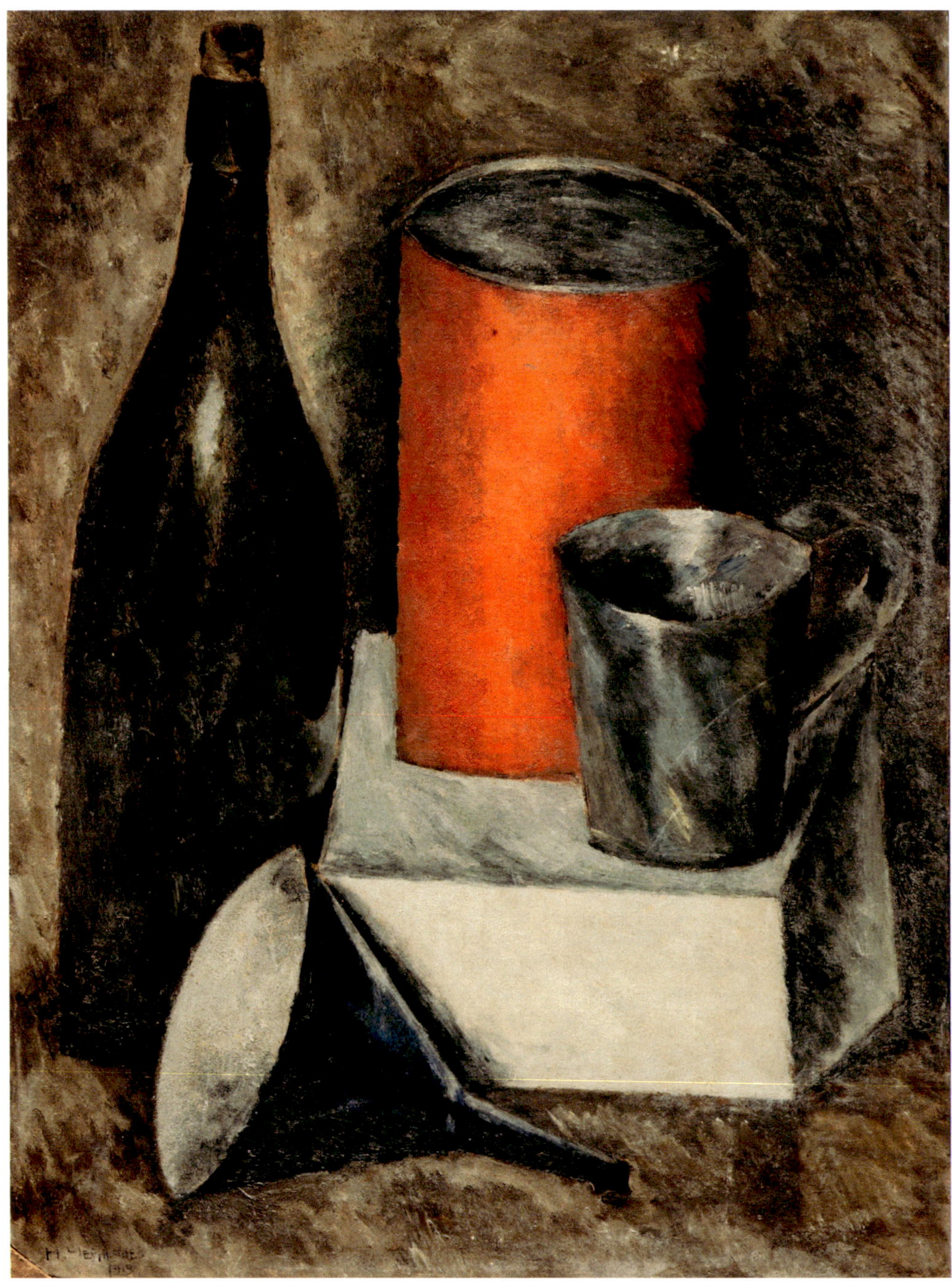

CHERNYSHEV Nikolai Mikhailovich | *Still Life with Red Bucket and a Bottle*
1919
Oil on canvas, 71 × 51.5 cm
The State Russian Museum, St Petersburg

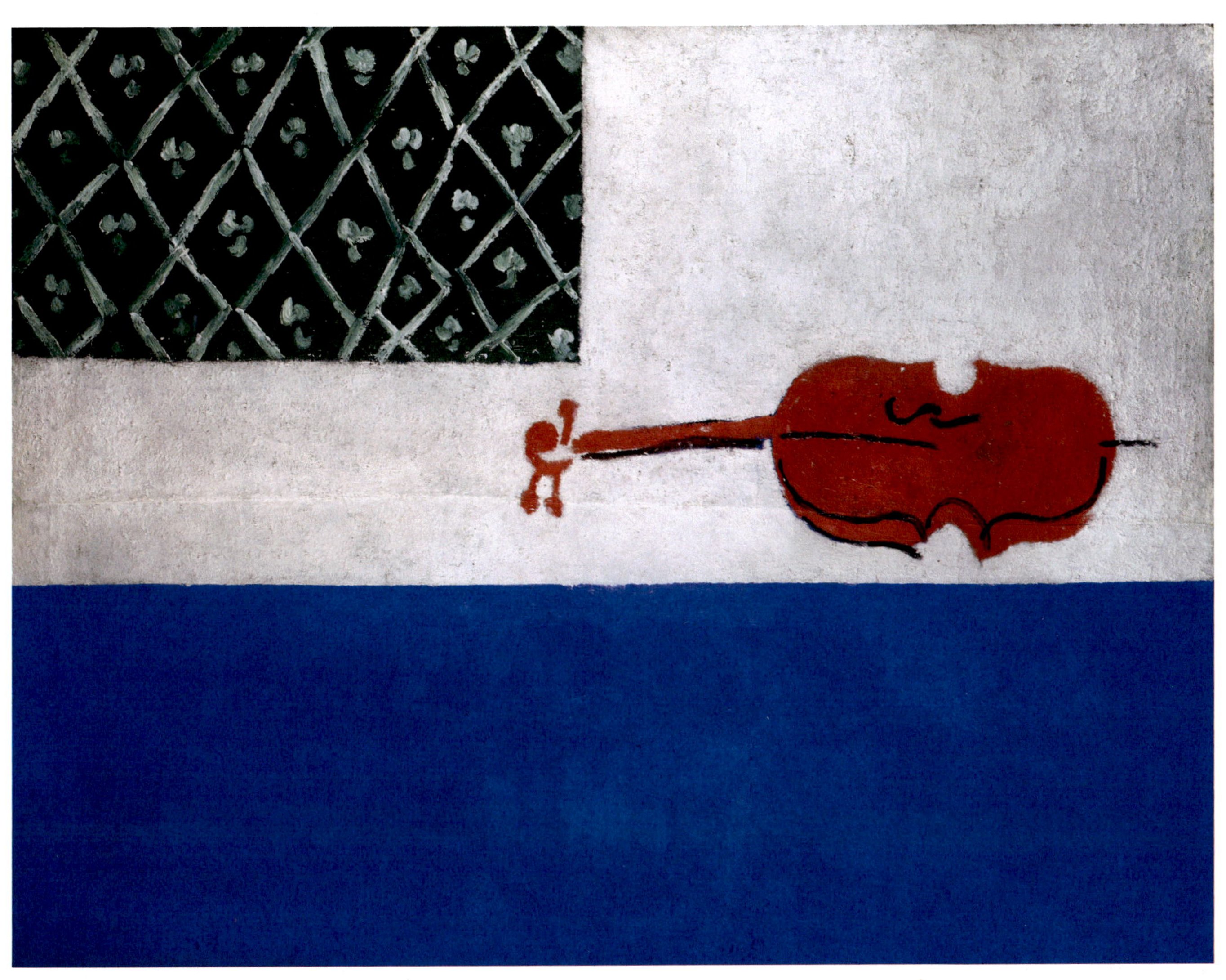

PUNI Ivan Albertovich | *Red Violin*
1919
Oil on canvas, 145 × 115 cm
The State Russian Museum, St Petersburg

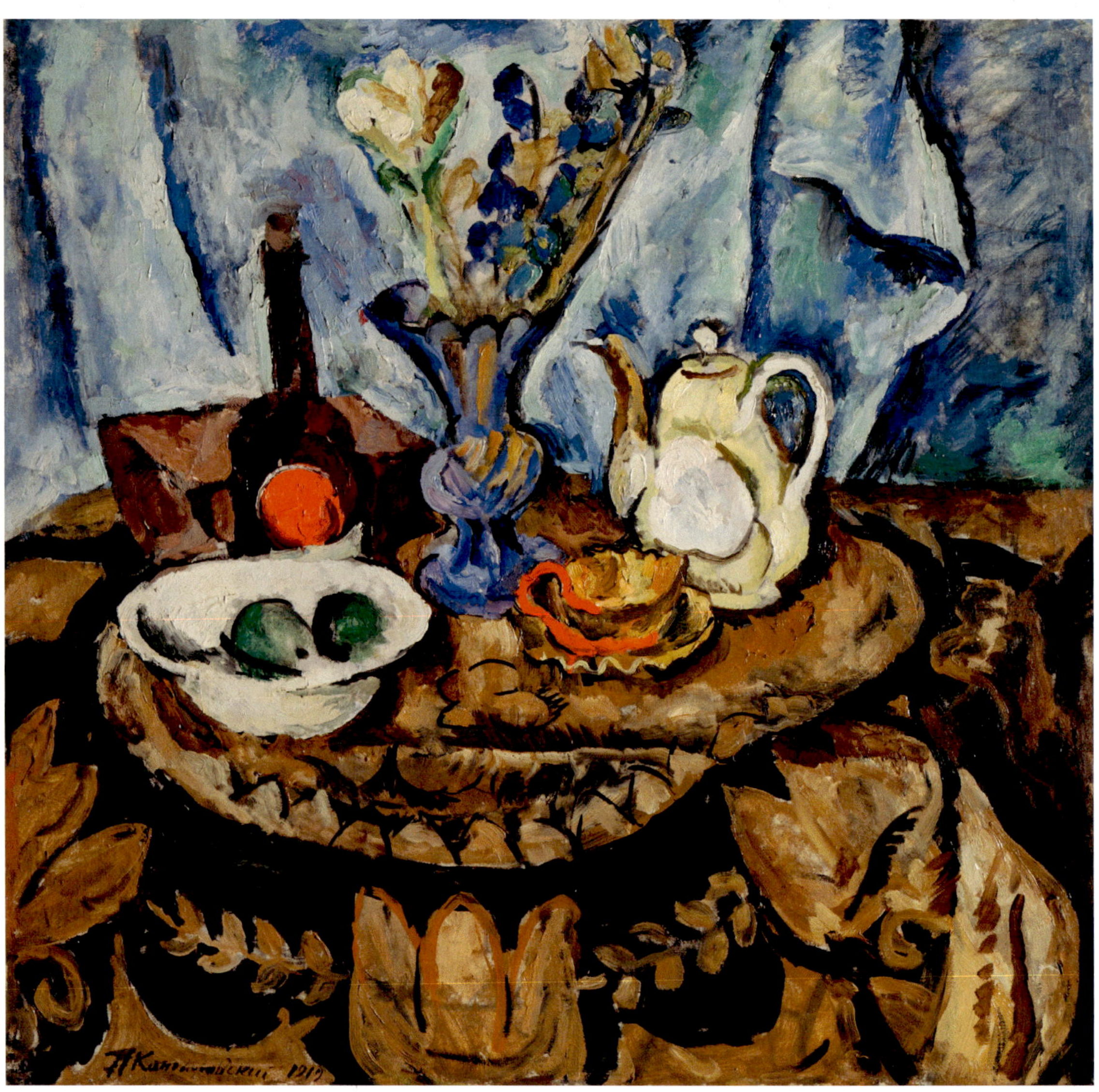

KONCHALOVSKY Petr Petrovich | *Flowers on a Table Cloth*
1919
Oil on canvas, 103.5 × 108 cm
The State Russian Museum, St Petersburg

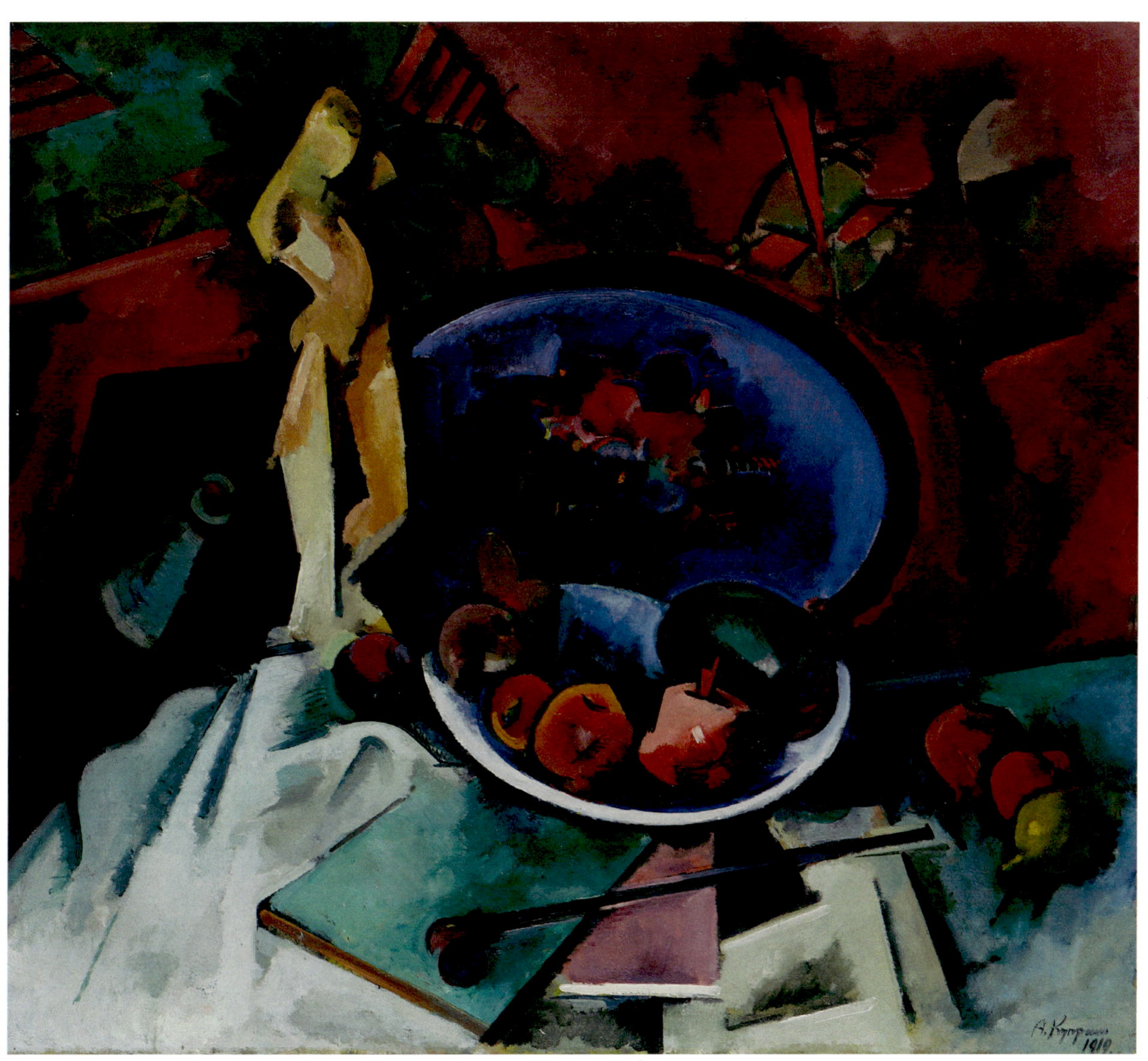

KUPRIN Aleksandr Vasilievich | *Still Life with the Sculpture by B. Korolev*
1919
Oil on canvas, 140 × 153 cm
The State Tretyakov Gallery, Moscow

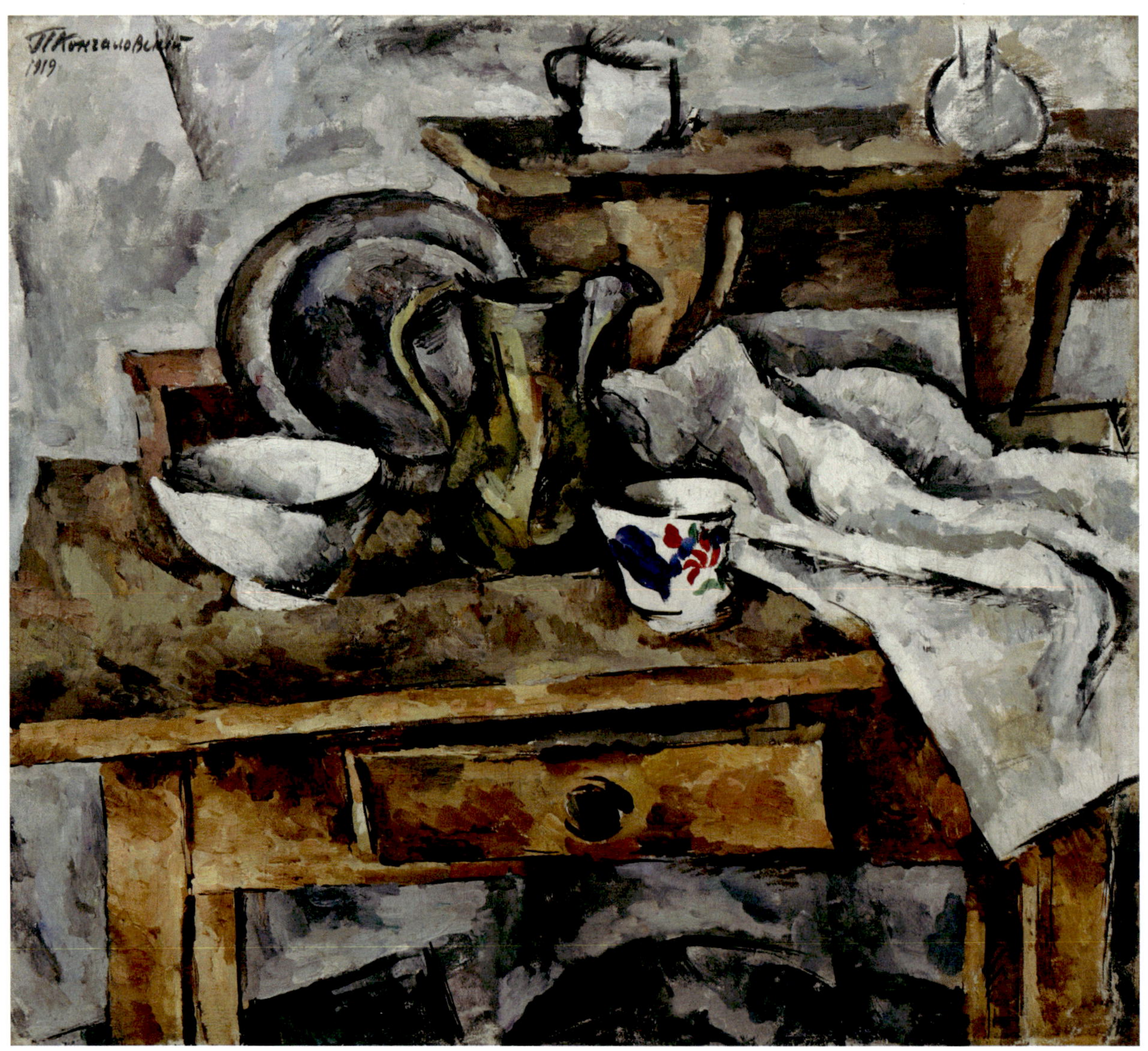

KONCHALOVSKY Petr Petrovich | *Still Life*
1919
Oil on canvas, 85.5 × 92.5 cm
Tula Regional Art Museum

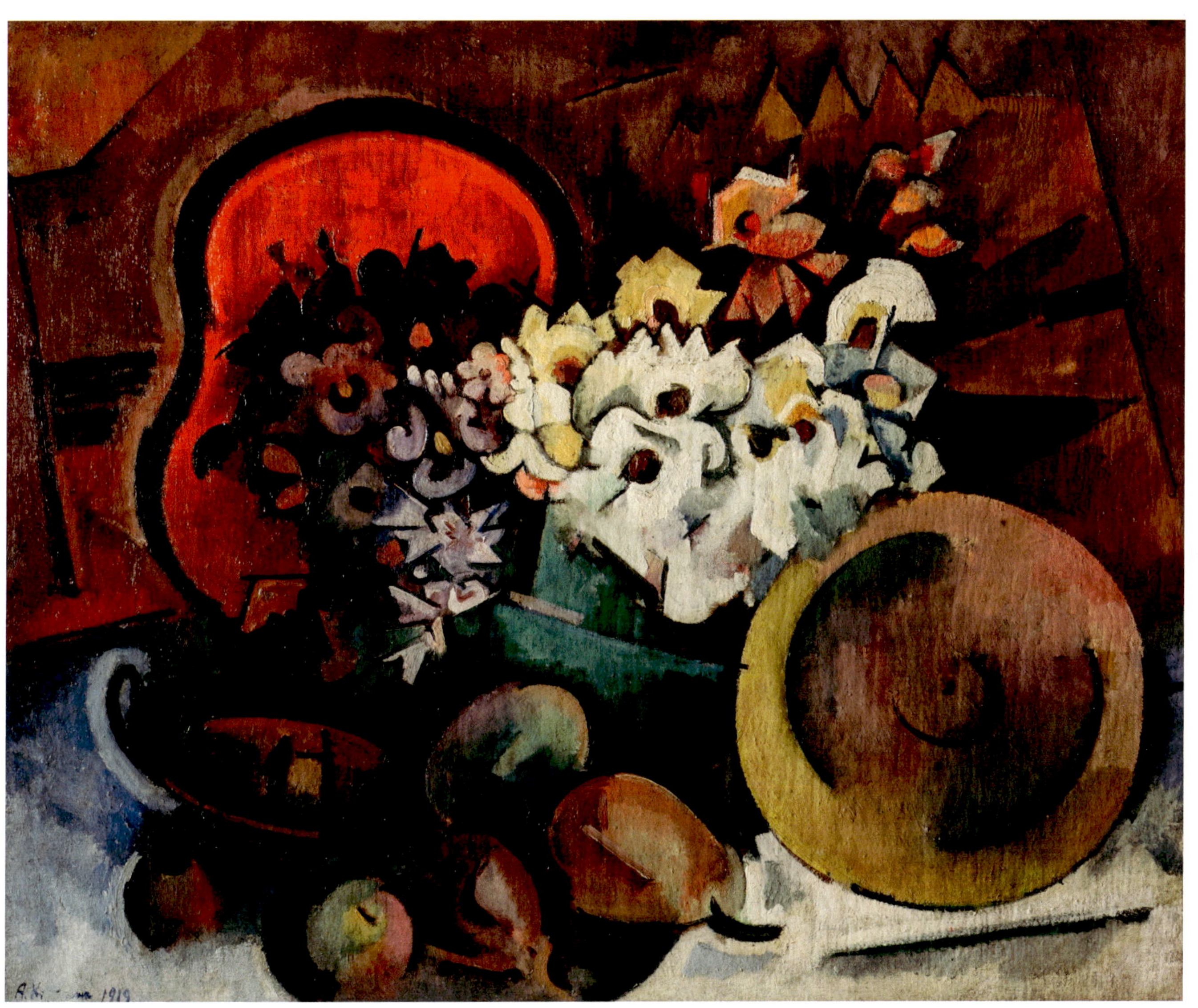

KUPRIN Aleksandr Vasilievich | *Big Still Life with Artificial Flowers, Red Tray and Wooden Plate*
1919
Oil on canvas, 140 × 168 cm
The State Russian Museum, St Petersburg

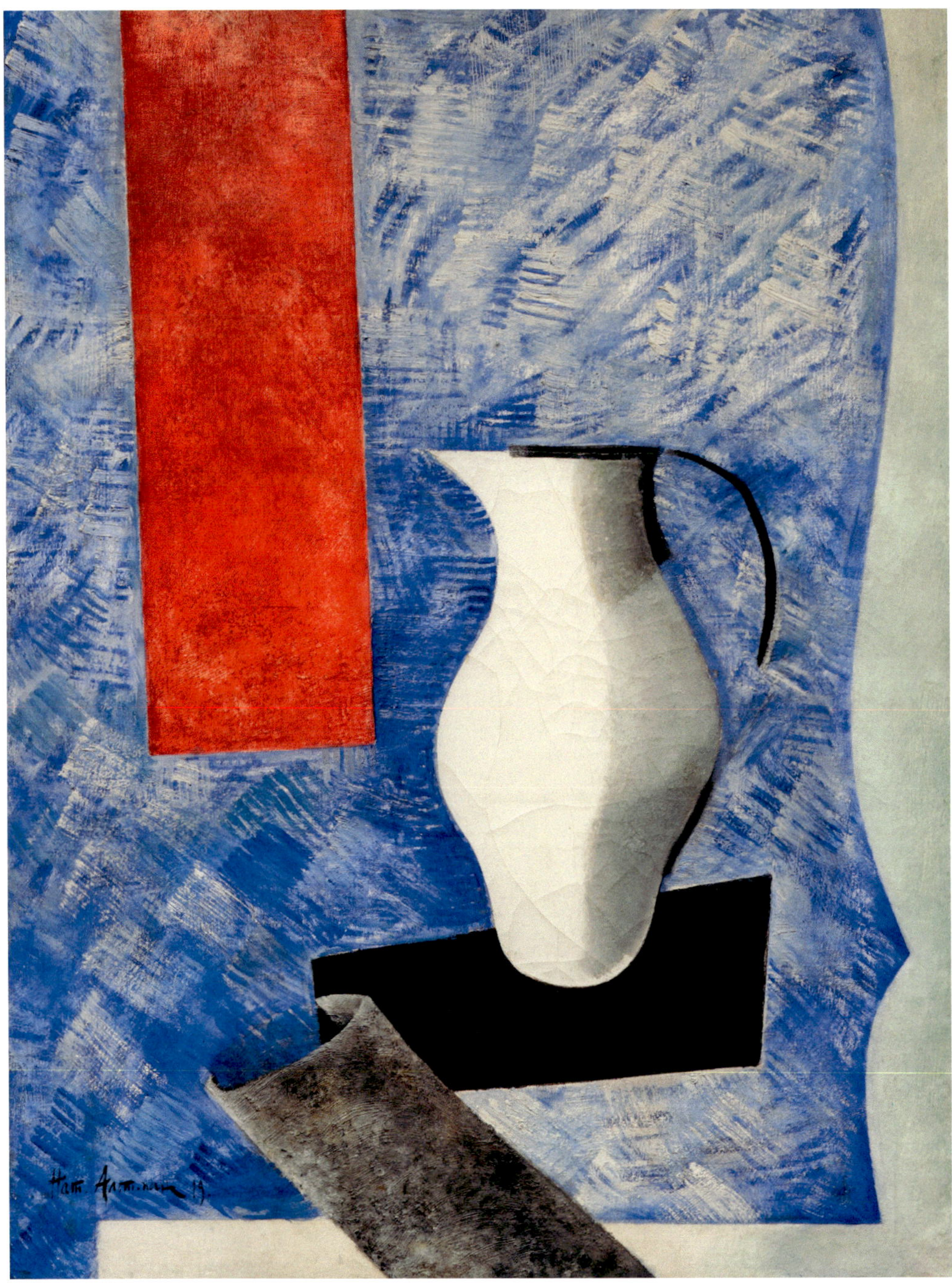

ALTMAN Nathan Isaevich | *Materialistic Art, Still Life with White Jug*
1919
Oil and enamel on canvas, 84.5 × 62 cm
The State Russian Museum, St Petersburg

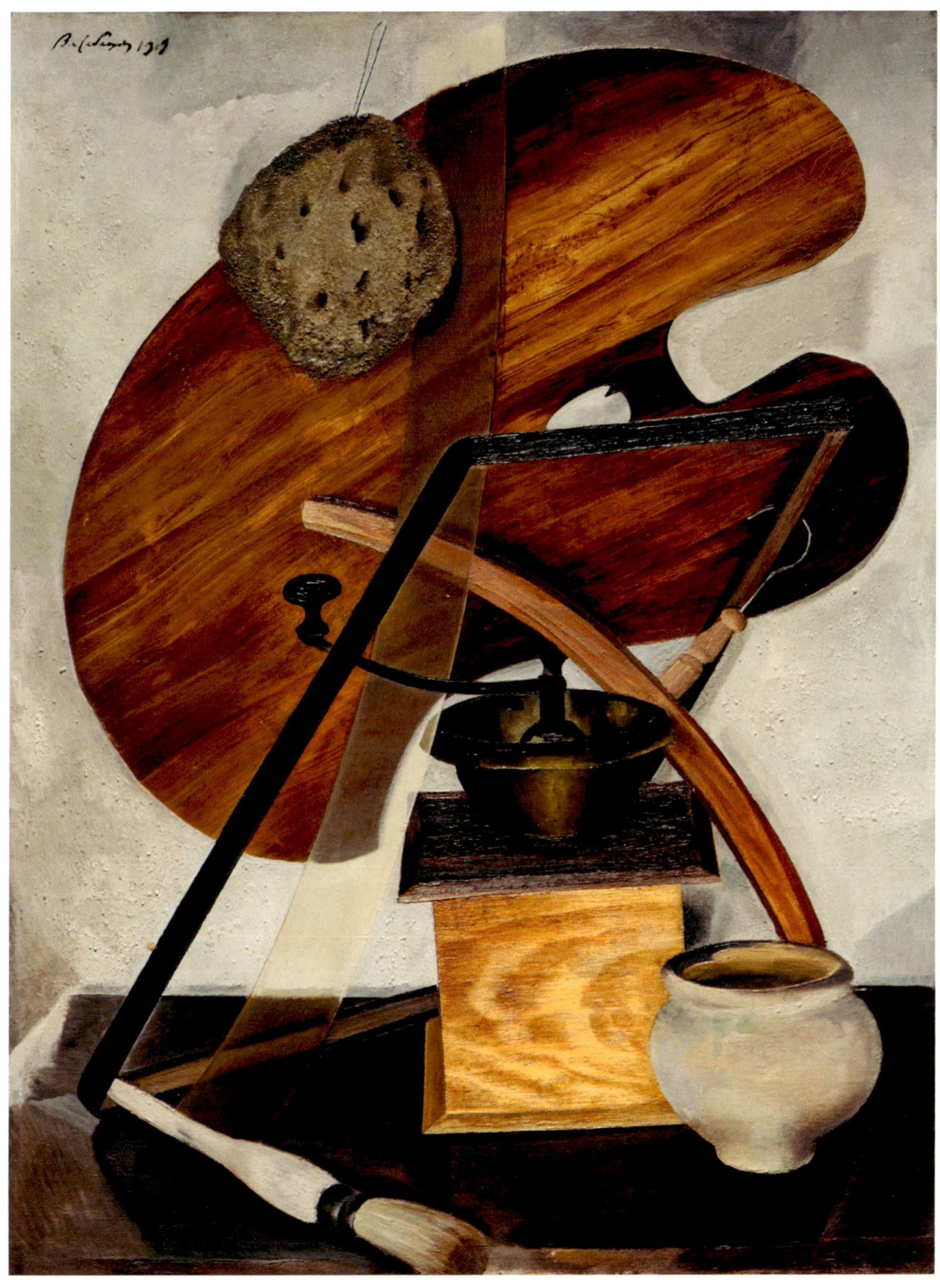

LEBEDEV Vladimir Vasilyevich | *Still Life with Palette*
1919
Oil on canvas, 90 × 65.5 cm
The State Russian Museum, St Petersburg

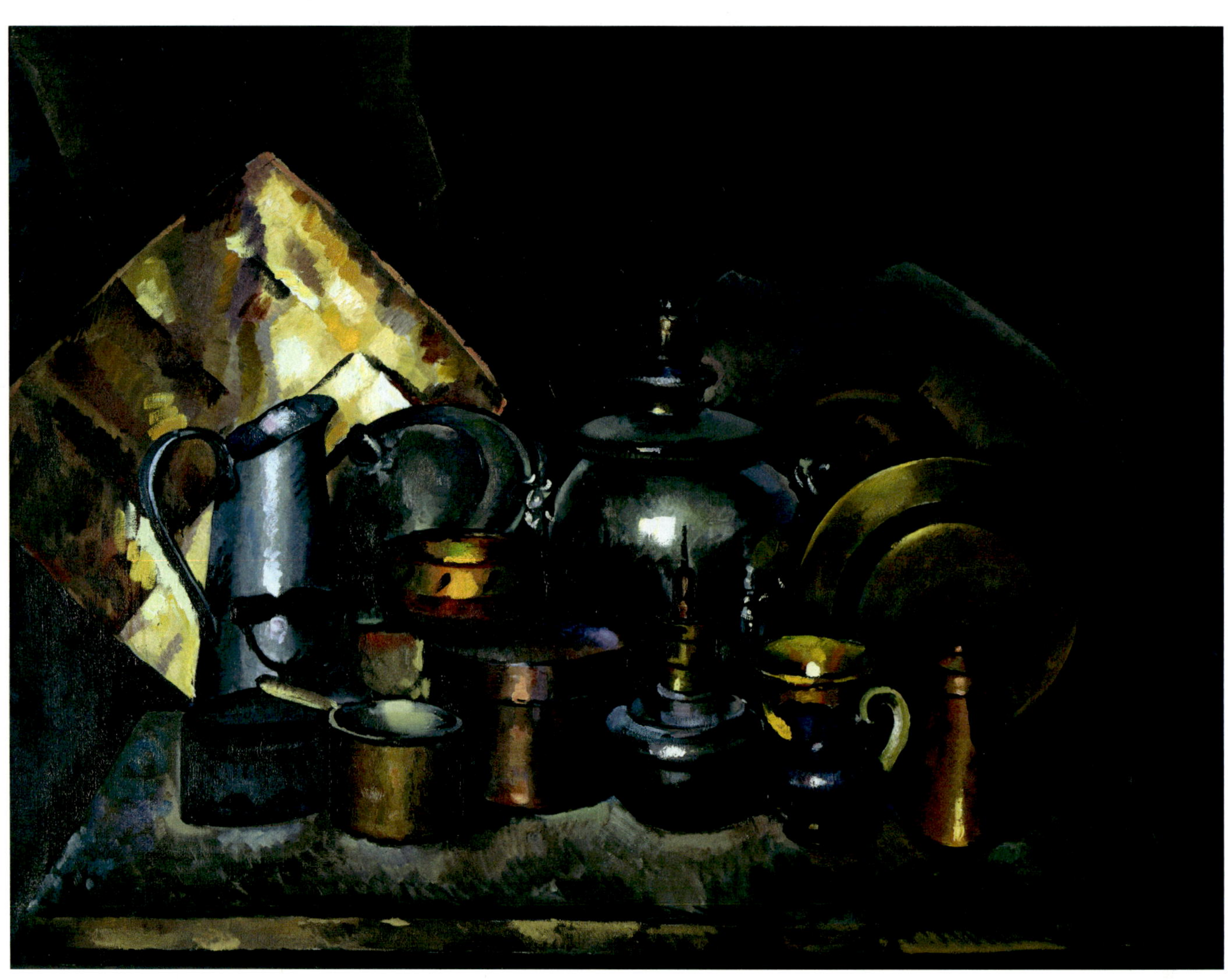

MASHKOV Ilya Ivanovich | *Still Life with Samovar*
1919
Oil on cardboard, 142 × 180 cm
The State Russian Museum, St Petersburg

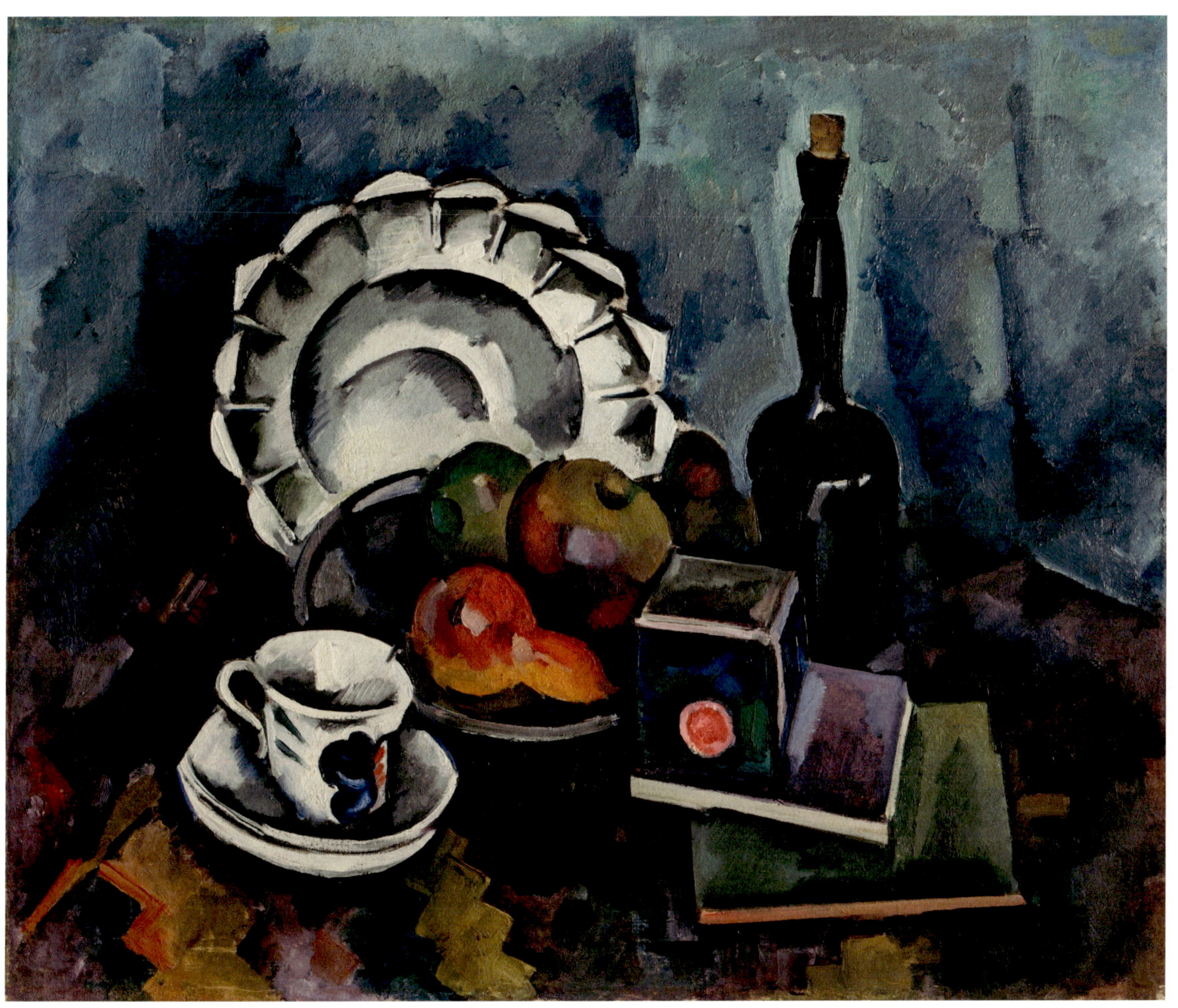

KUPRIN Aleksandr Vasilievich | *Still Life, Crockery and Fruit*
1919
Oil on canvas, 81 × 96 cm
The State Russian Museum, St Petersburg

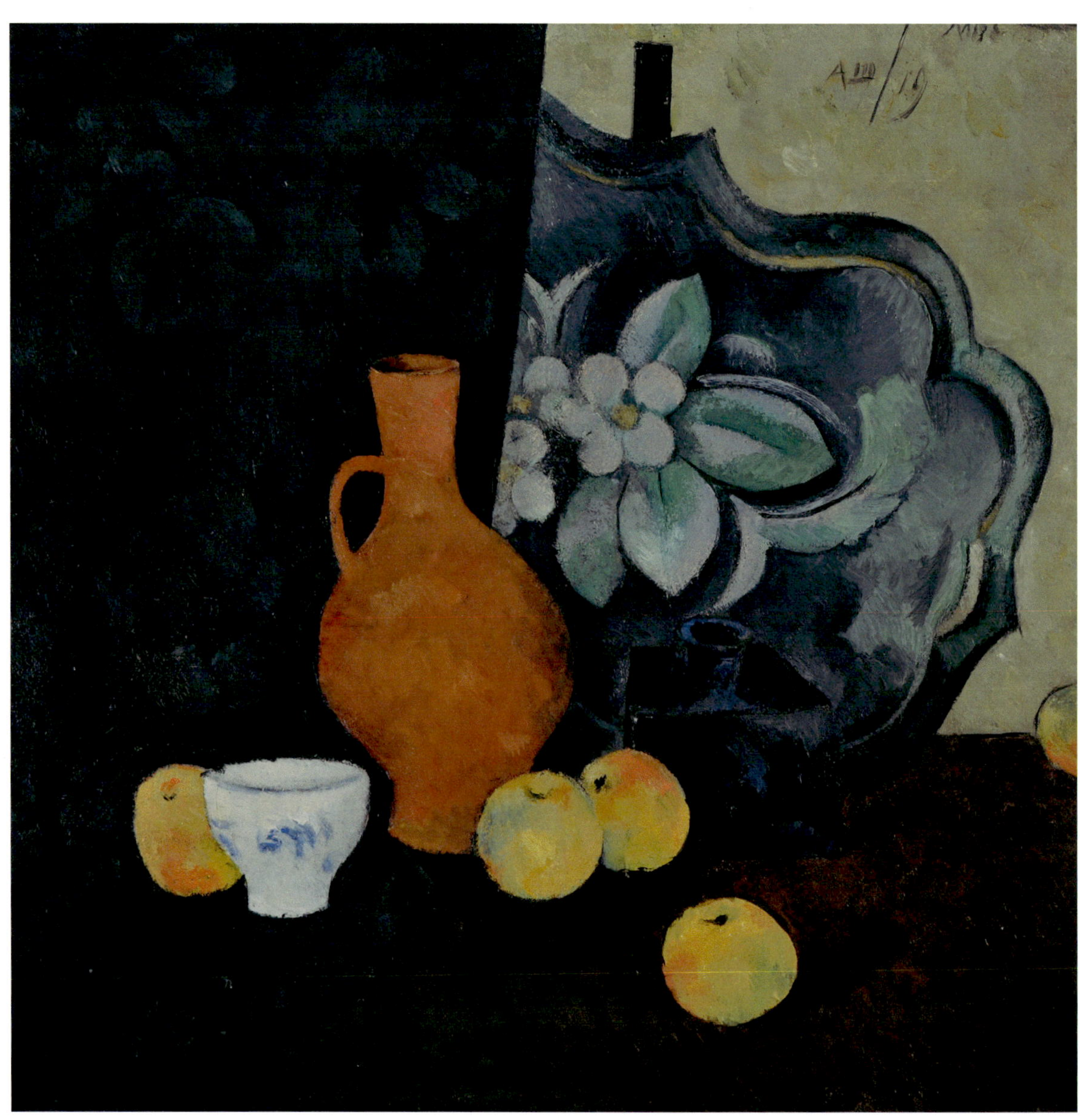

SHEVCHENKO Aleksandr Vasilievich | *Still Life with Yellow Jug*
1919
Oil on cardboard, 75 × 74 cm
The State Russian Museum, St Petersburg

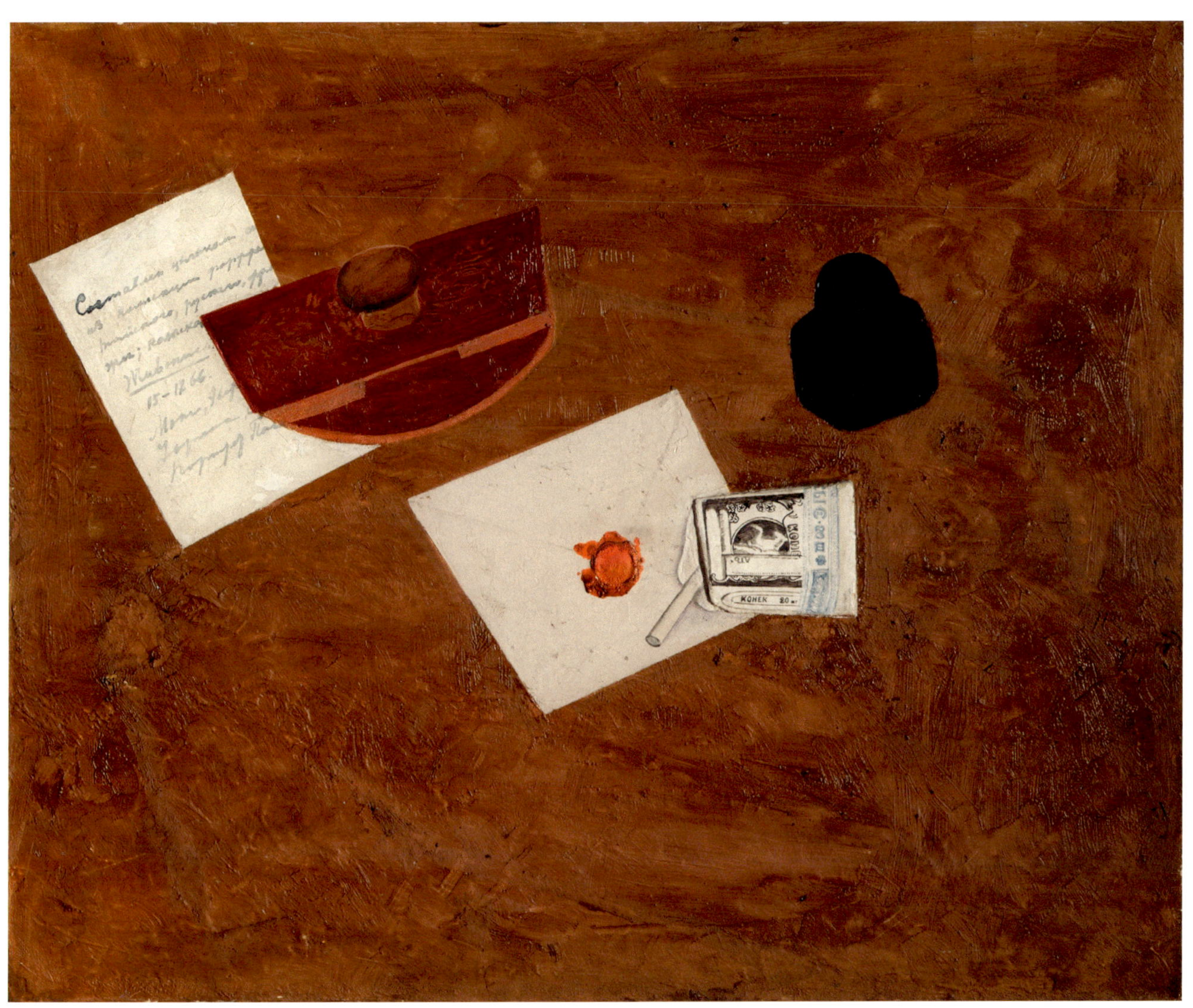

SHTERENBERG David Petrovich | *Desk*
1920
Oil on canvas, 46 × 65 cm
The State Russian Museum, St Petersburg

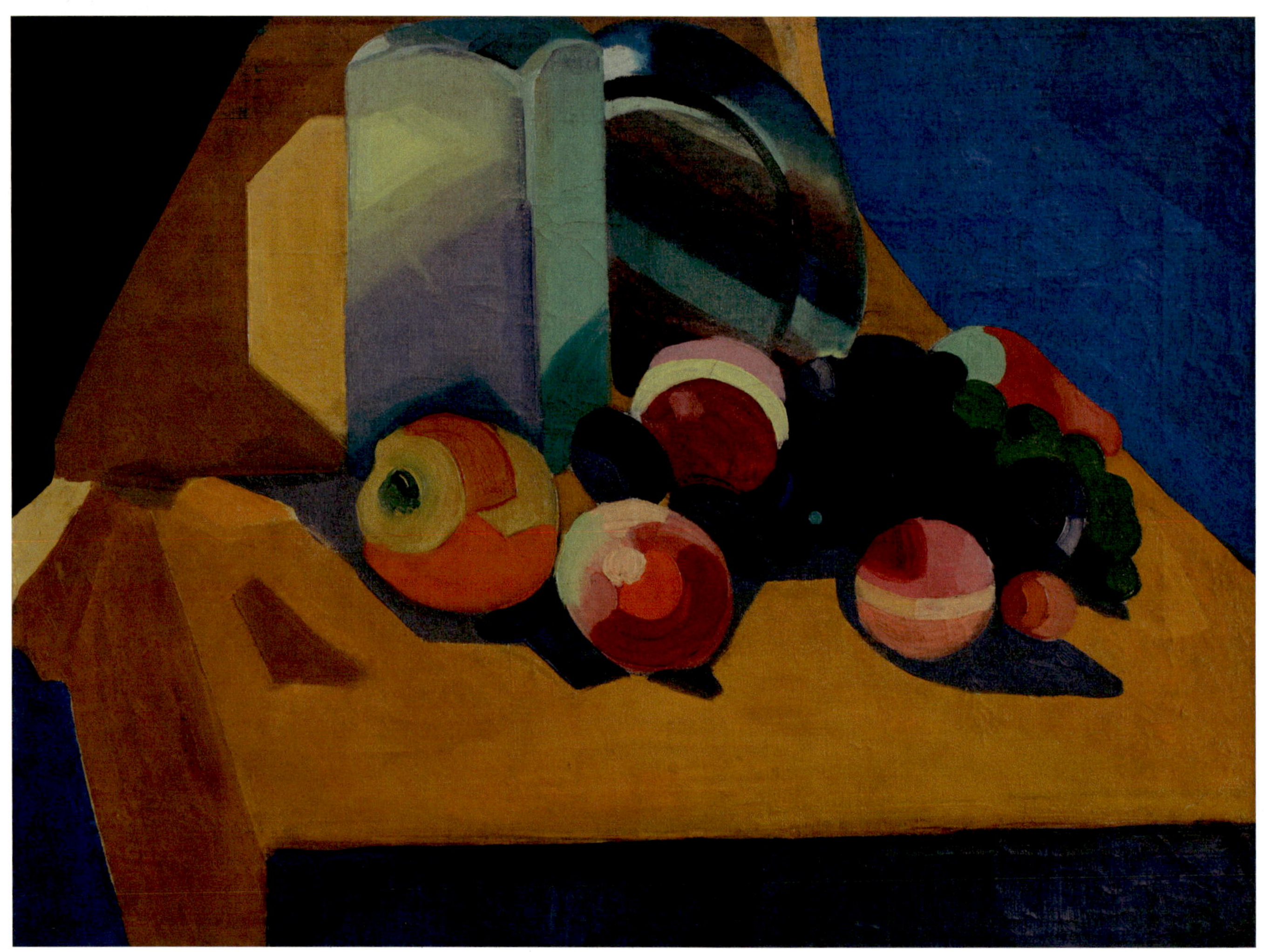

SAMOKHVALOV Alexander Nikolayevich | *Still Life*
1920s
Oil on canvas, 53.5 × 72 cm
Samara Regional Art Museum

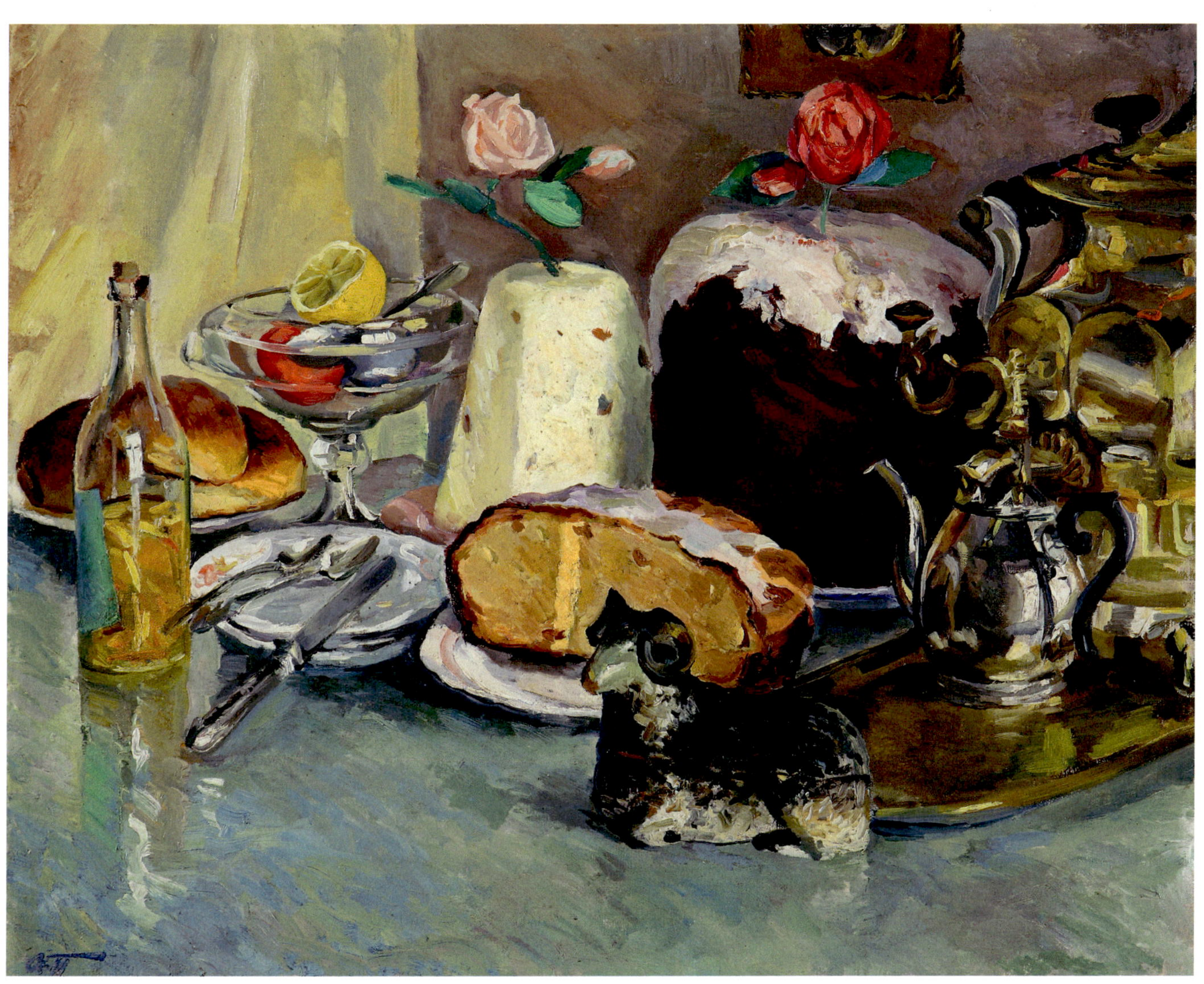

PLASTOV Arkady Alexandrovich | *Easter Still Life*
1920s
Oil on canvas, 51 × 63 cm
Private collection

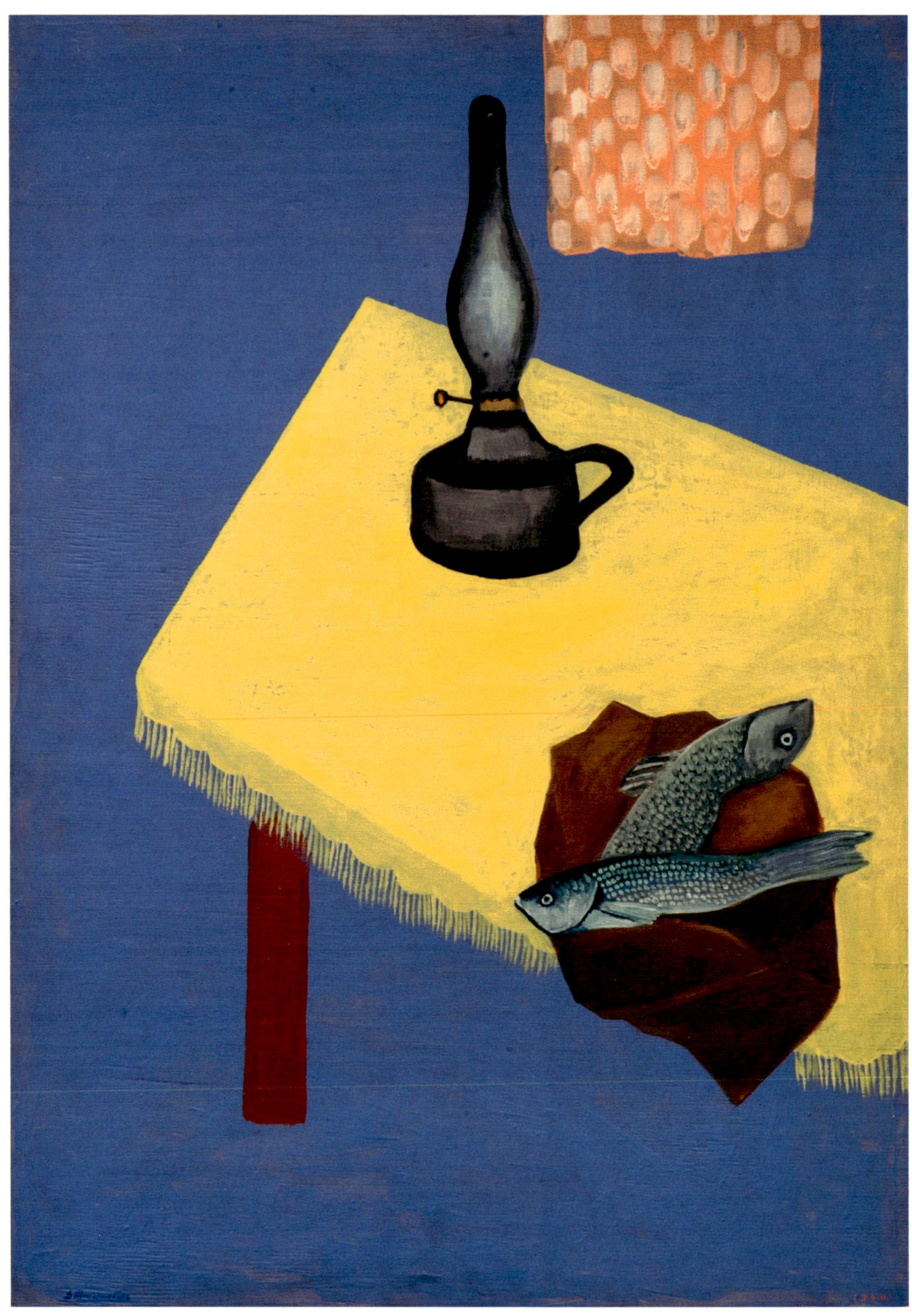

SHTERENBERG David Petrovich | *Still Life with Lamp and Herring*
1920
Oil on canvas, 89.5 × 62.5 cm
The State Russian Museum, St Petersburg

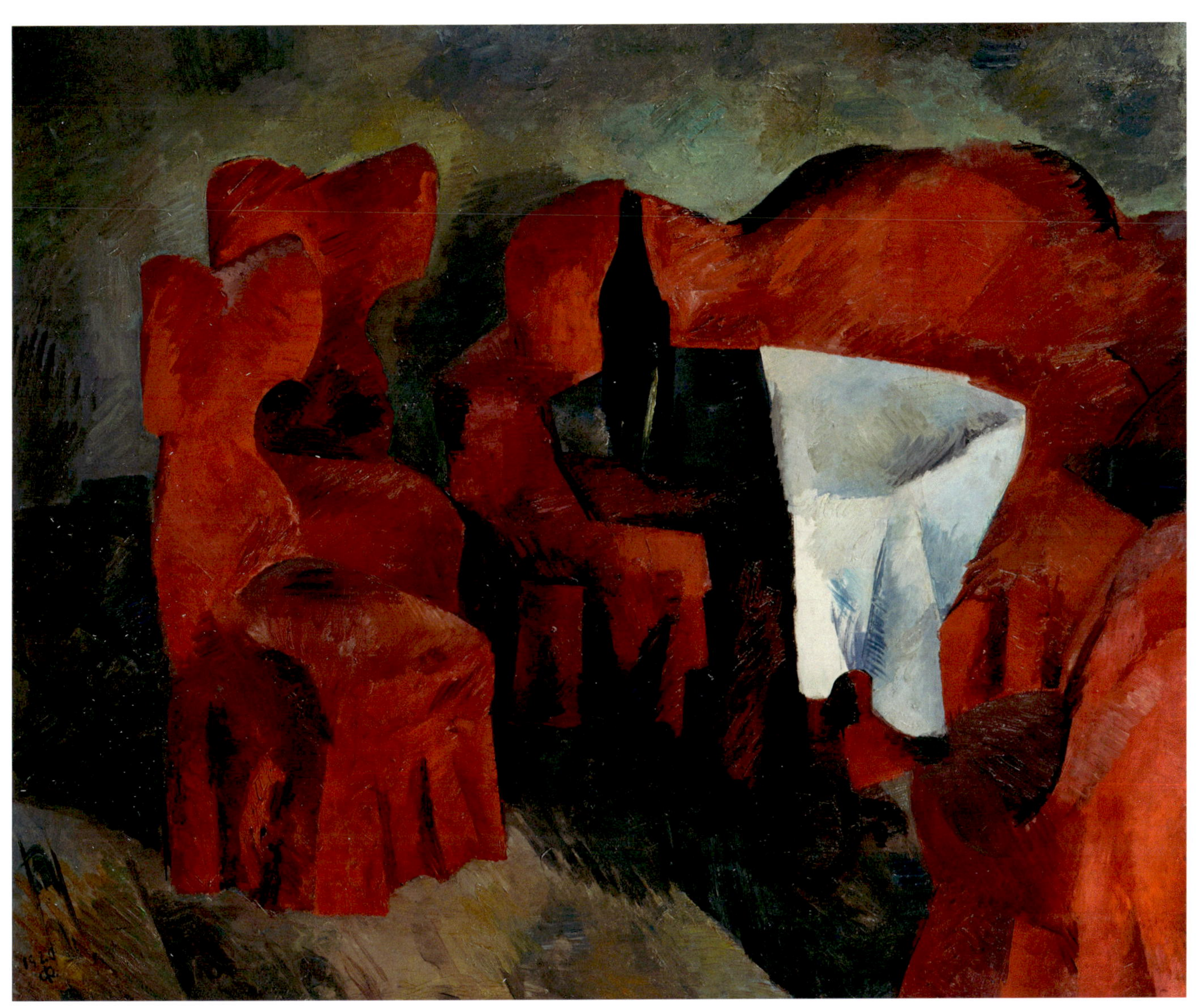

FALK Robert Rafailovich | *Red Furniture*
1920
Oil on canvas, 105 × 123 cm
The State Tretyakov Gallery, Moscow

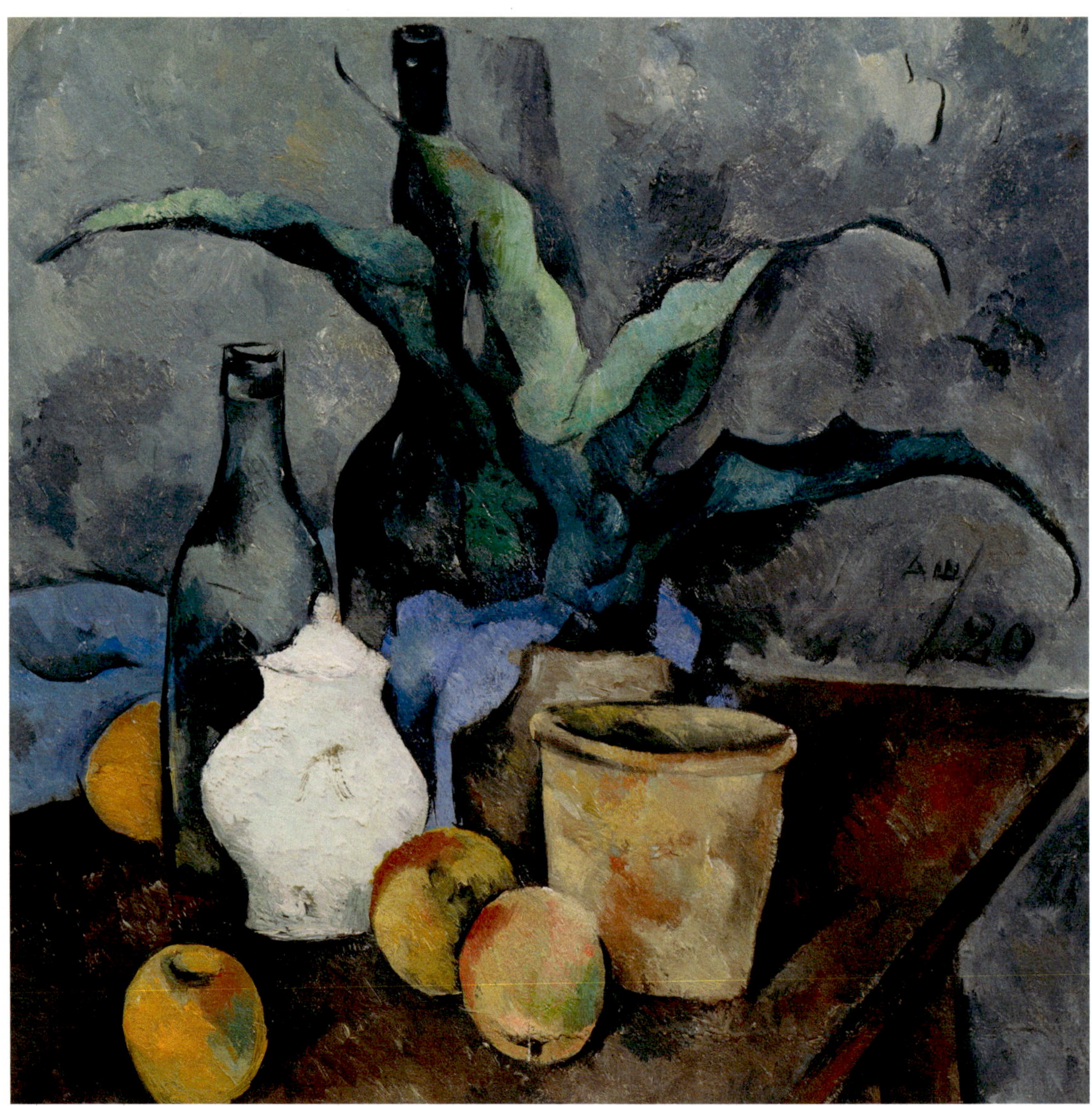

SHEVCHENKO Aleksandr Vasilievich | *Still Life*
1920
Oil on cardboard, 53 × 52.4 cm
Tula Regional Art Museum

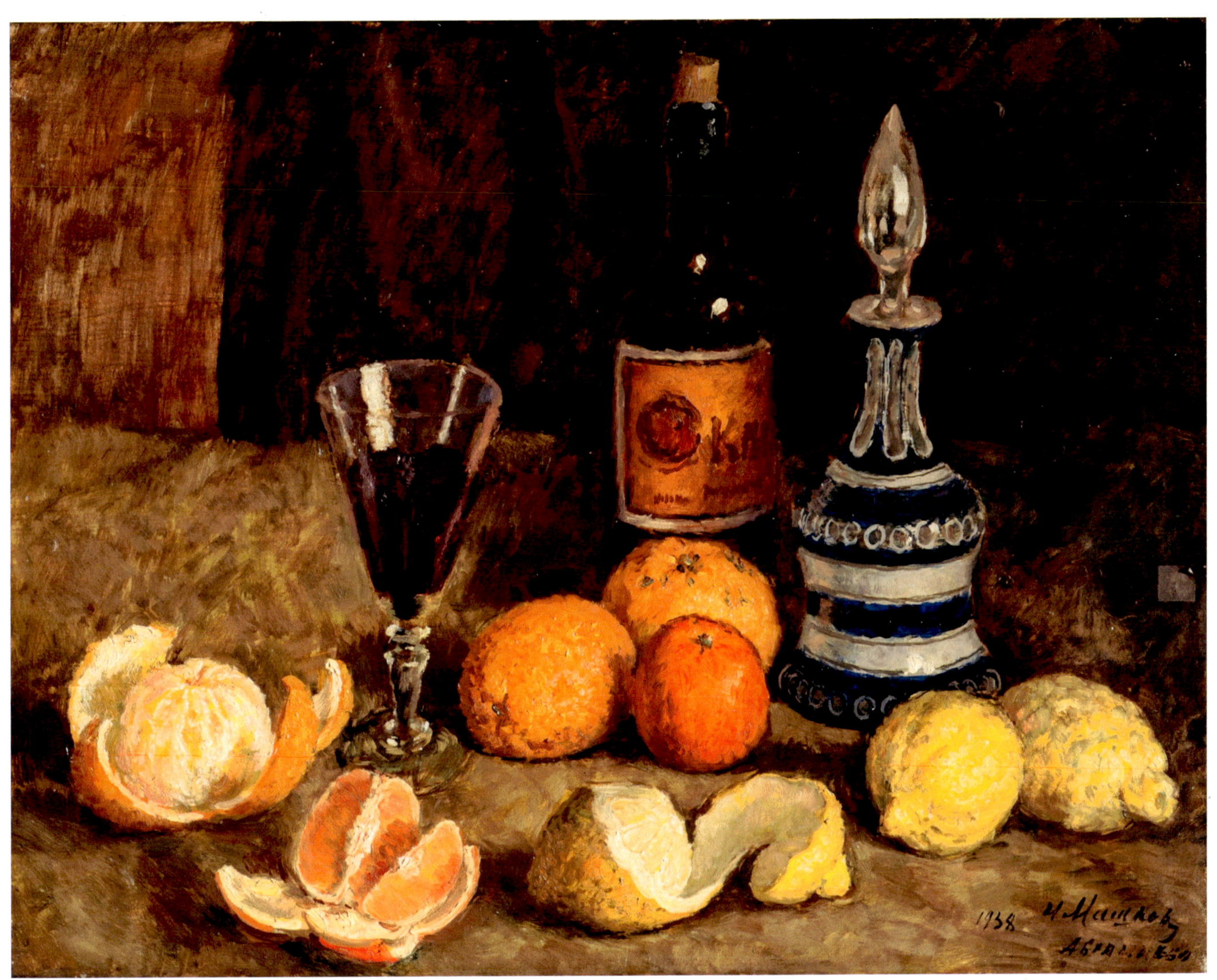

MASHKOV Ilya Ivanovich | *Still Life, Oranges, Fruits and Wine*
1920
Oil on canvas, 56 × 70 cm
The State Russian Museum, St Petersburg

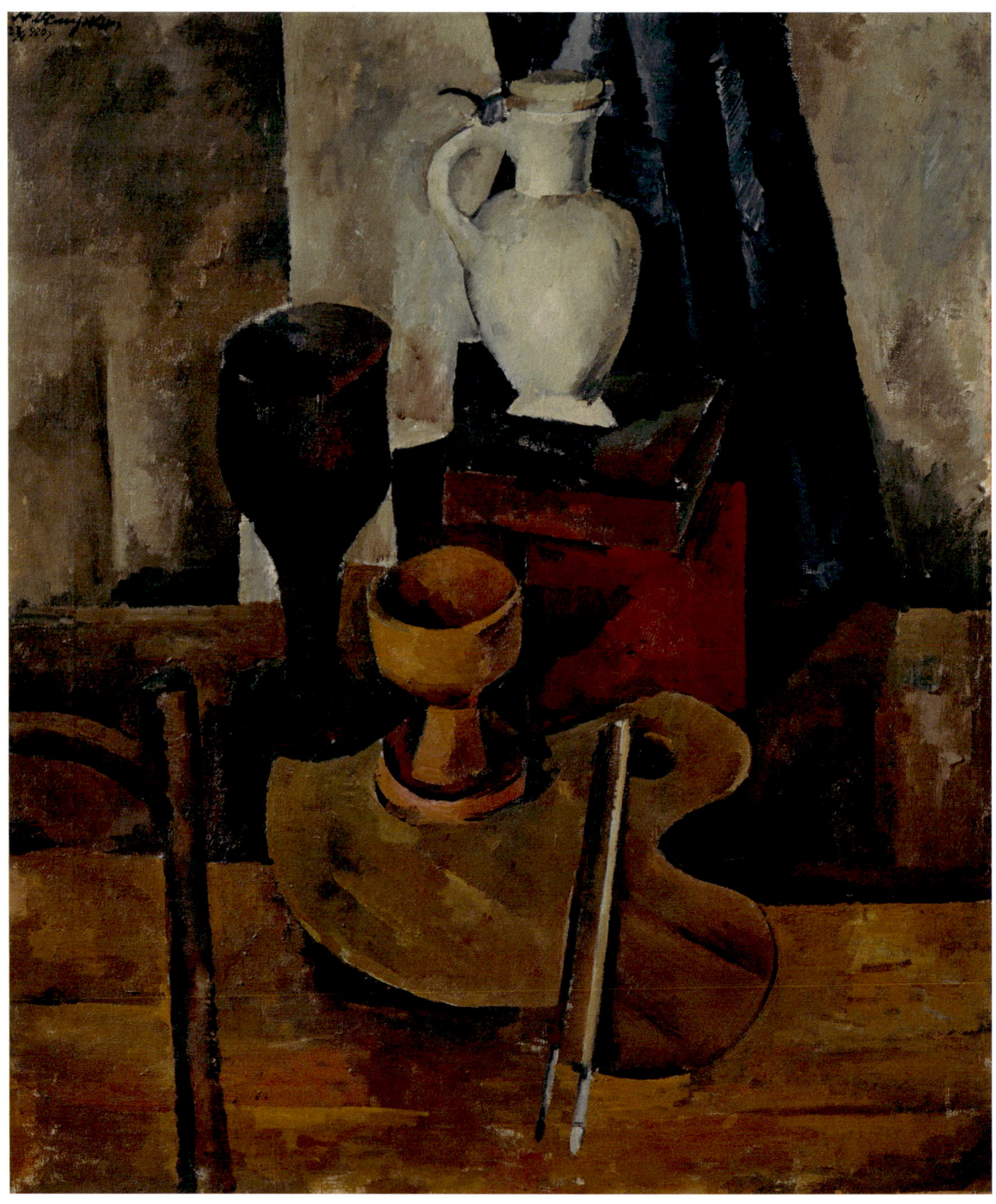

OSMERKIN Alexander Alexandrovich | *Still Life with Palette*
1920
Oil on canvas, 108 × 90 cm
Tula Regional Art Museum

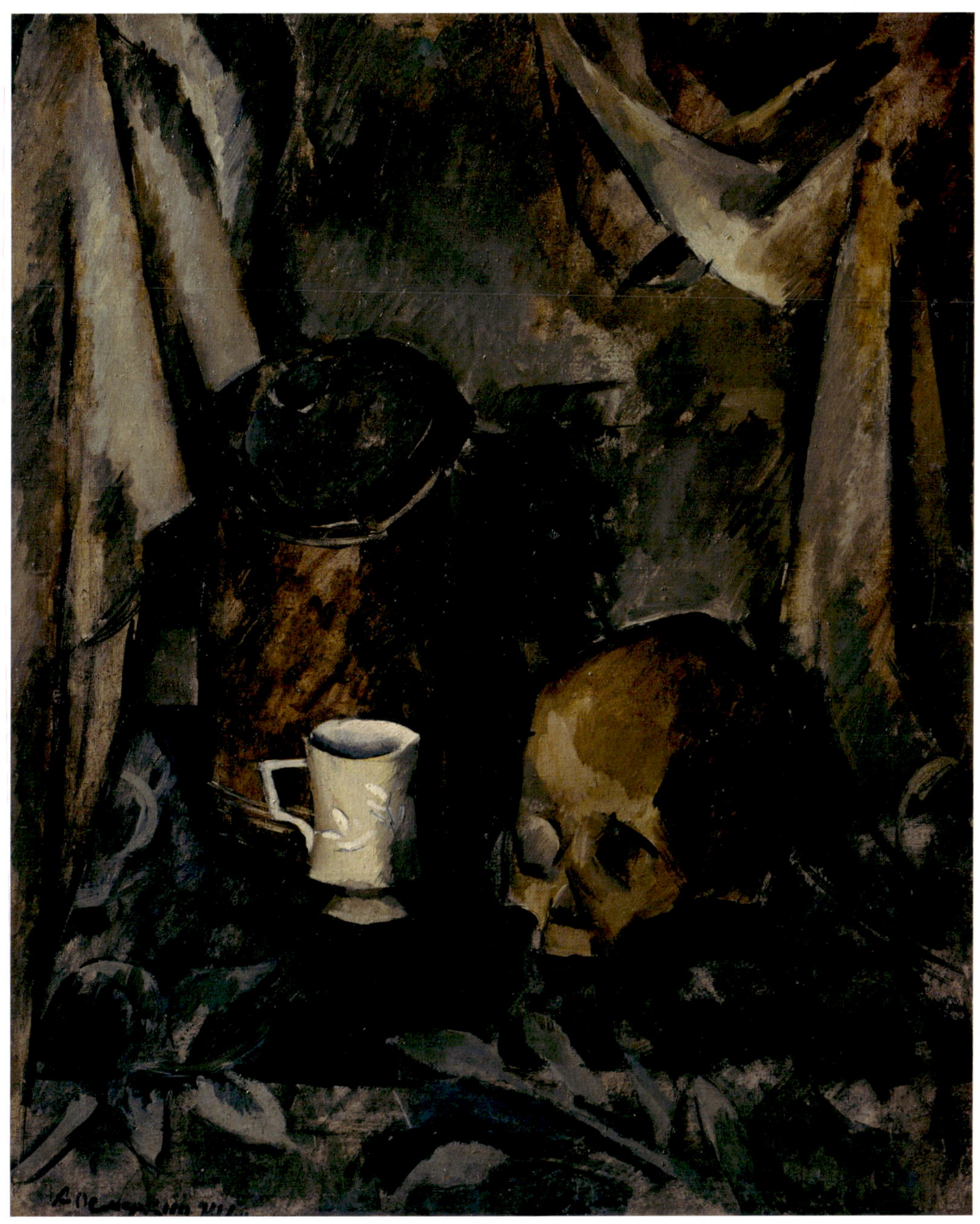

OSMERKIN Alexander Alexandrovich | *Still Life with a Skull*
1921
Oil on canvas, 82 × 64.5 cm
The State Russian Museum, St Petersburg

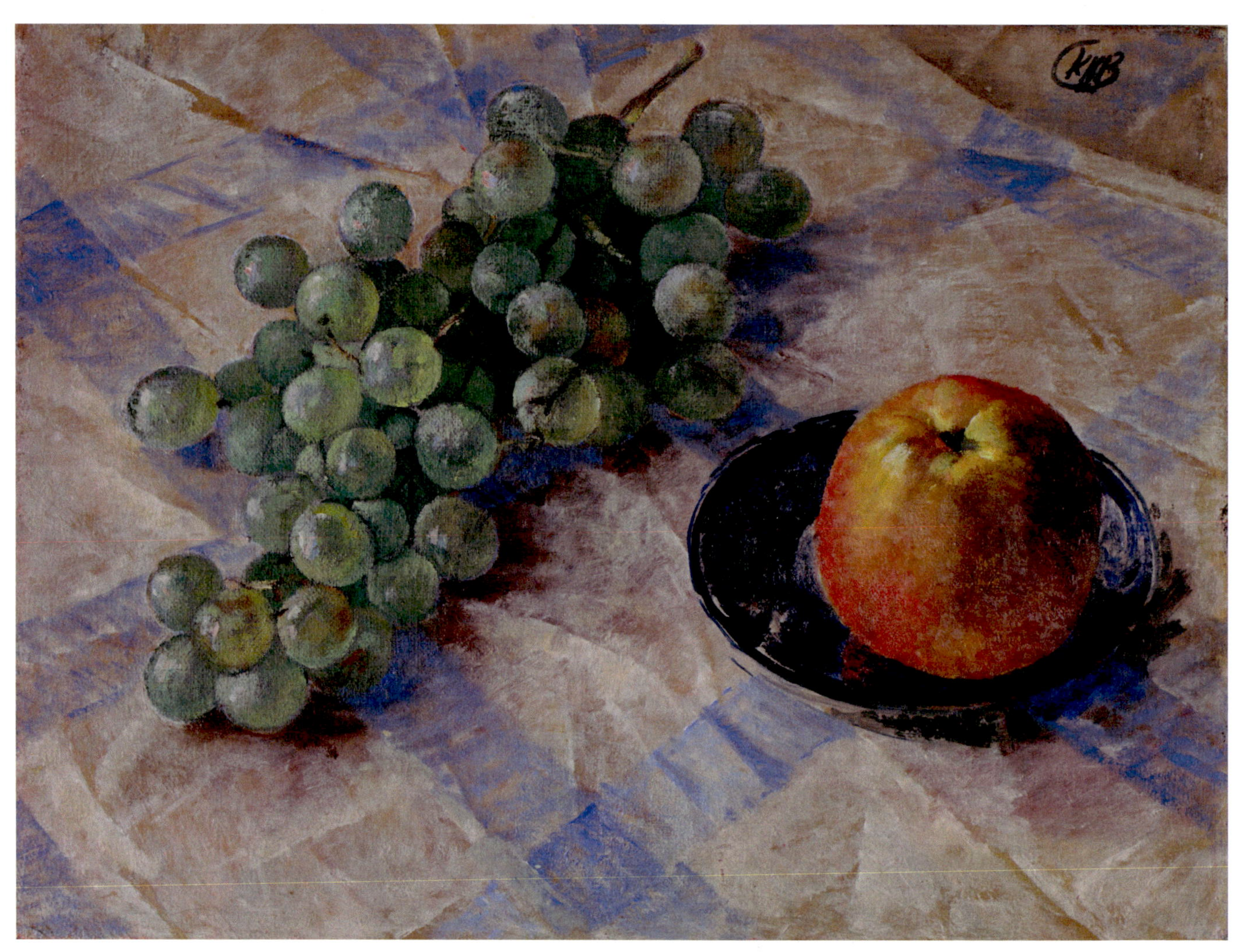

PETROV-VODKIN Kuzma Sergeevich | *Grapes and Apple*
1921
Oil on canvas, 37.5 × 48 cm
Perm State Art Gallery

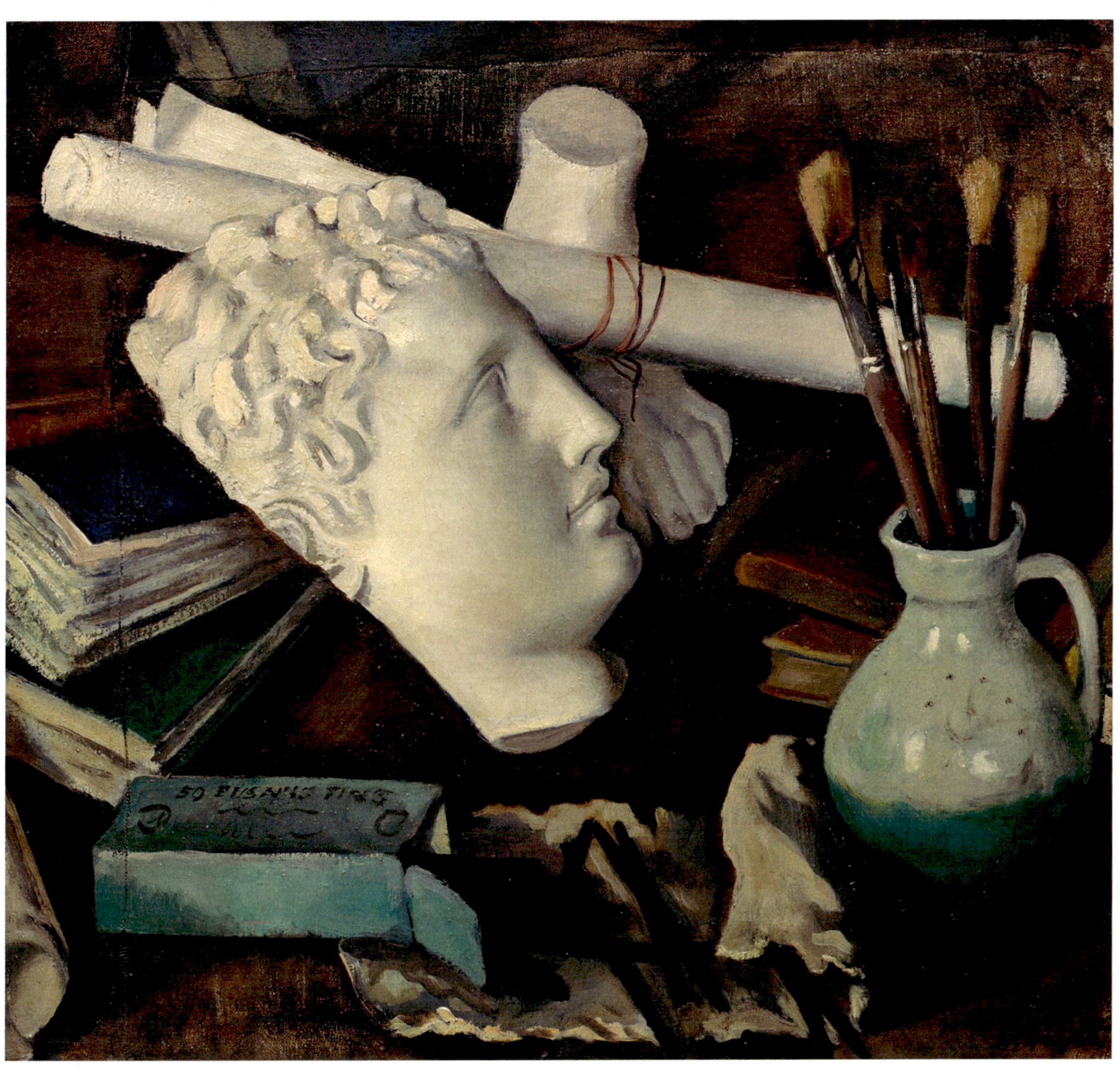

SEREBRIAKOVA Zinaida Yevgenyevna | *Still Life with Art Paraphernalia*
1922
Oil on canvas, 59 × 62.2 cm
Yaroslavl Art Museum

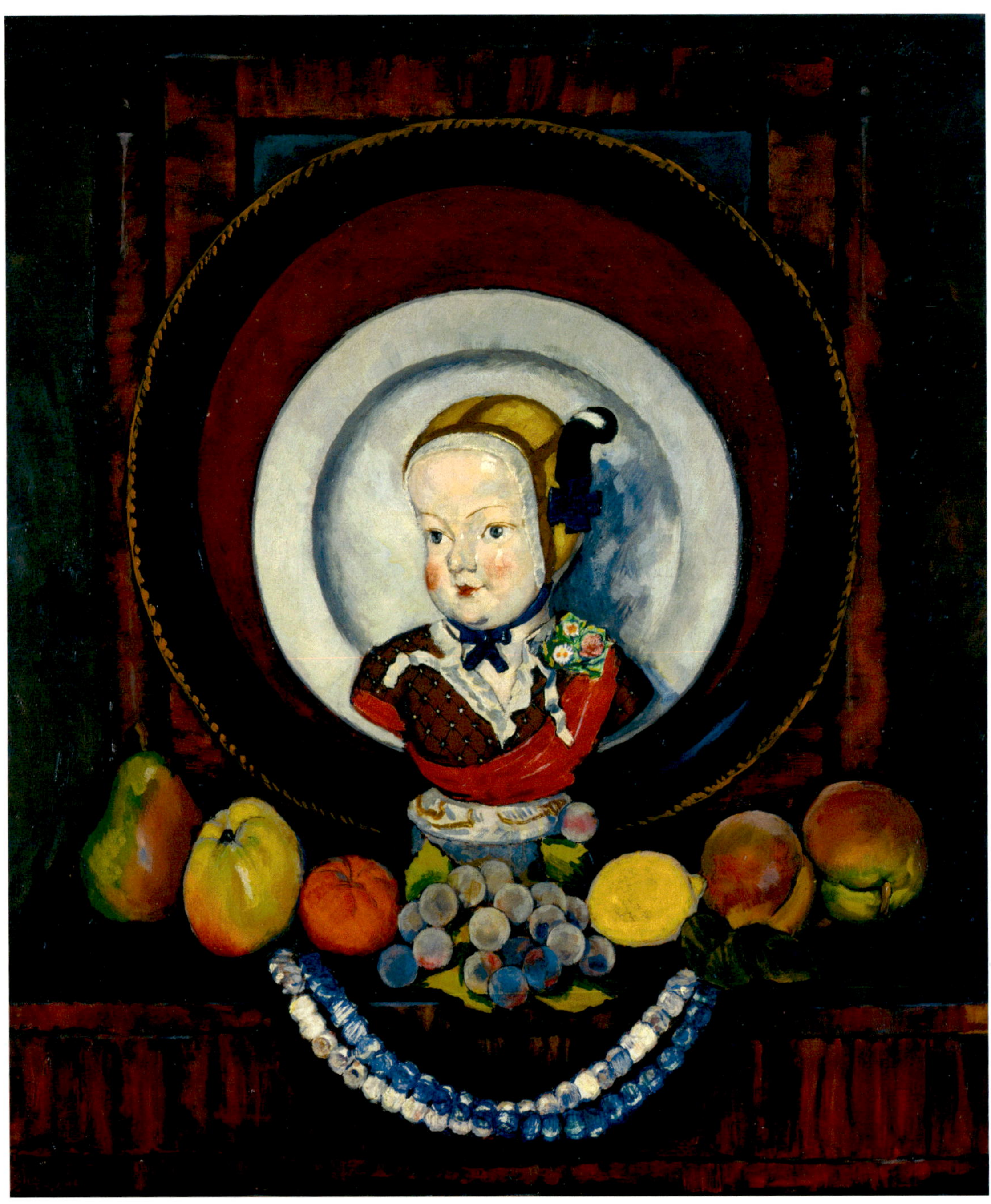

MASHKOV Ilya Ivanovich | *Still Life with a Doll*
1922
Oil on canvas, 96 × 76 cm
Kiev National Picture Gallery

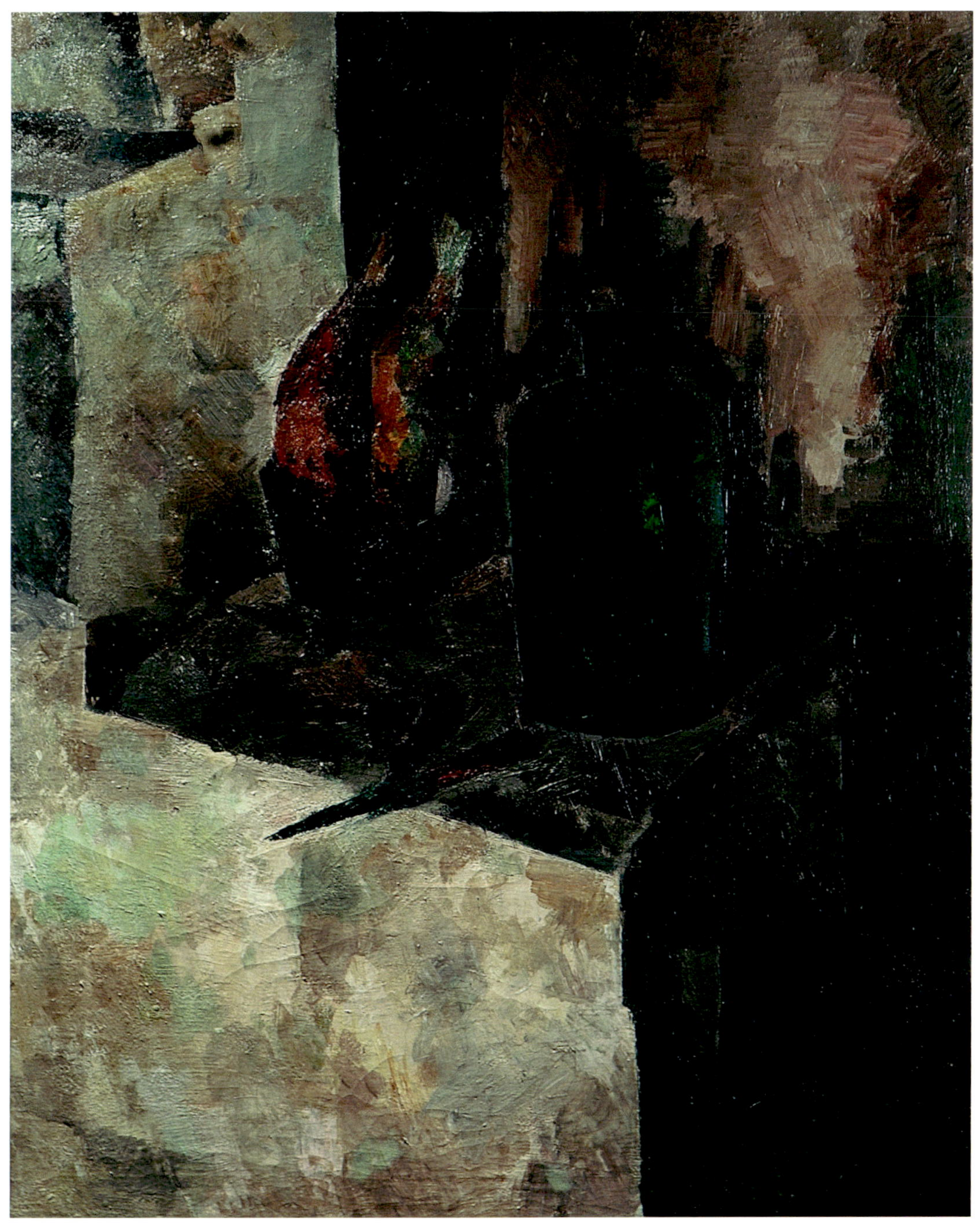

FALK Robert Rafailovich | *Stove*
1922
Oil on canvas, 115 × 90 cm
Yaroslavl Art Museum

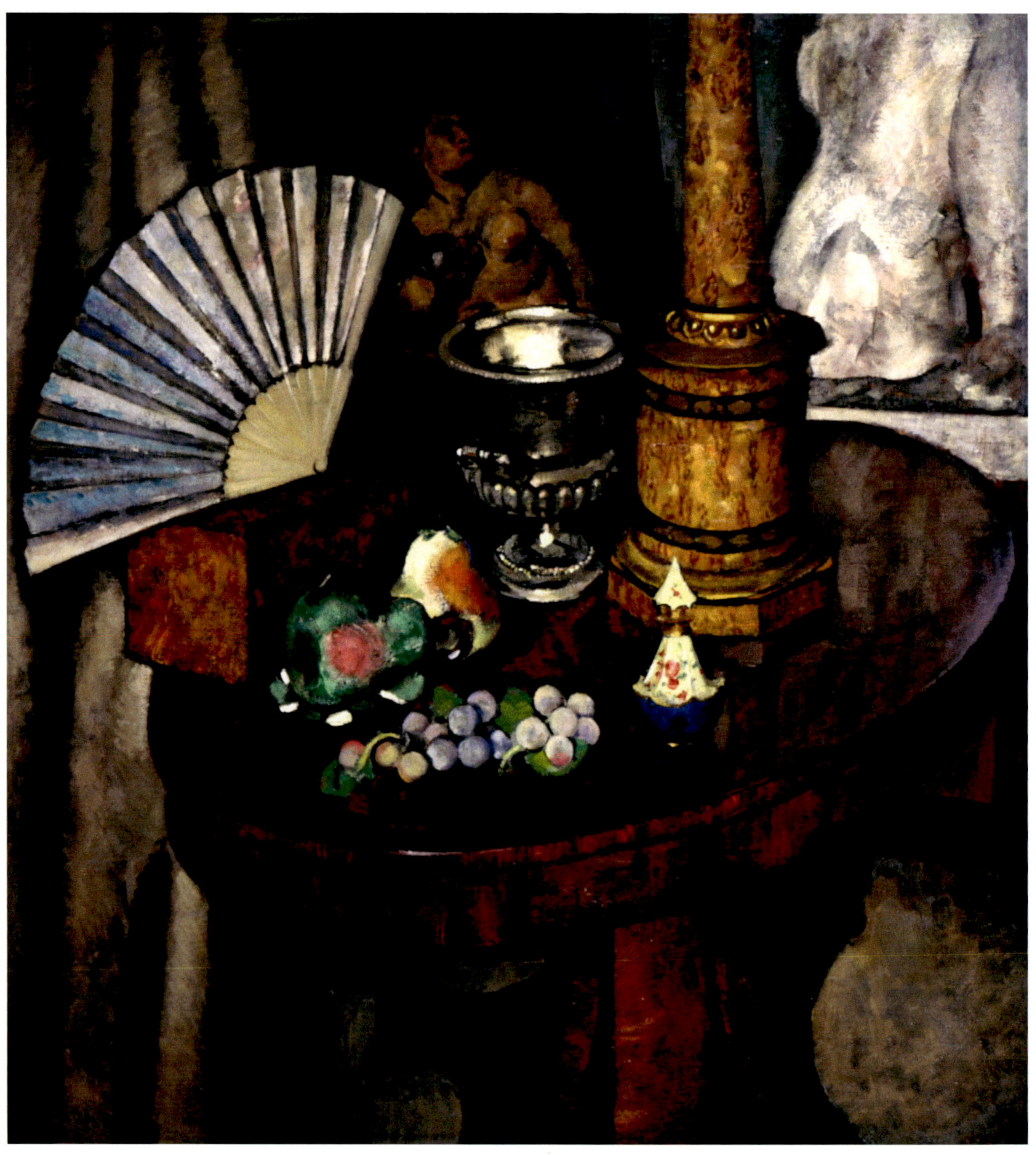

MASHKOV Ilya Ivanovich | *Still Life with Fan*
1922
Oil on canvas, 145 × 127.5 cm
The State Russian Museum, St Petersburg

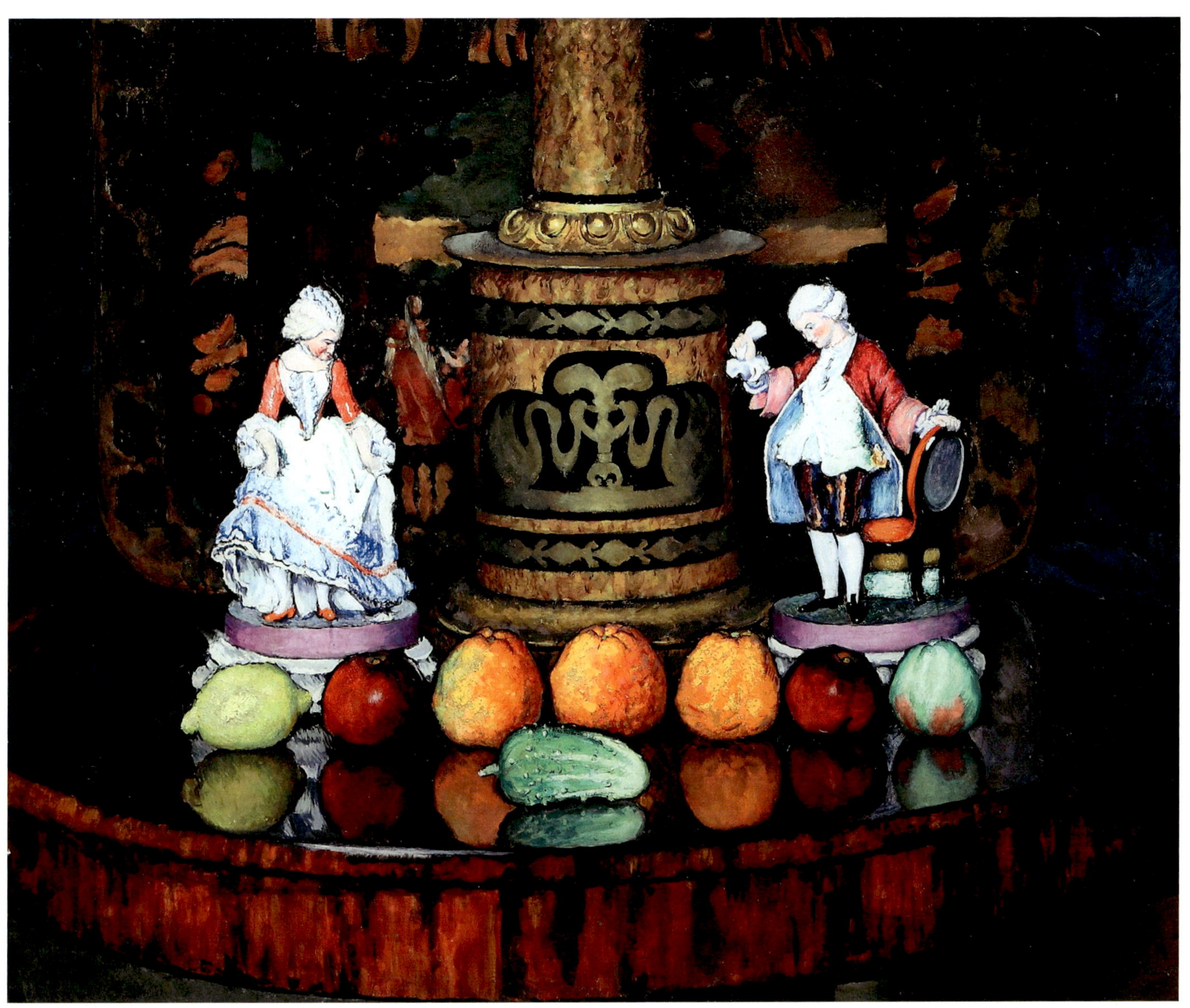

MASHKOV Ilya Ivanovich | *Still Life with Figurines*
1922
Oil on canvas, 97.9 × 113.5 cm
Yaroslavl Art Museum

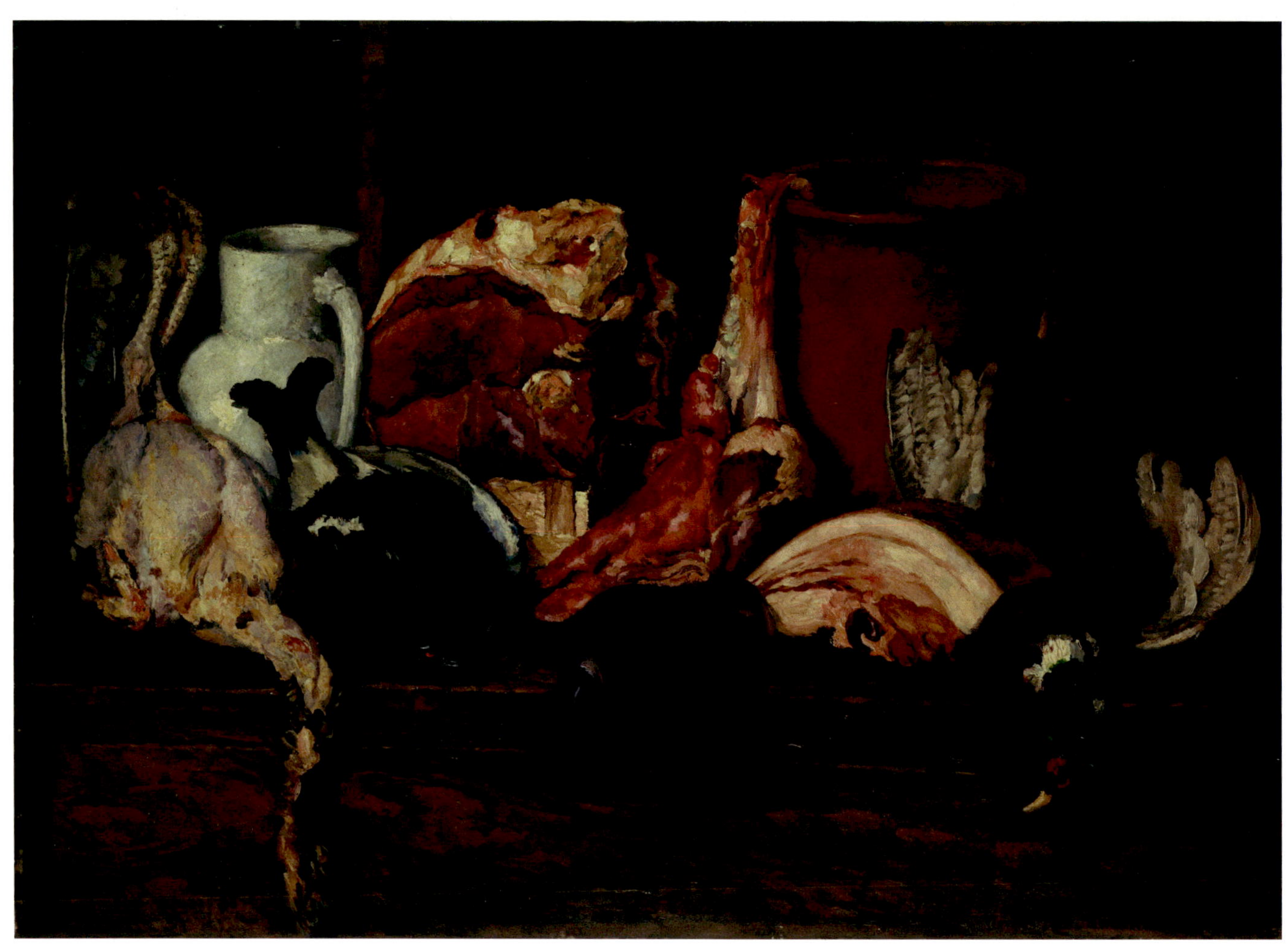

MASHKOV Ilya Ivanovich | *Moscow Food, Meat and Game*
1924
Oil on canvas, 87 × 120 cm
The State Tretyakov Gallery, Moscow

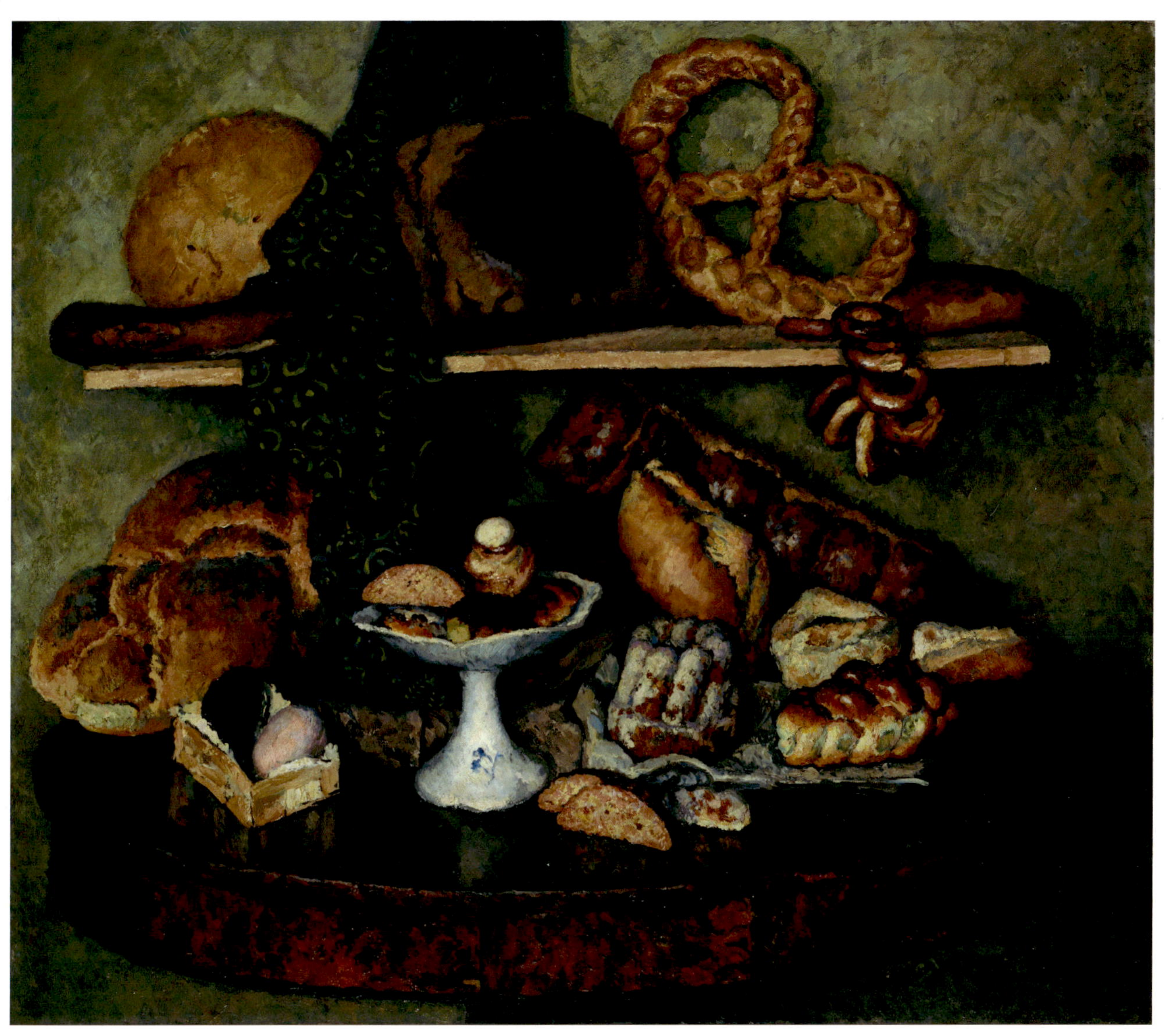

MASHKOV Ilya Ivanovich | *Moscow Food, Bread*
1924
Oil on canvas, 129 × 145 cm
The State Tretyakov Gallery, Moscow

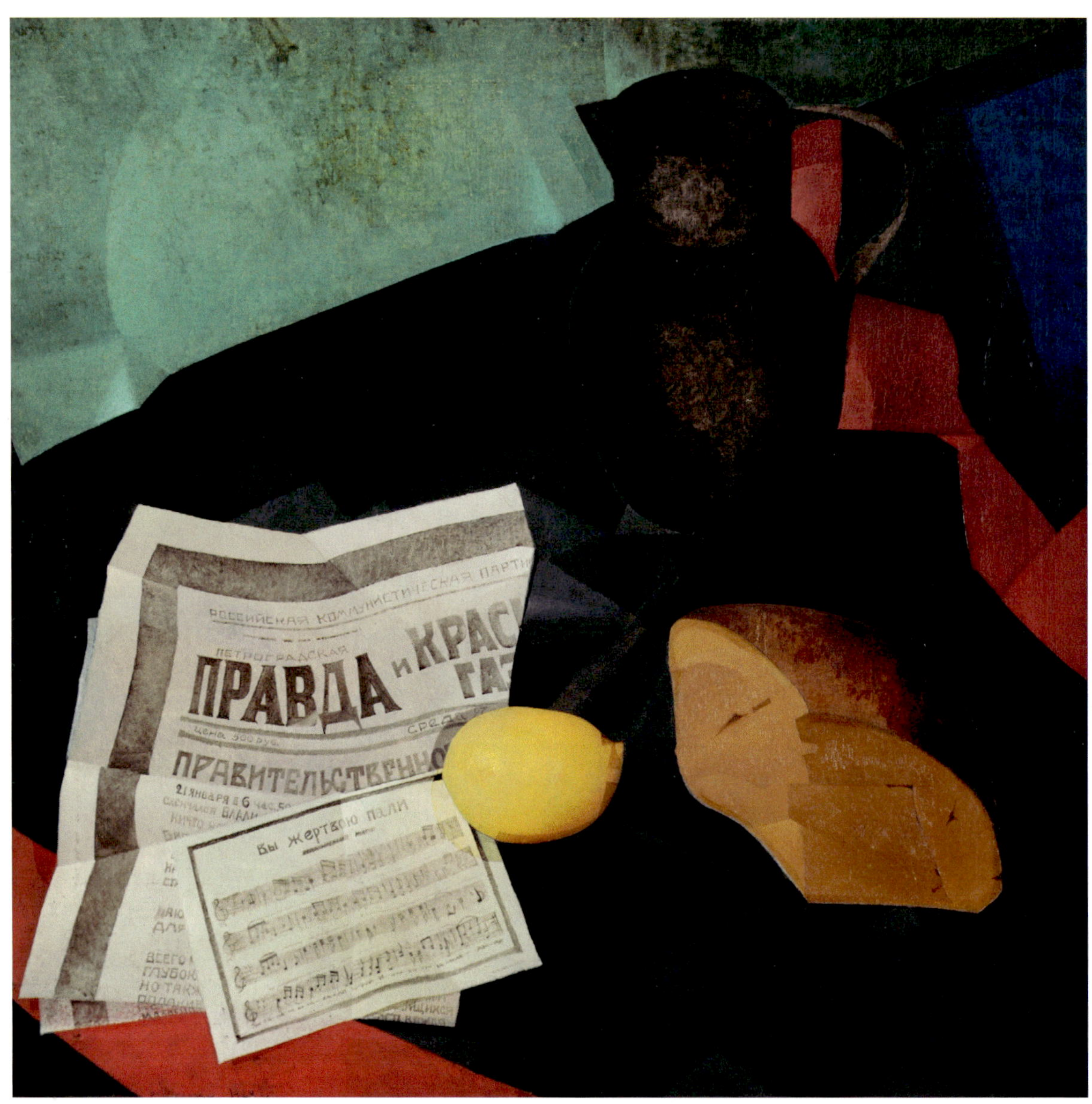

MALAGIS Vladimir Ilyich | *Still Life 'Mourning'*
1924
Oil on canvas, 74 × 74 cm
The State Russian Museum, St Petersburg

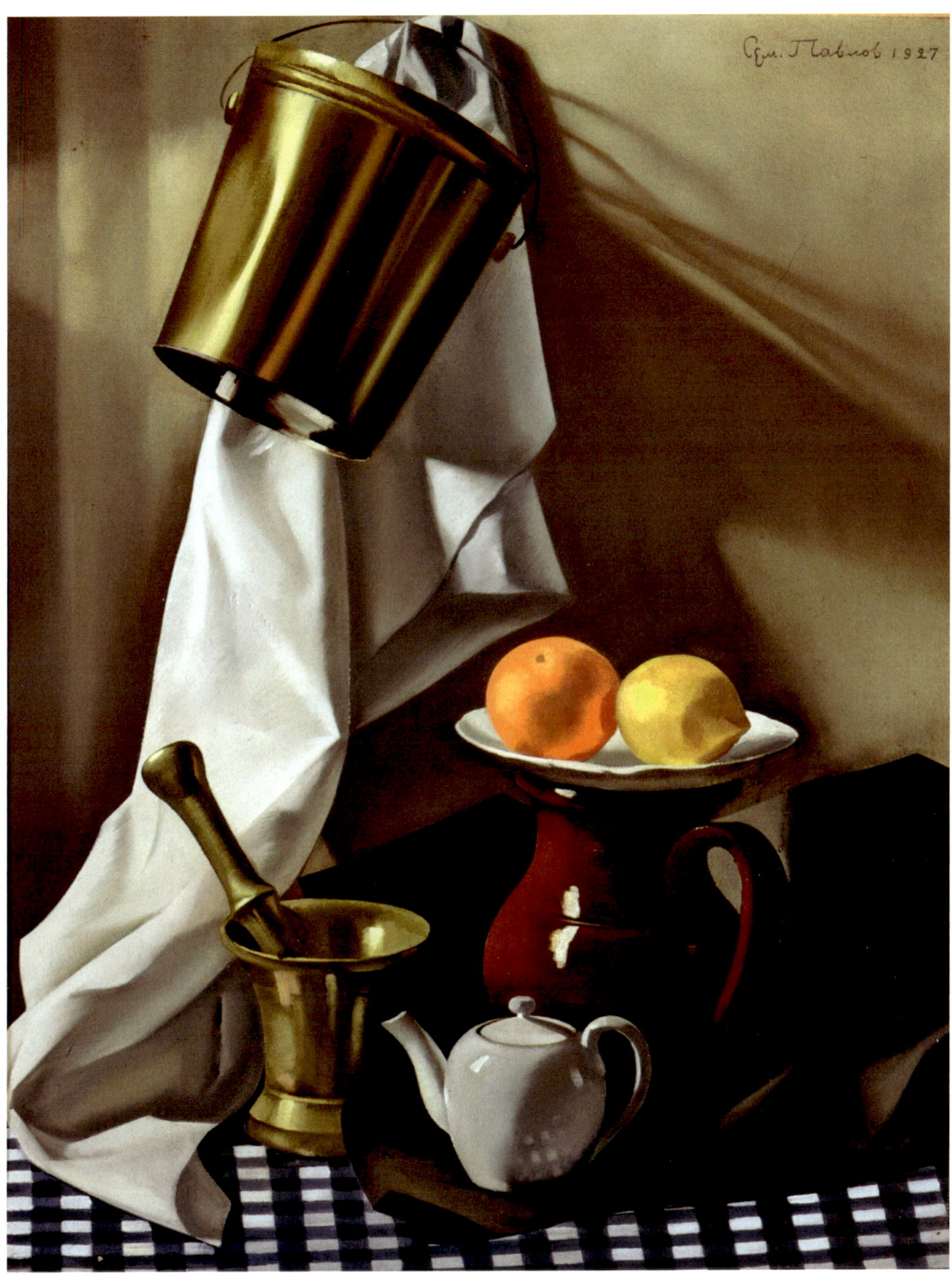

PAVLOV Semyon Andreevich | *Still Life*
1927
Oil on canvas, 86 × 66 cm
The State Russian Museum, St Petersburg

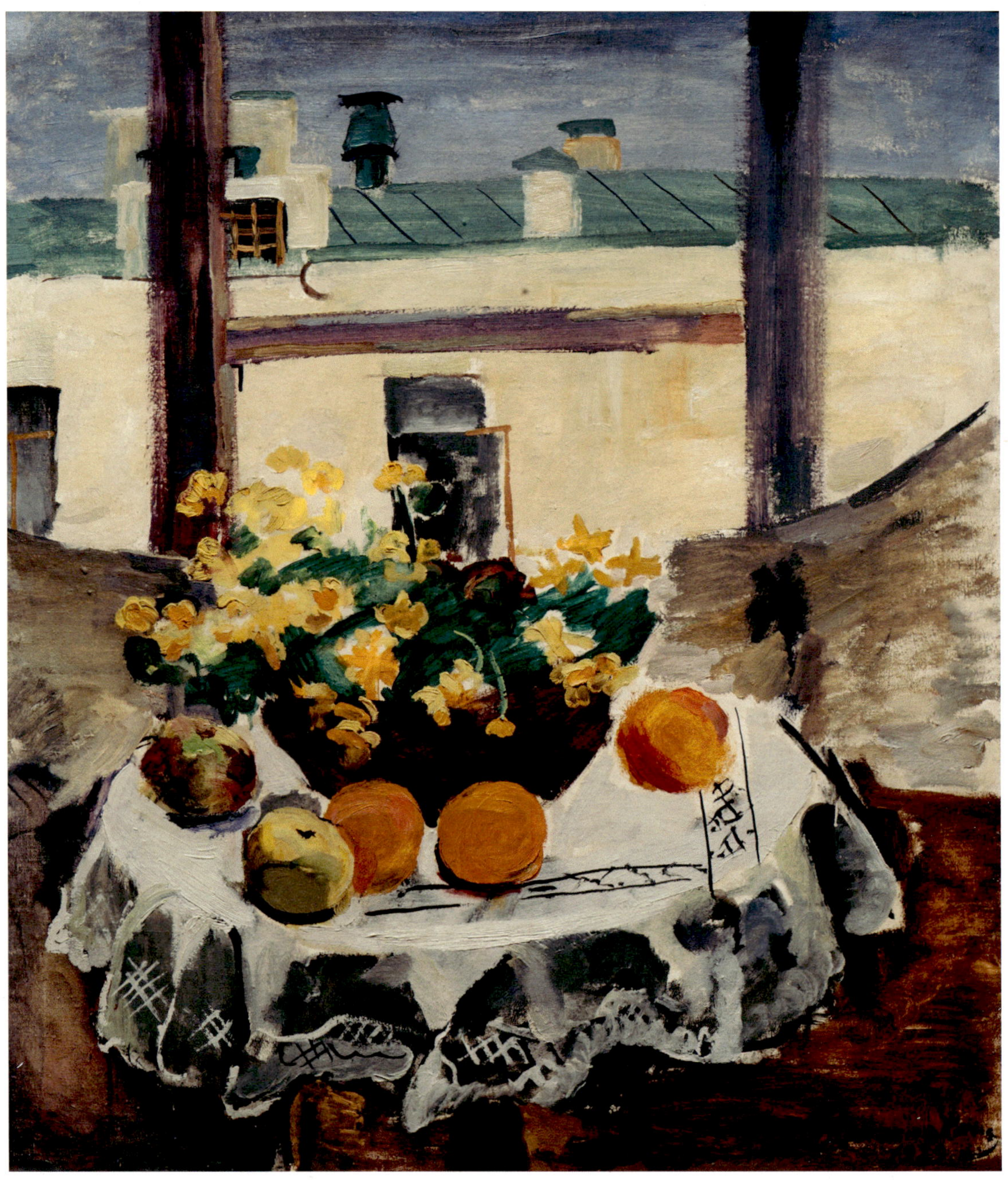

KONCHALOVSKY Petr Petrovich | *Table with Fruit and Yellow Flowers*
1929
Oil on canvas, 96 × 82 cm
The State Russian Museum, St Petersburg

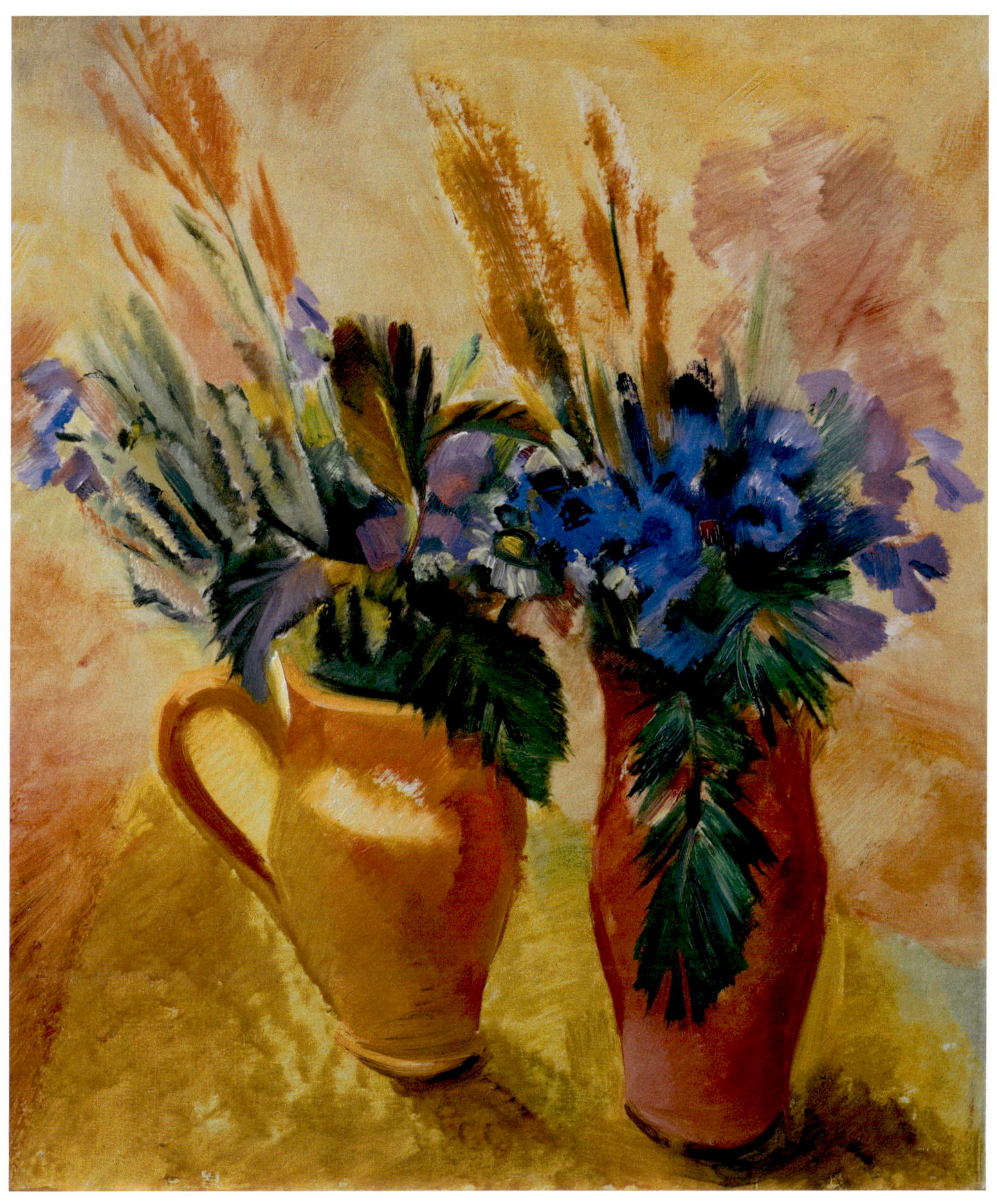

TYRSA Nikolai Andreevich | *Flowers in Two Vases*
1930
Oil on canvas, 53.5 × 44.5 cm
The State Russian Museum, St Petersburg

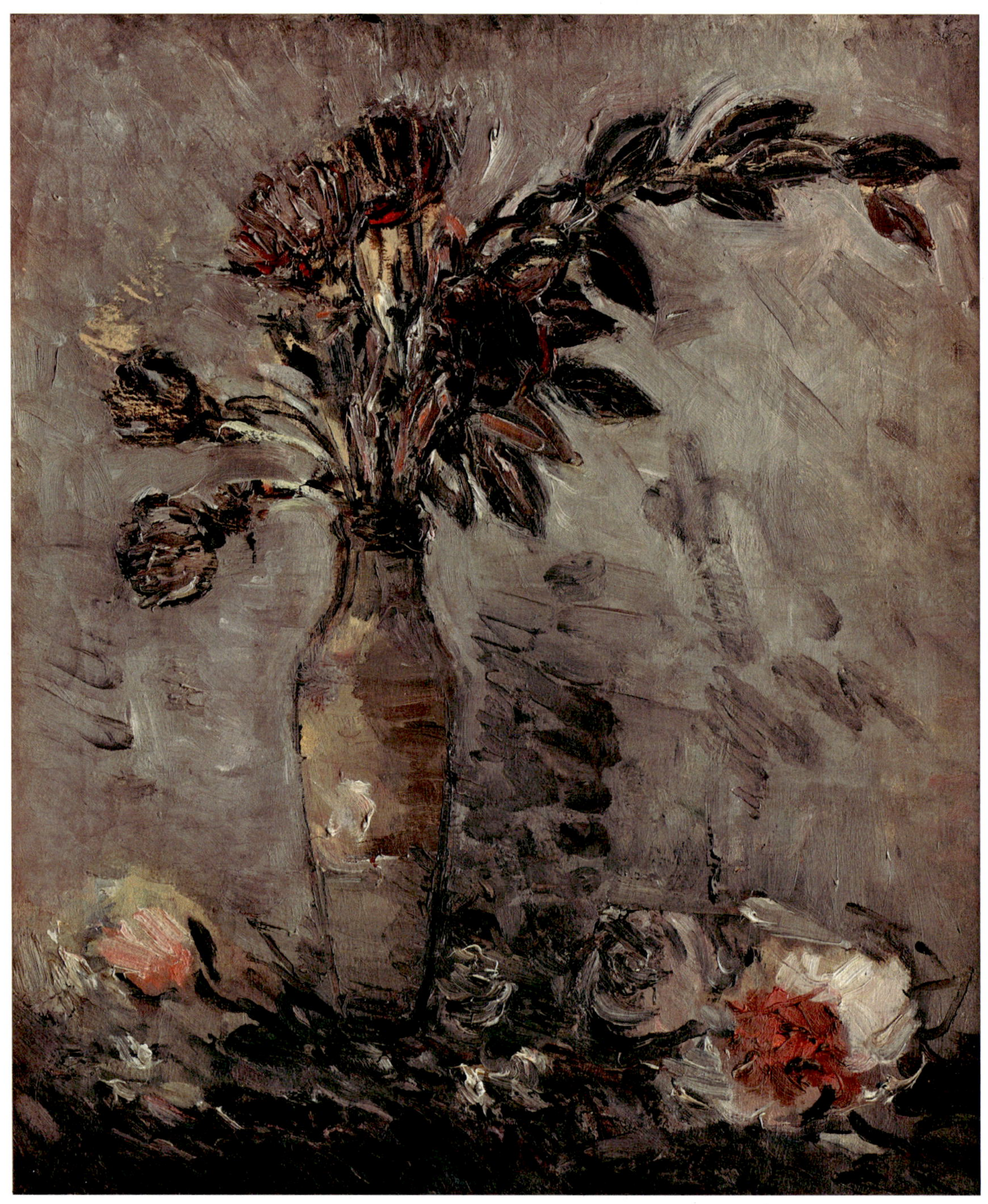

SOKOLOV Mikhail Ksenofontovitch | *Still Life, Flowers*
1930s
Oil on canvas, 62 × 50.2 cm
Yaroslavl Art Museum

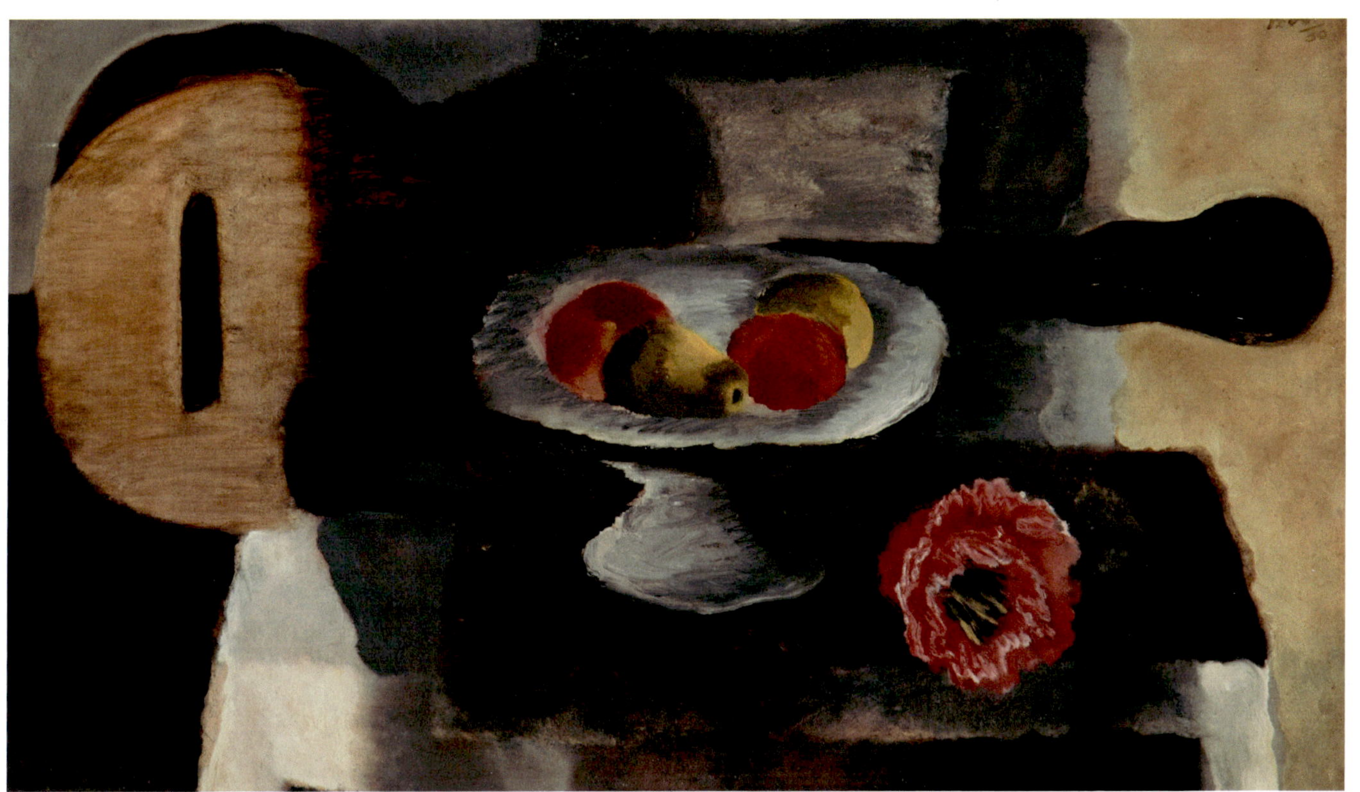

LEBEDEV Vladimir Vasilyevich | *Guitar and Poppy*
1930
Oil on cardboard, 46 × 77 cm
The State Russian Museum, St Petersburg

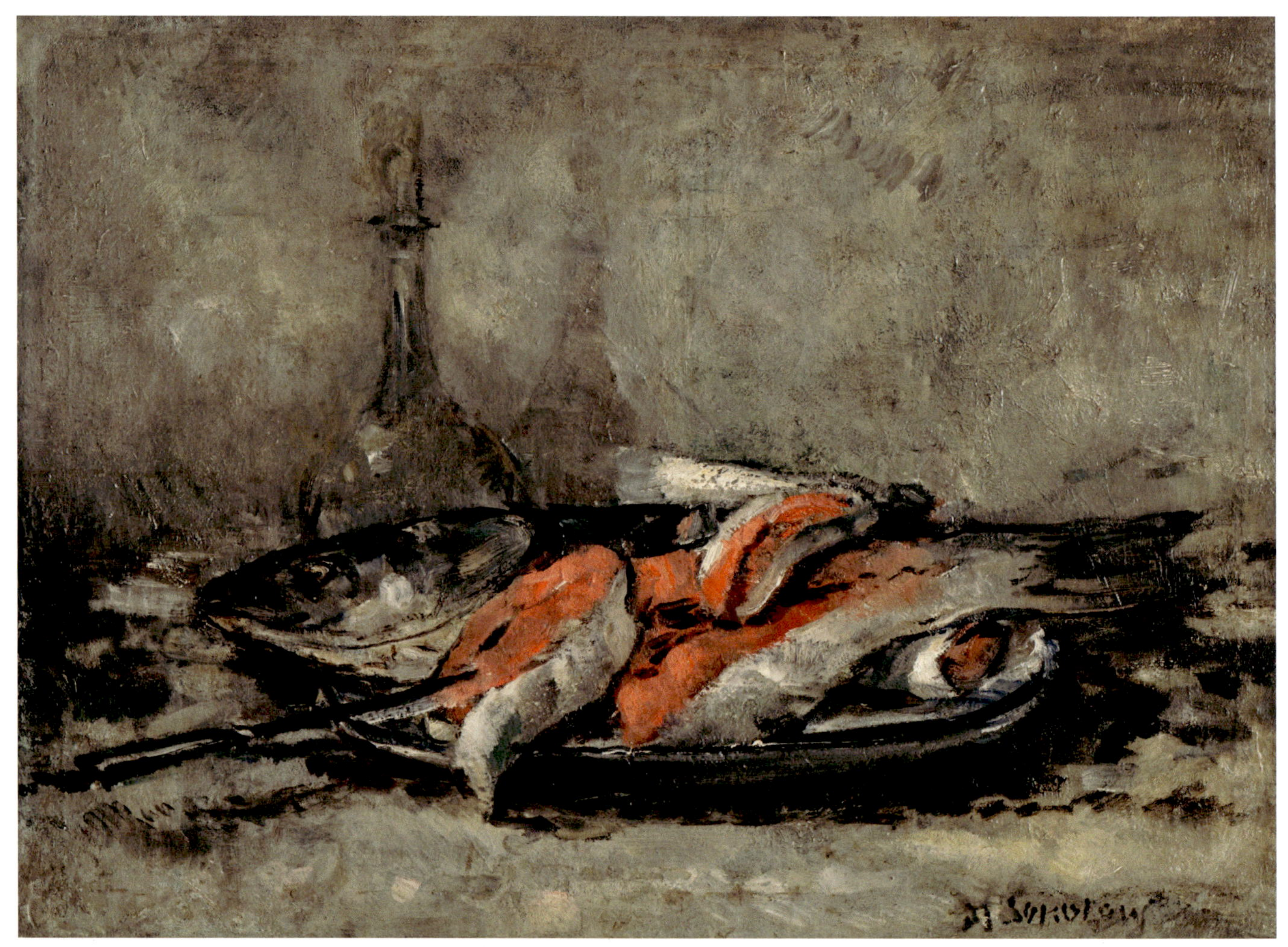

SOKOLOV Mikhail Ksenofontovitch | *Still Life with Fish*
1930s
Oil on canvas, 52.7 × 70.5 cm
The State Russian Museum, St Petersburg

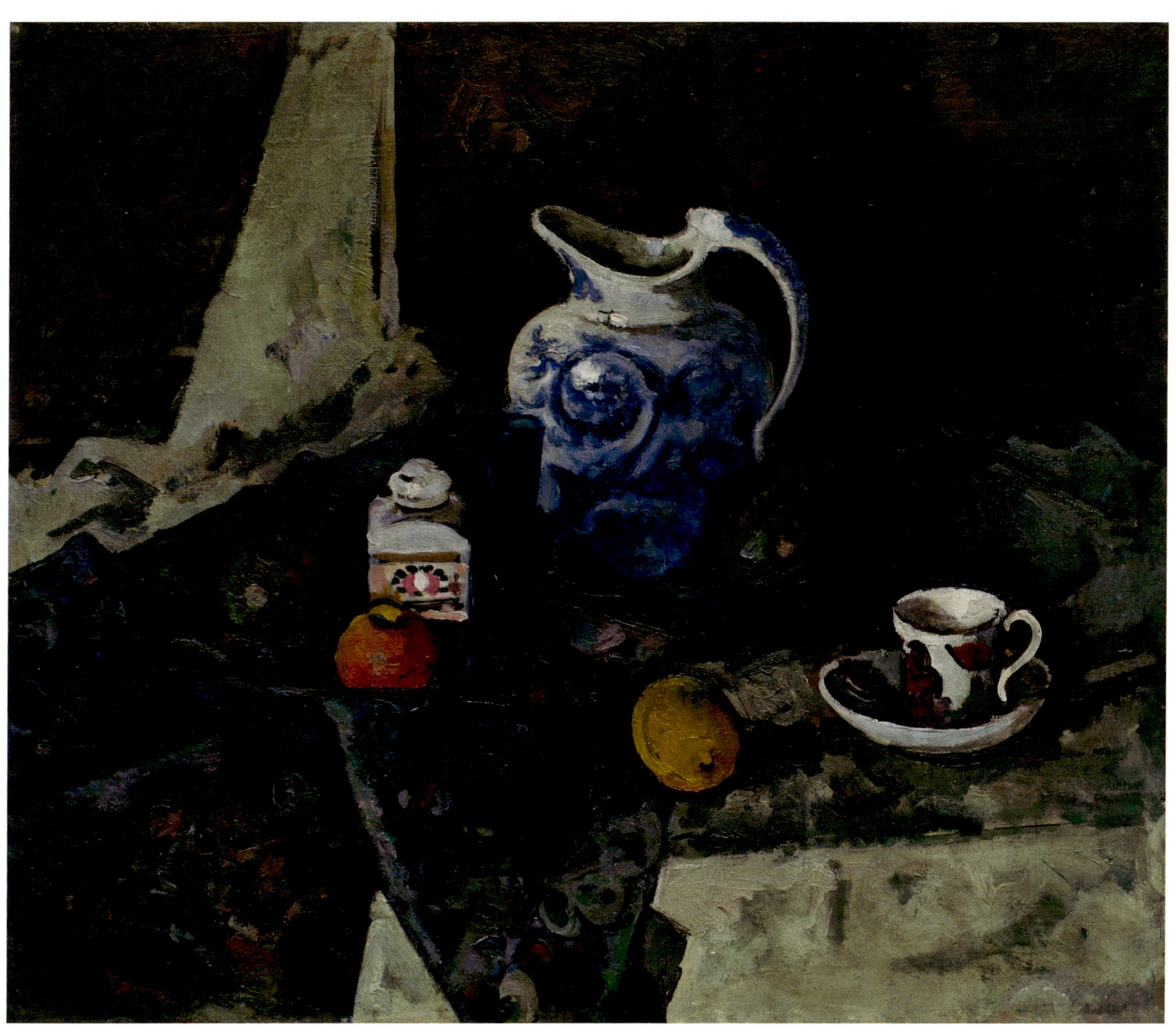

KUPRIN Aleksandr Vasilievich | *Still Life with a Blue Jug*
1931
Oil on canvas, 100 × 115 cm
Irkutsk Regional ArtMuseum named after
V. P. Sukachov

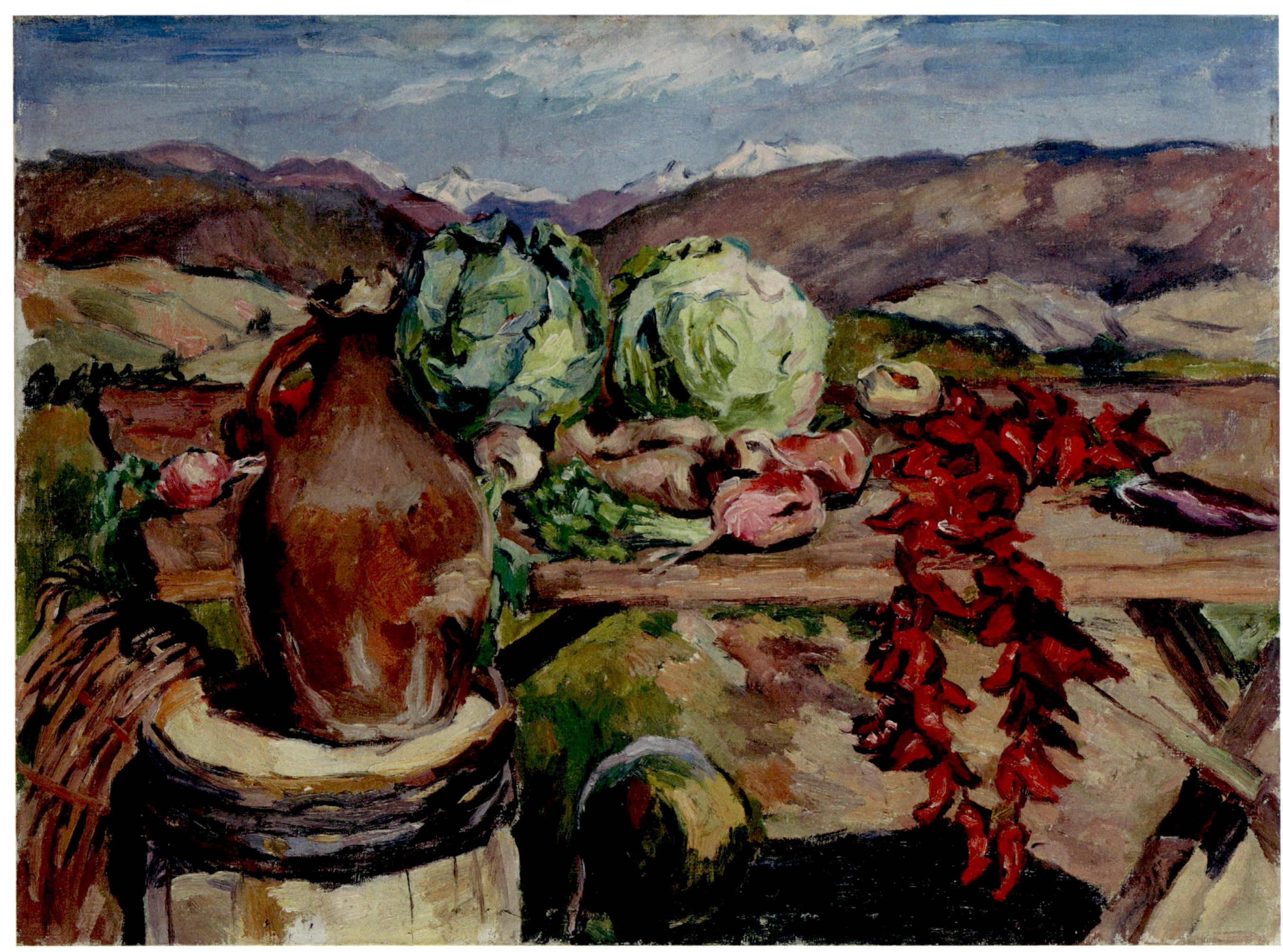

LENTULOV Aristarkh Vasilyevich | *Vegetables*
1932
Oil on canvas, 76 × 103 cm
The State Tretyakov Gallery, Moscow

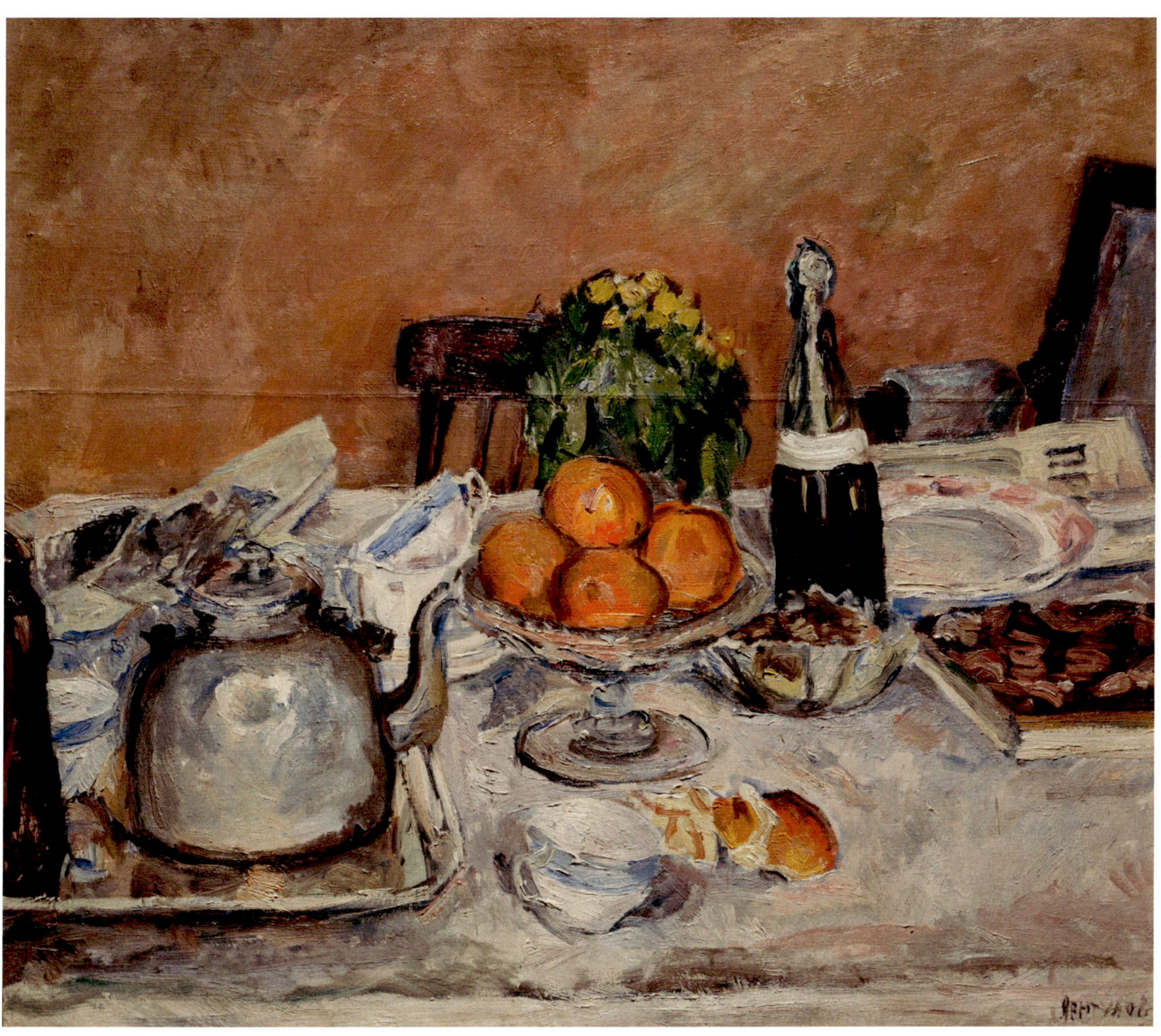

LENTULOV Aristarkh Vasilyevich | *Celebratory Table*
1932
Oil on canvas, 85.5 × 95.5 cm
The State Russian Museum, St Petersburg

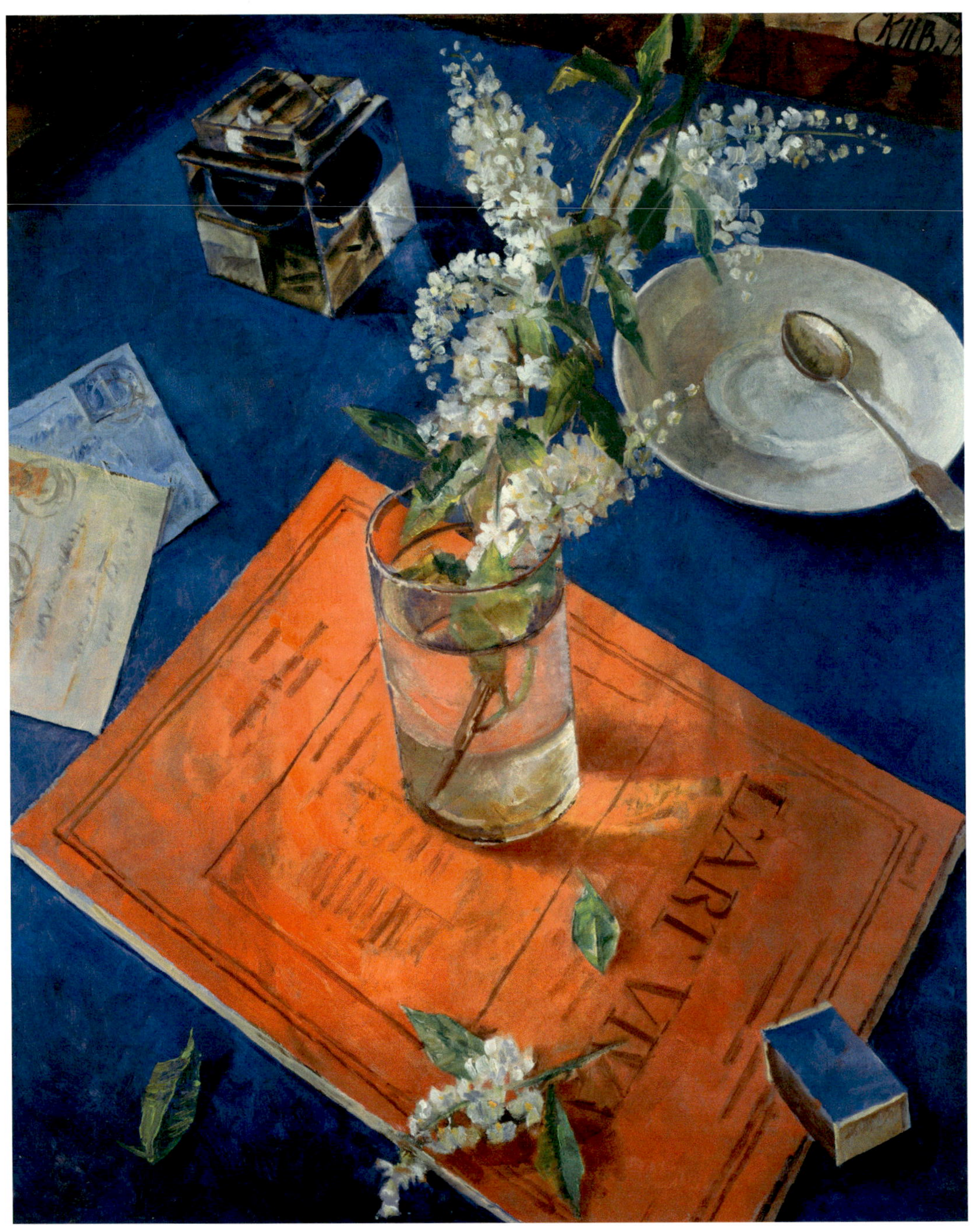

PETROV-VODKIN Kuzma Sergeevich | *Bird Cherry Blossom in a Glass*
1932
Oil on canvas, 73 × 60 cm
The State Russian Museum, St Petersburg

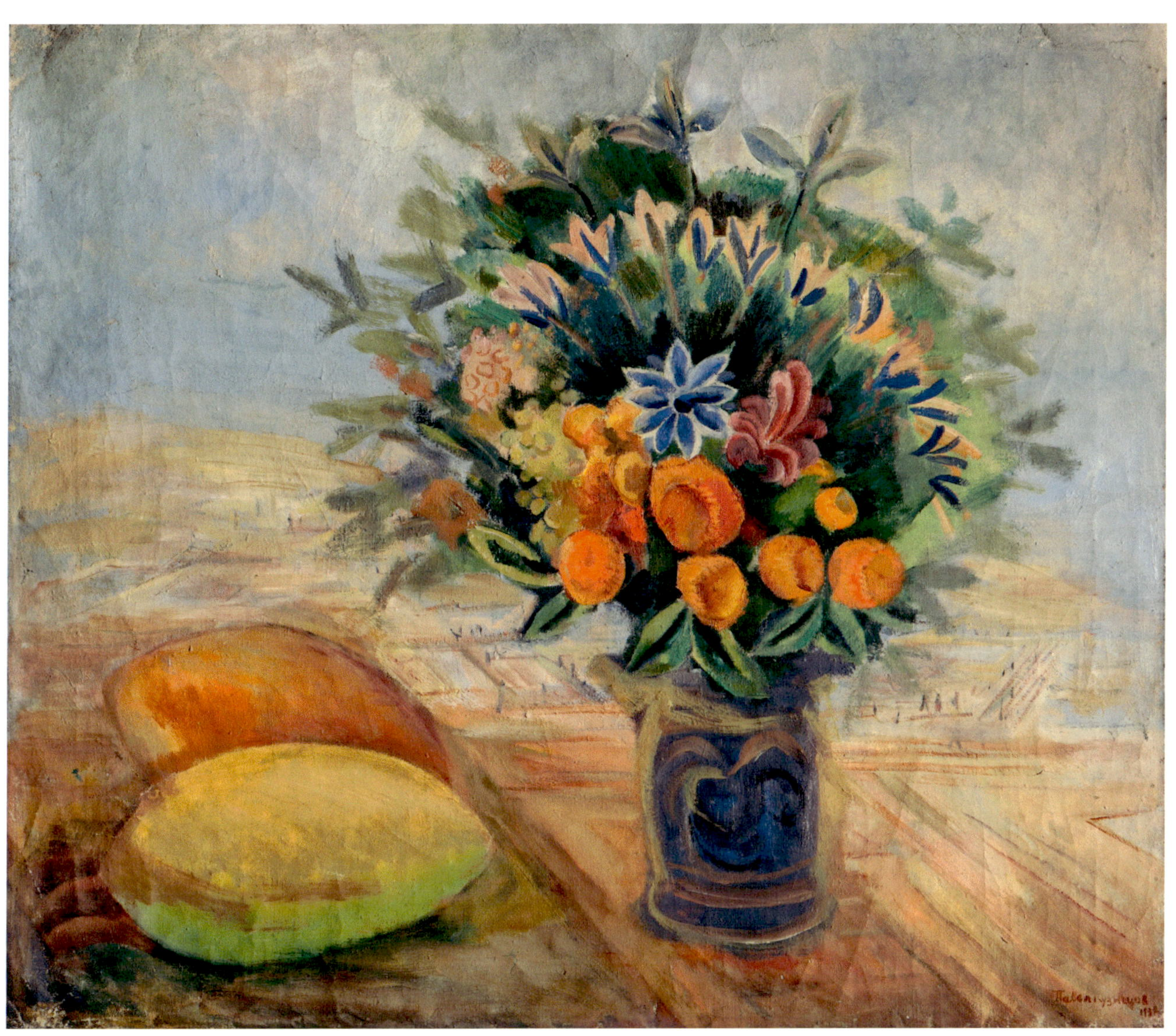

KUZNETZOV Pavel Varfolomevich | *Flowers and Melons*
1932
Oil on canvas, 78 × 90 cm
The State Russian Museum, St Petersburg

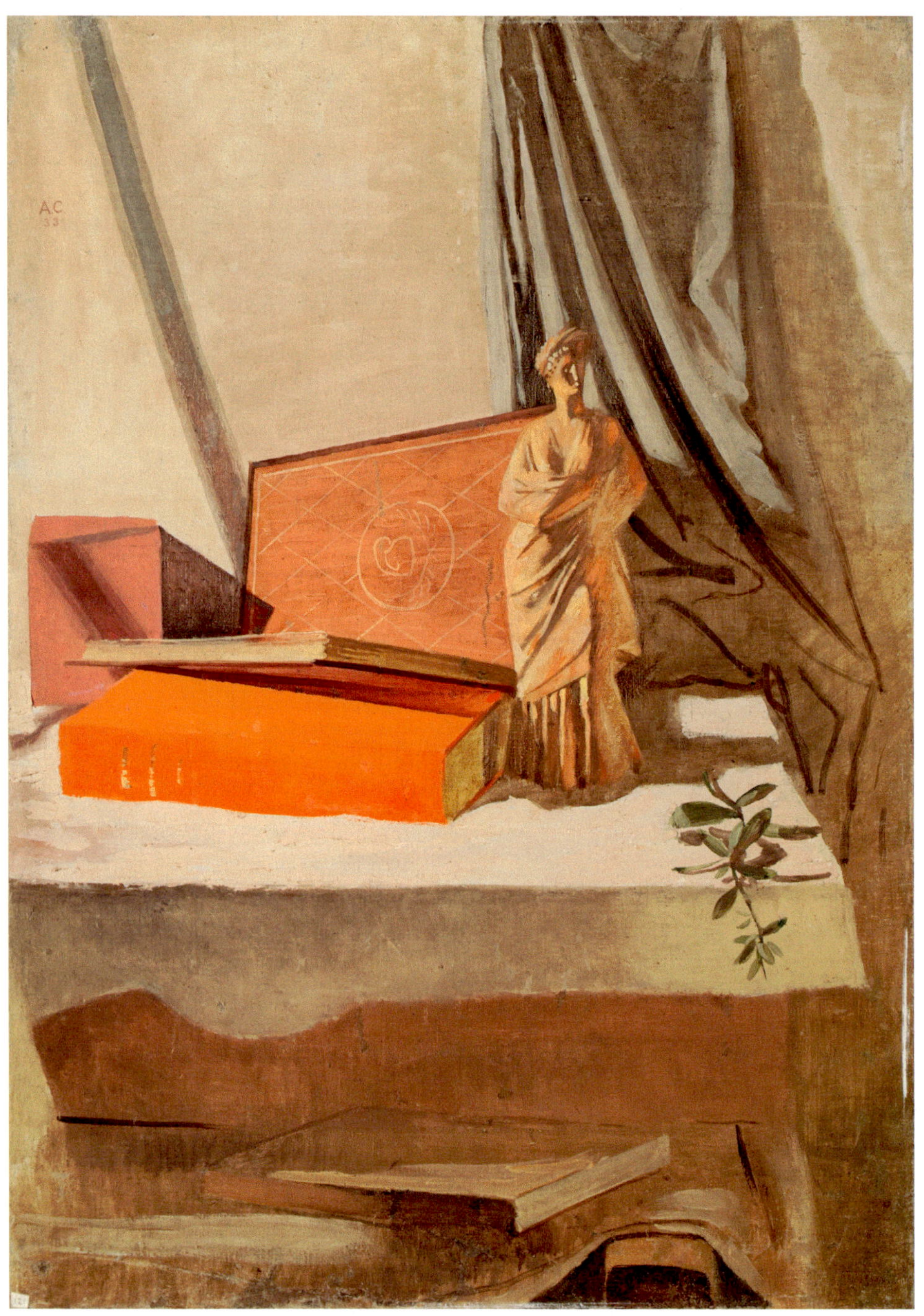

SAMOKHVALOV Alexander Nikolayevich | *Still Life with Sculpture*
1933
Oil on canvas, 97.5 × 67.5 cm
The State Russian Museum, St Petersburg

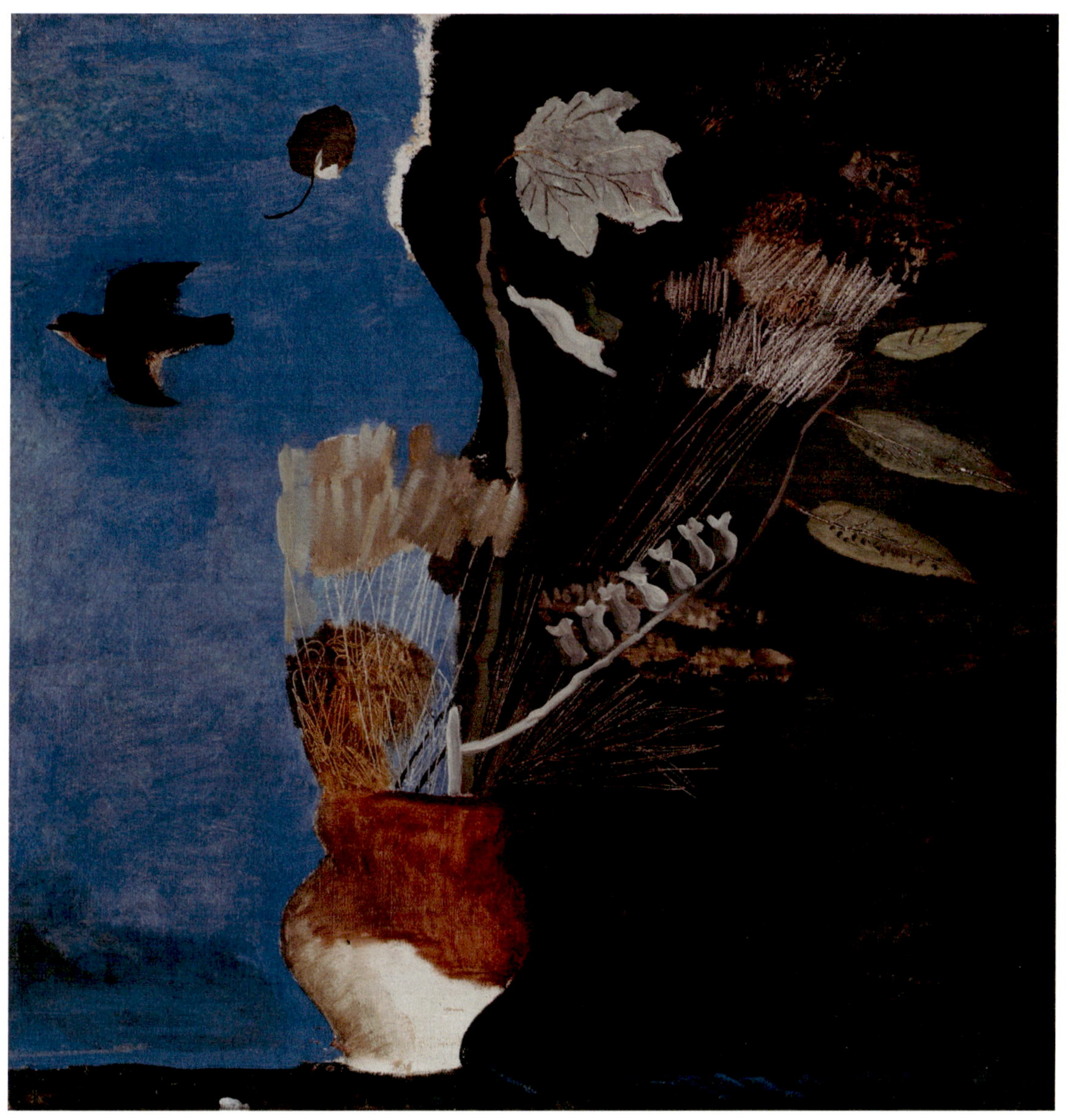

DEINEKA Aleksandr Aleksandrovich | *Dried Leaves*
1933
Oil on canvas, 66 × 61.5 cm
Kursk State Picture Gallery named after A. A. Deineka

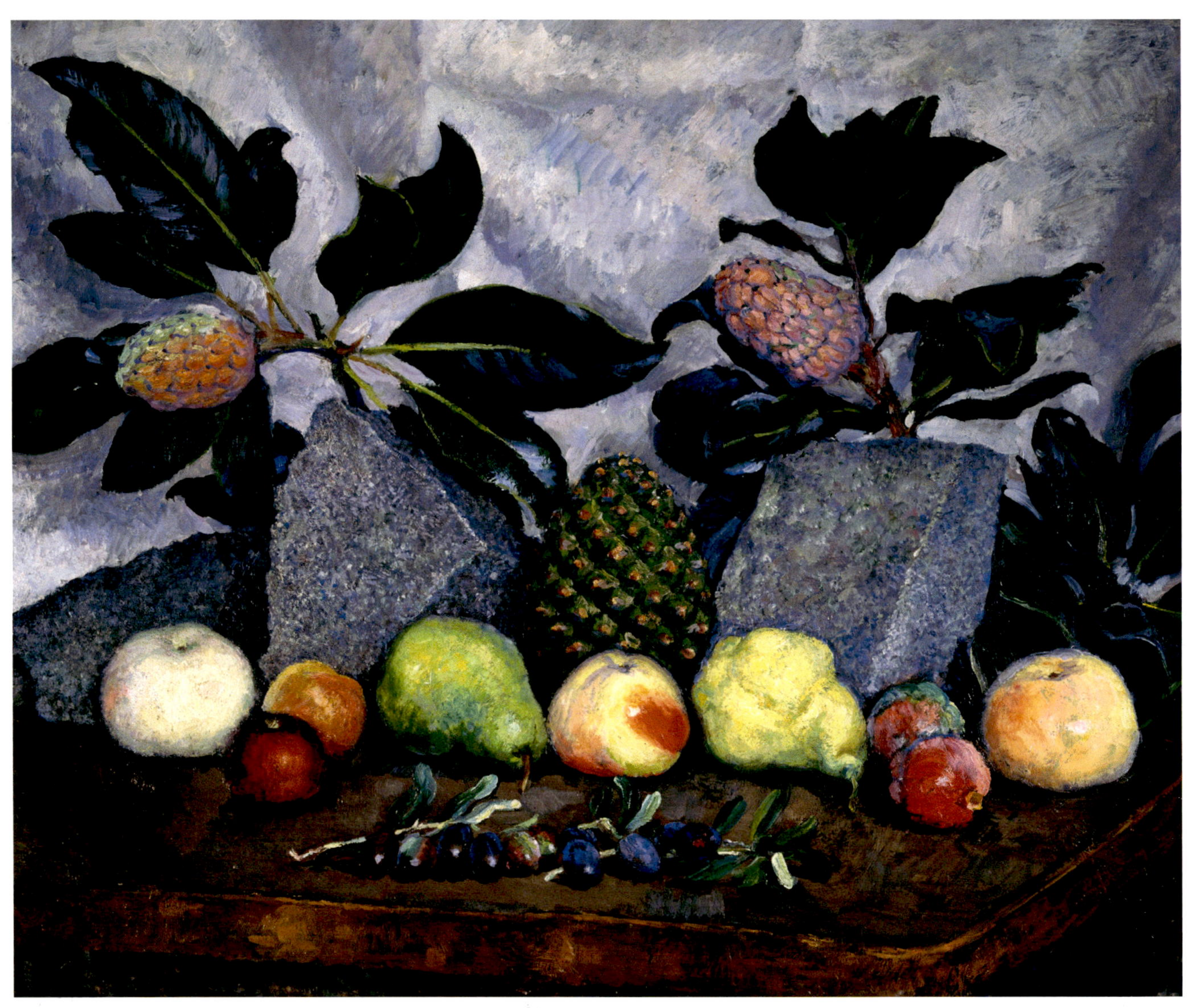

MASHKOV Ilya Ivanovich | *Still Life with Magnolias*
1934
Oil on canvas, 81.5 × 97 cm
The State Russian Museum, St Petersburg

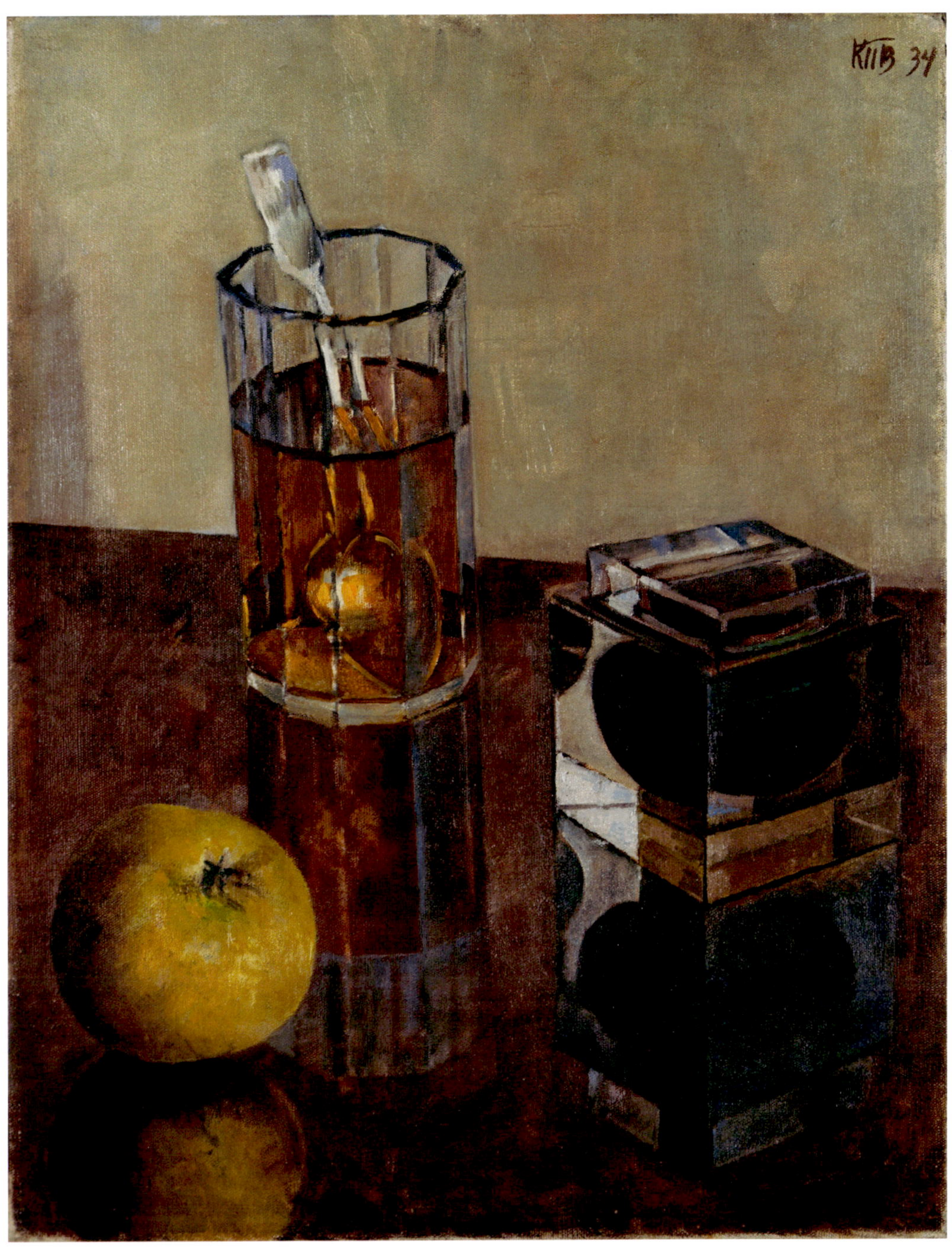

PETROV-VODKIN Kuzma Sergeevich | *Still Life with Inkwell*
1934
Oil on canvas, 48 × 37 cm
The State Russian Museum, St Petersburg

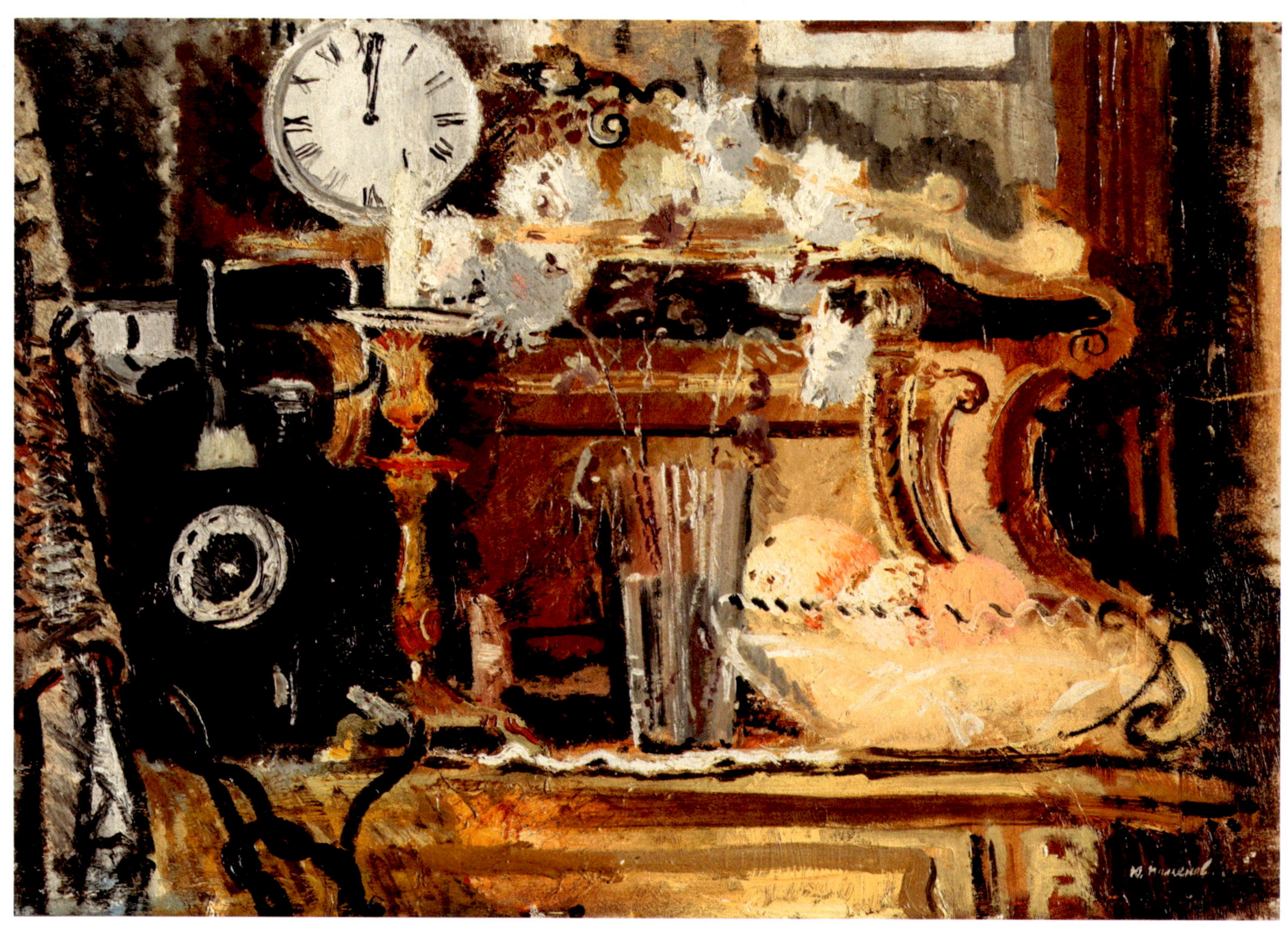

PIMENOV Yury Ivanovich | *Still Life with a Phone*
1934
Oil on canvas on cardboard, 52 × 75 cm
The State Russian Museum, St Petersburg

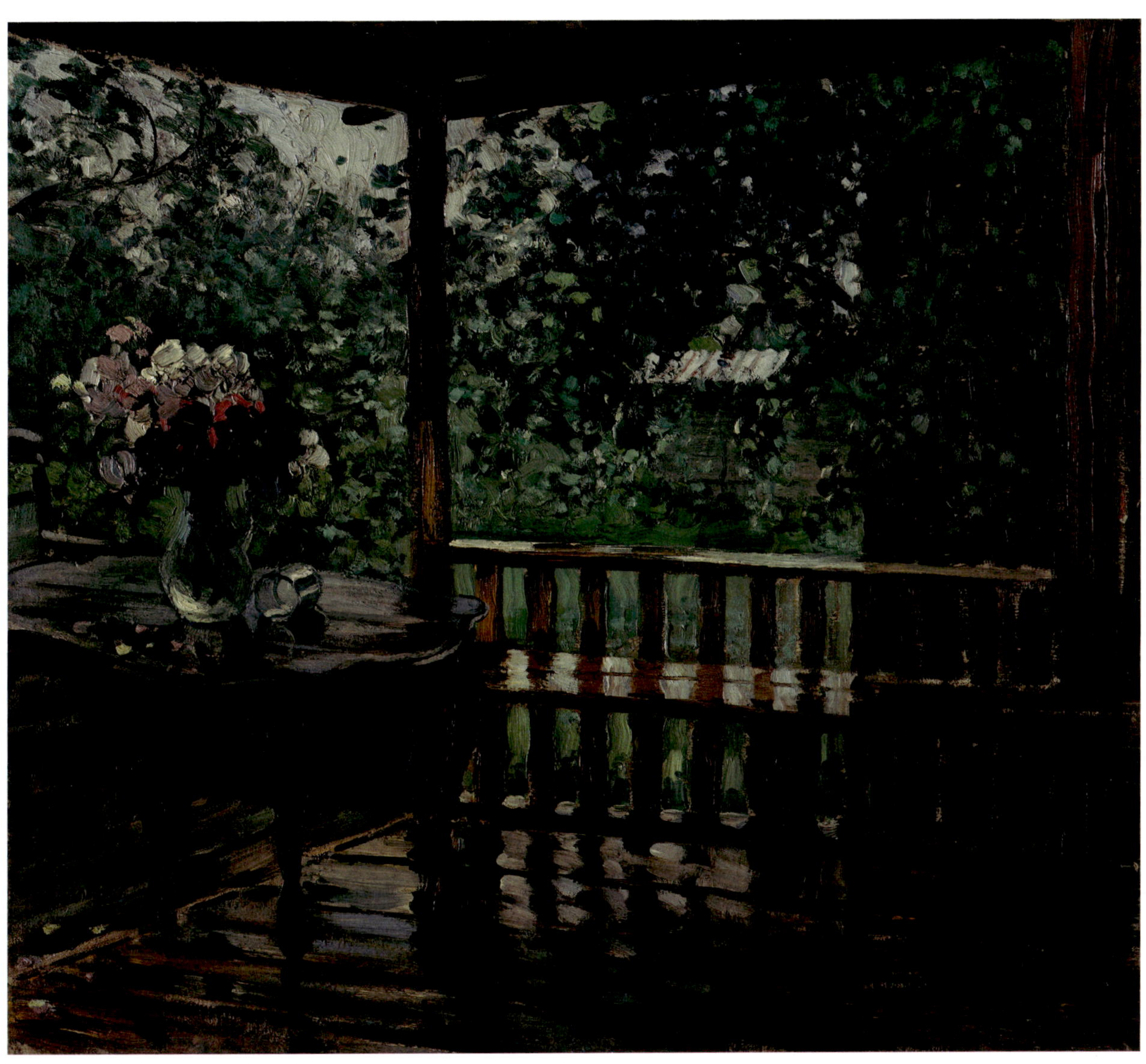

GERASIMOV Aleksandr Mikhaylovich | *After the Rain*
1935
Oil on canvas, 78 × 85 cm
The State Tretyakov Gallery, Moscow

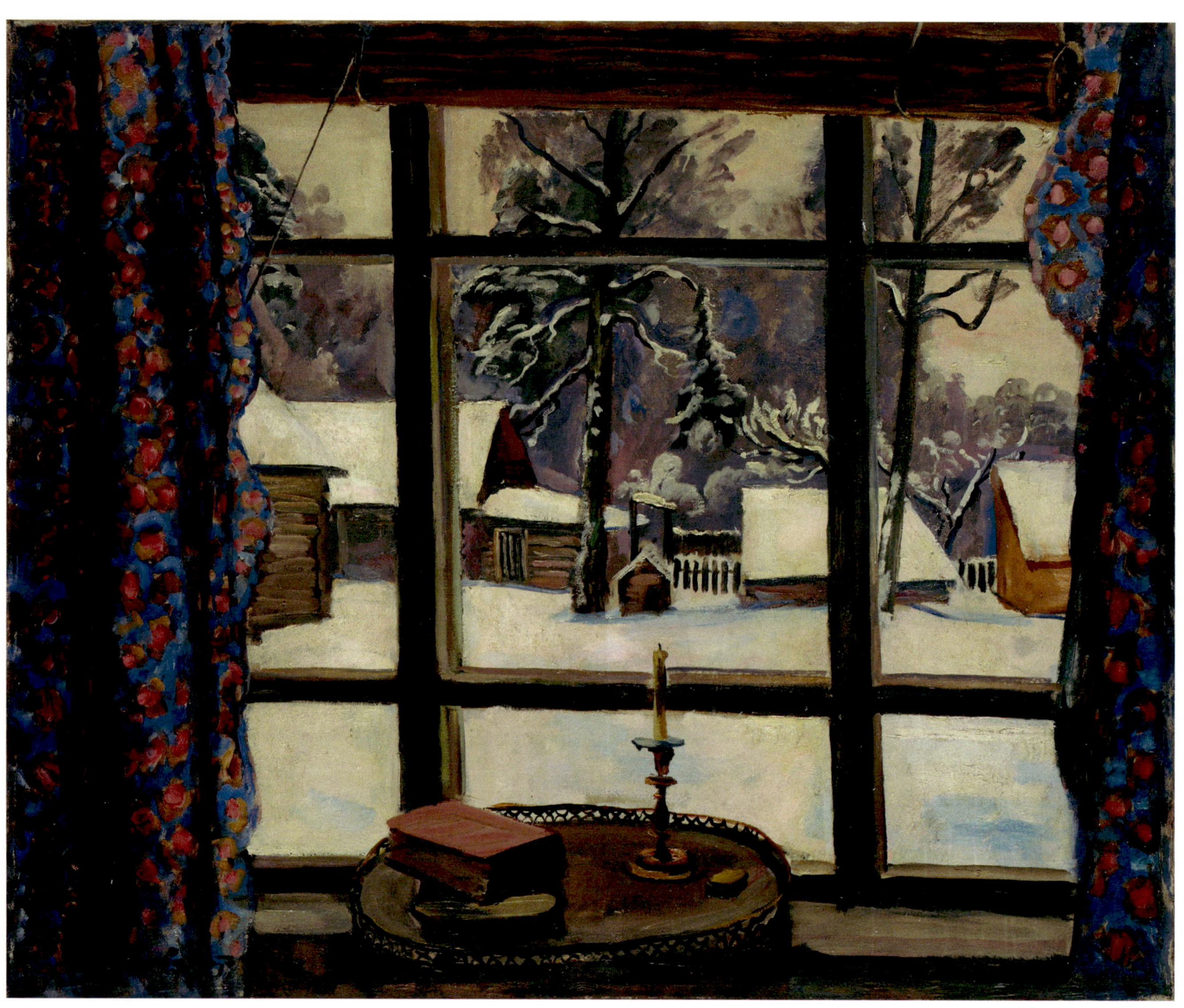

KONCHALOVSKY Petr Petrovich | *Poet's Window*
1935
Oil on canvas, 122 × 134 cm
The State Tretyakov Gallery, Moscow

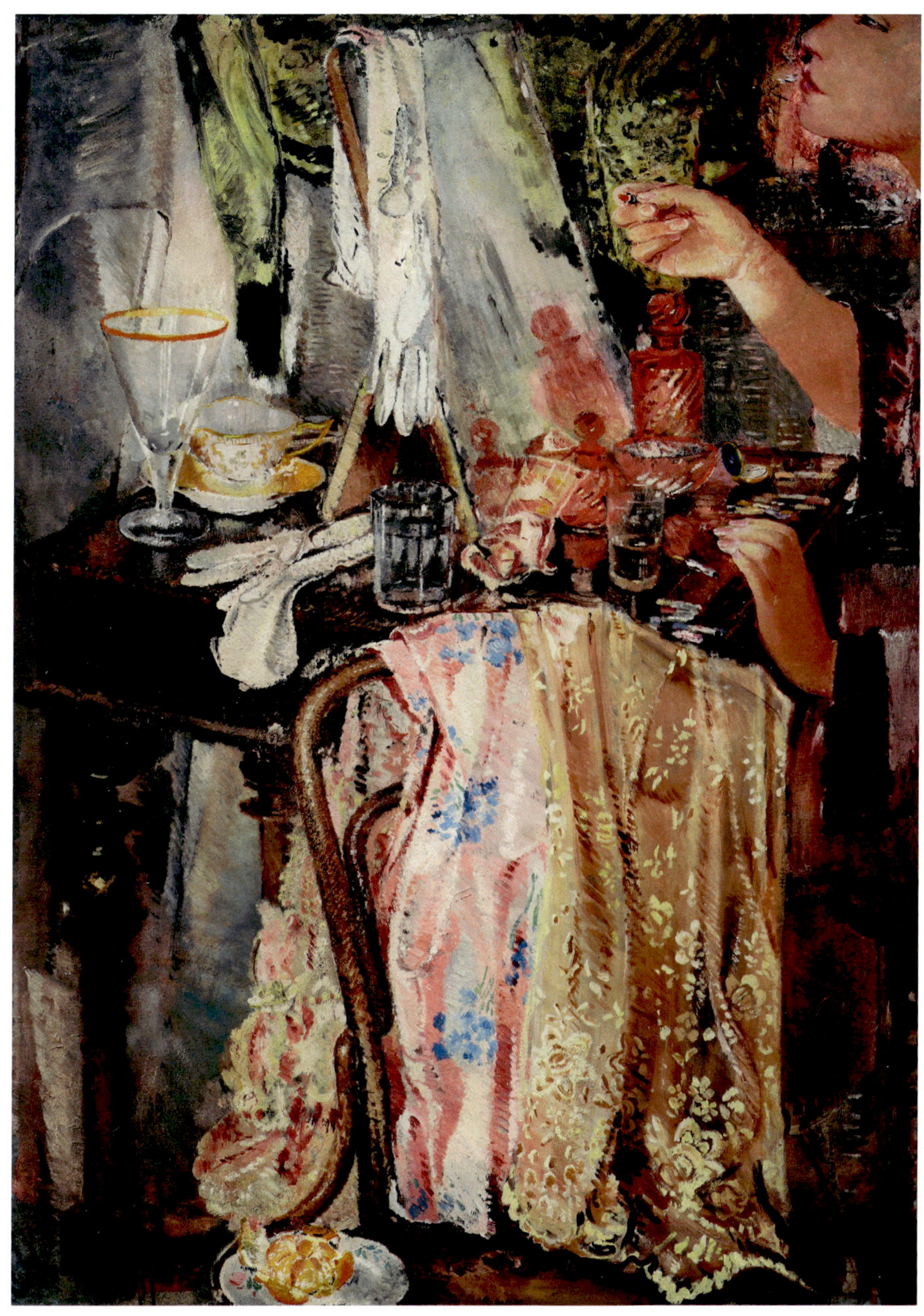

PIMENOV Yury Ivanovich | *Actress*
1935
Oil on canvas, 125.5 × 89 cm
The State Tretyakov Gallery, Moscow

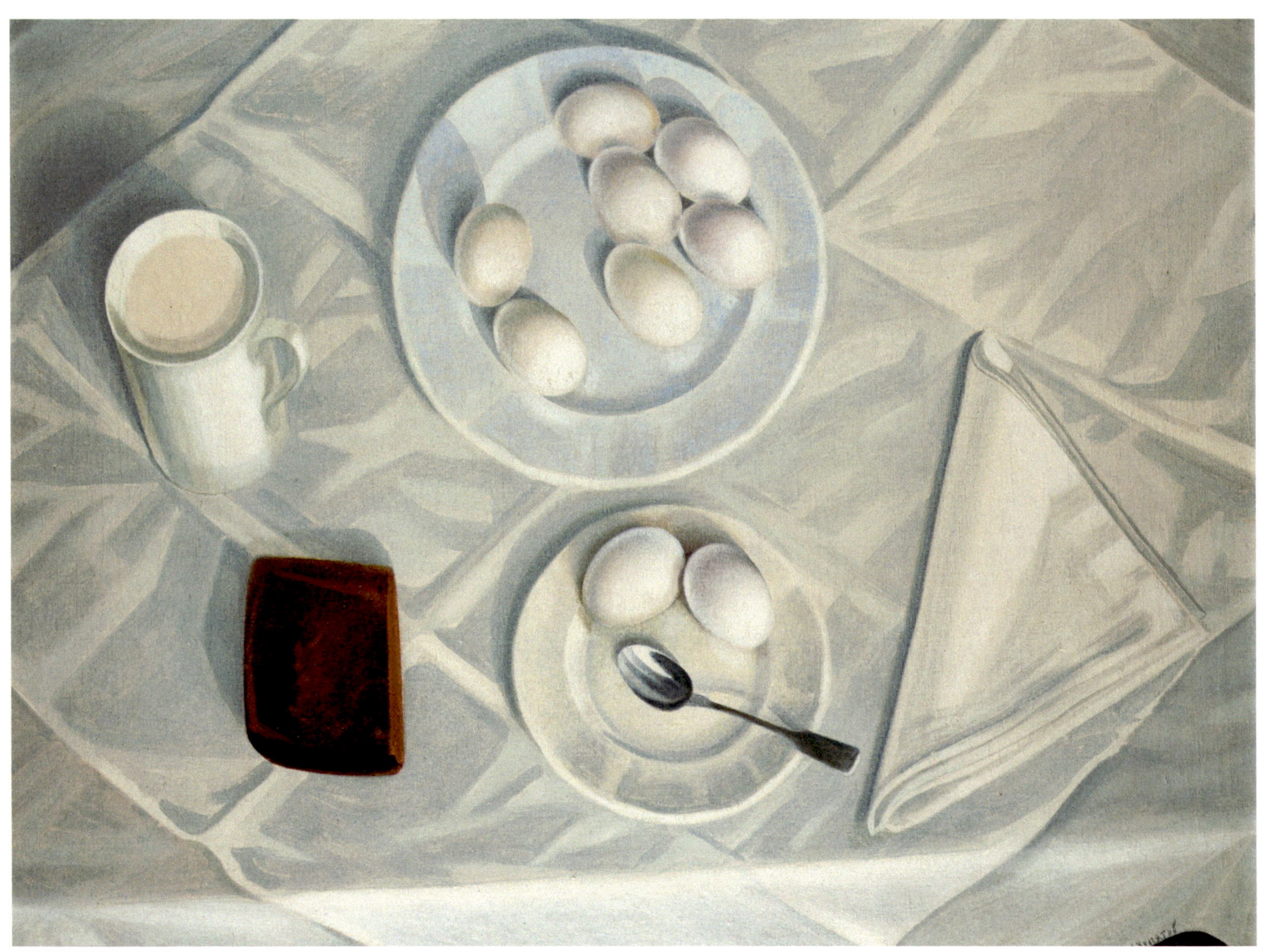

CHUPYATOV Leonid Terentievich | *White Still Life*
1936
Oil on canvas, 59.5 × 75.3 cm
The State Russian Museum, St Petersburg

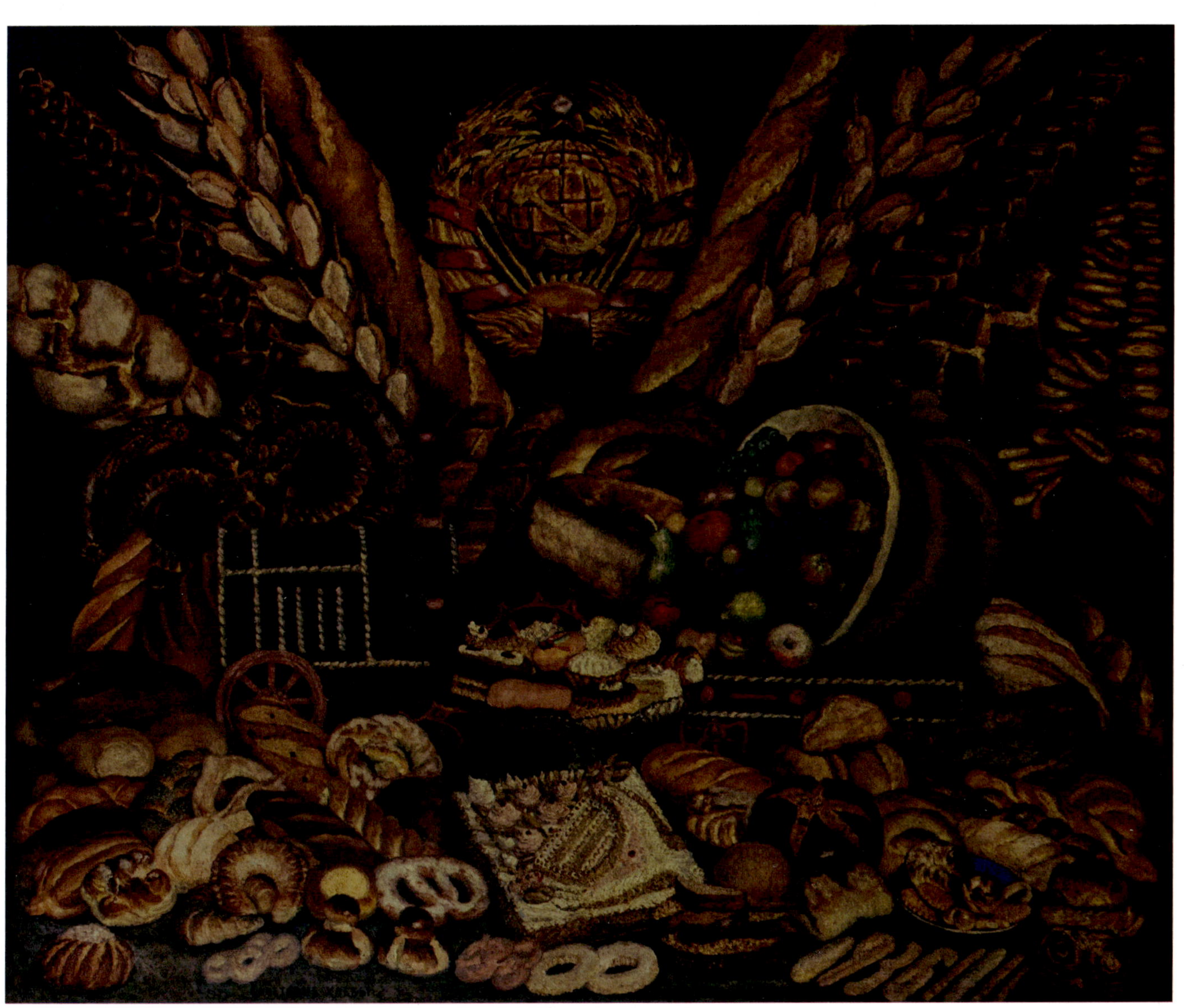

MASHKOV Ilya Ivanovich | *Soviet Bread*
1936
Oil on canvas, 145 × 175 cm
The State Museum of Fine Arts of Tatarstan Republic,
Kazan

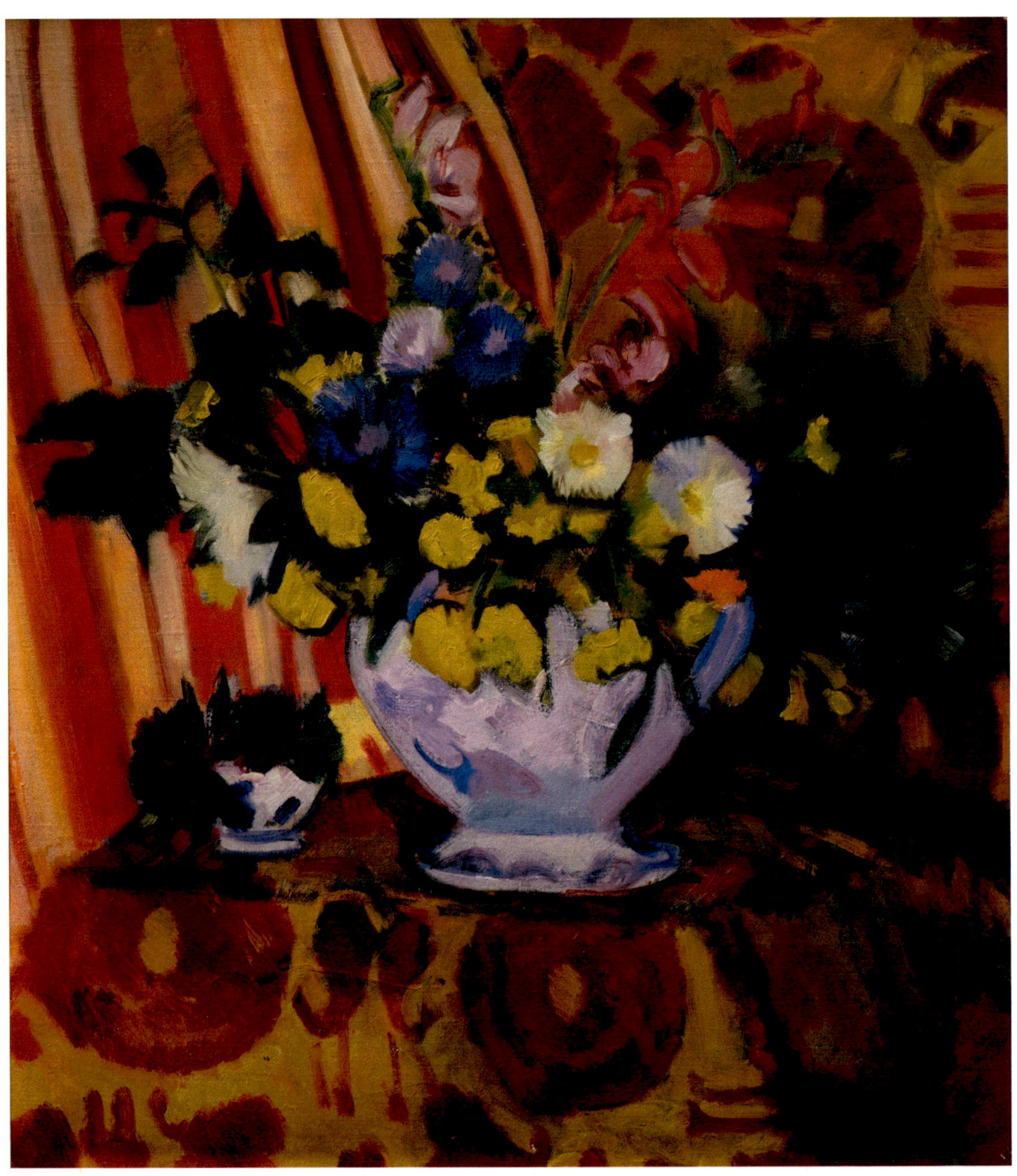

TYRSA Nikolai Andreevich | *Bouquet in a Shallow Vase*
1936
Oil on canvas, 76 × 66 cm
The State Russian Museum, St Petersburg

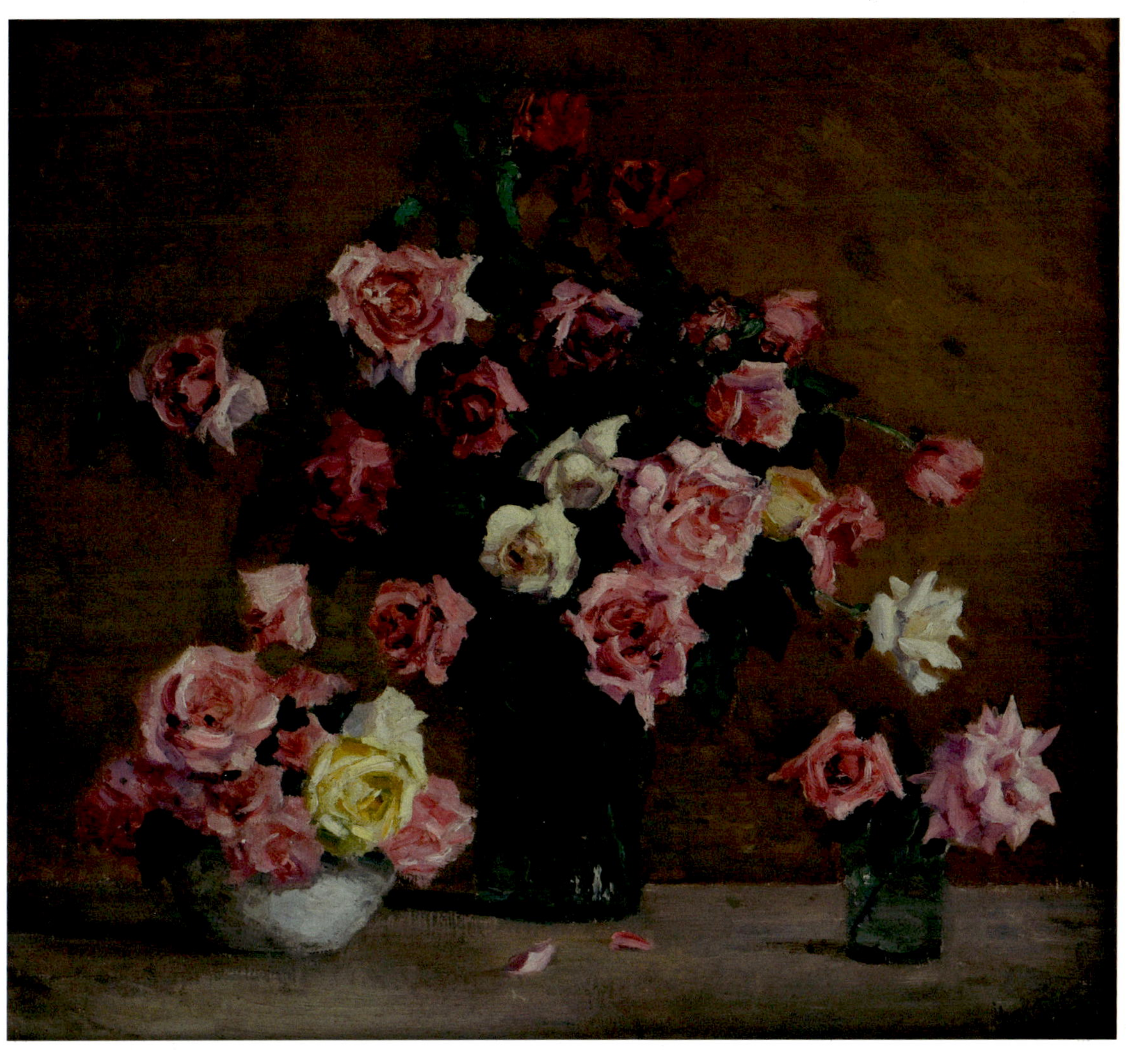

GRABAR Igor Emmanuilovich | *Rose Bouquet*
1937
Oil on canvas on board, 69.7 × 75.3 cm
Samara Regional Art Museum

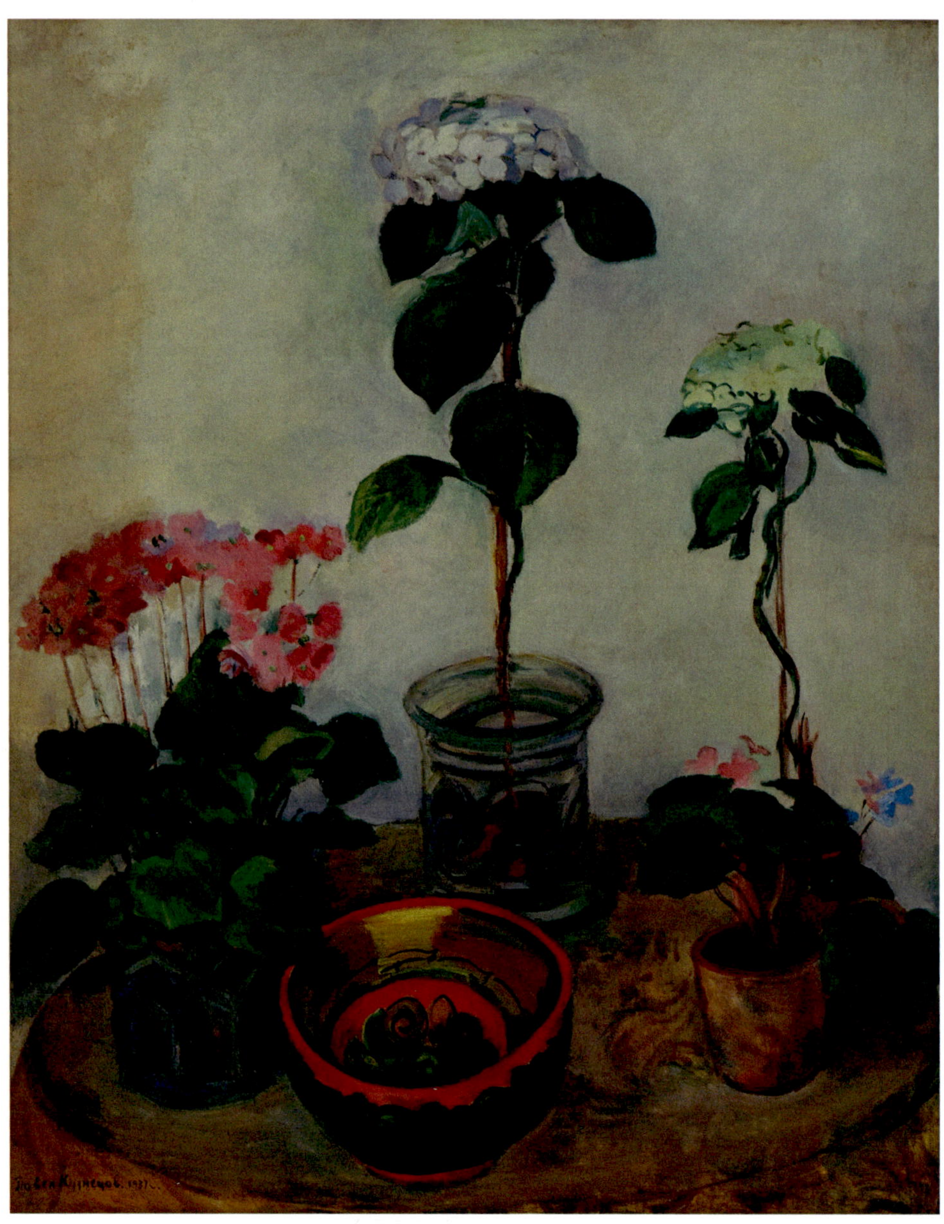

KUZNETSOV Pavel Varfolomevich | *Primroses and Hydrangeas*
1937
Oil on canvas, 101 × 79 cm
Samara Regional Art Museum

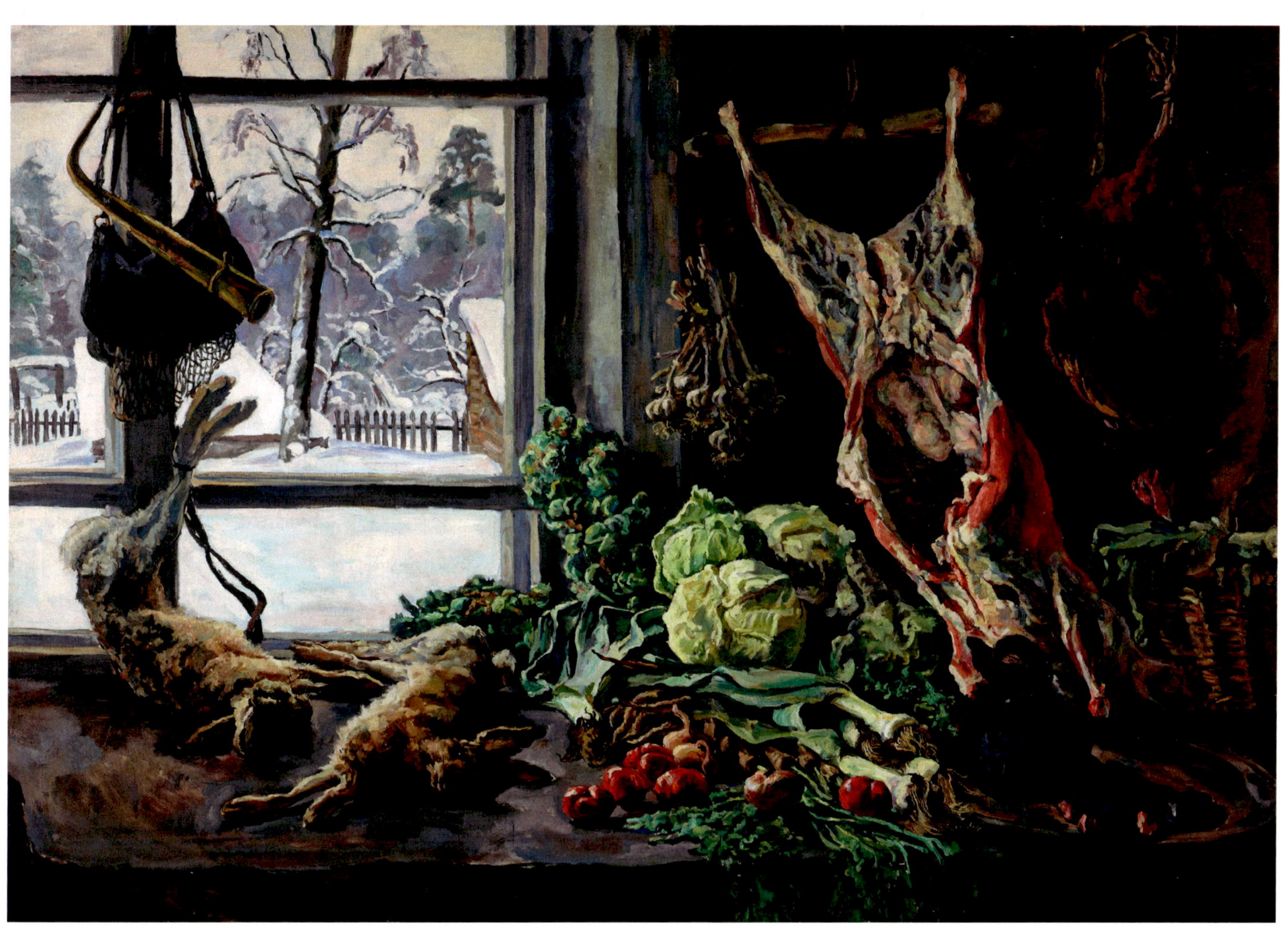

KONCHALOVSKY Petr Petrovich | *Meat, Game and Brussels Sprouts against a Window*
1937
Oil on canvas, 186 × 261 cm
The State Tretyakov Gallery, Moscow

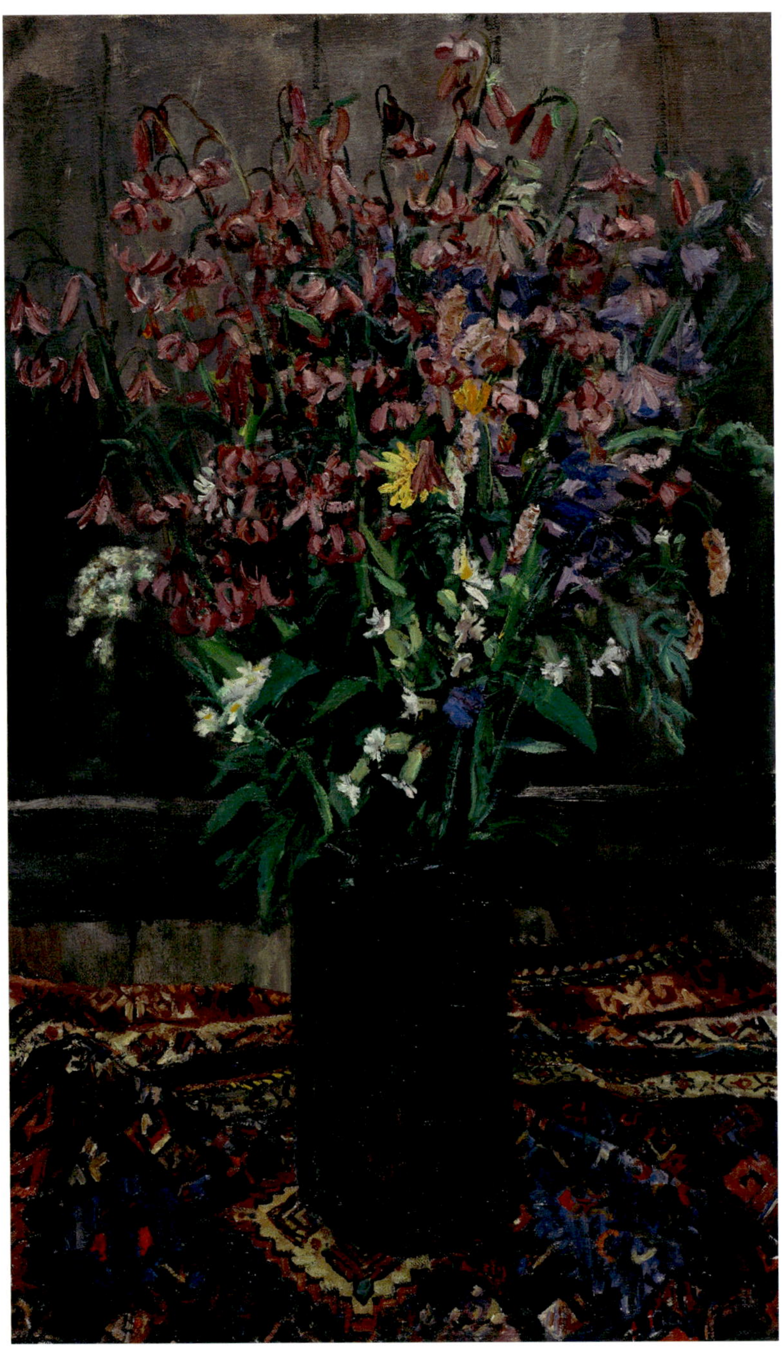

PLASTOV Arkady Alexandrovich │ *'Tsarskie Kudri' (Turk's Cap Lily)*
1937–38
Oil on canvas, 104 × 60.5 cm
Private collection

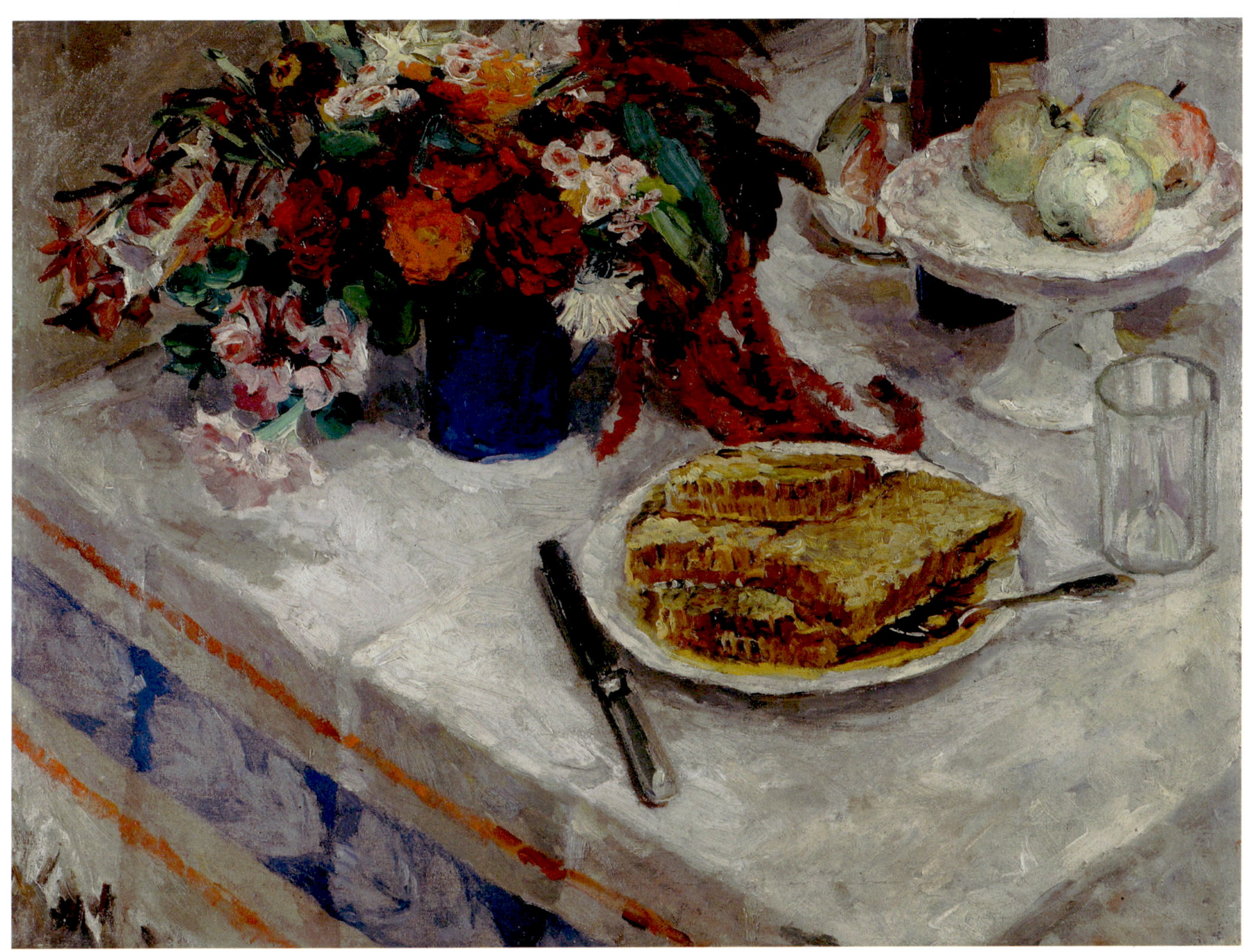

PLASTOV Arkady Alexandrovich | *Flowers and Honey*
1937–38
Oil on canvas, 62.5 × 74 cm
Private collection

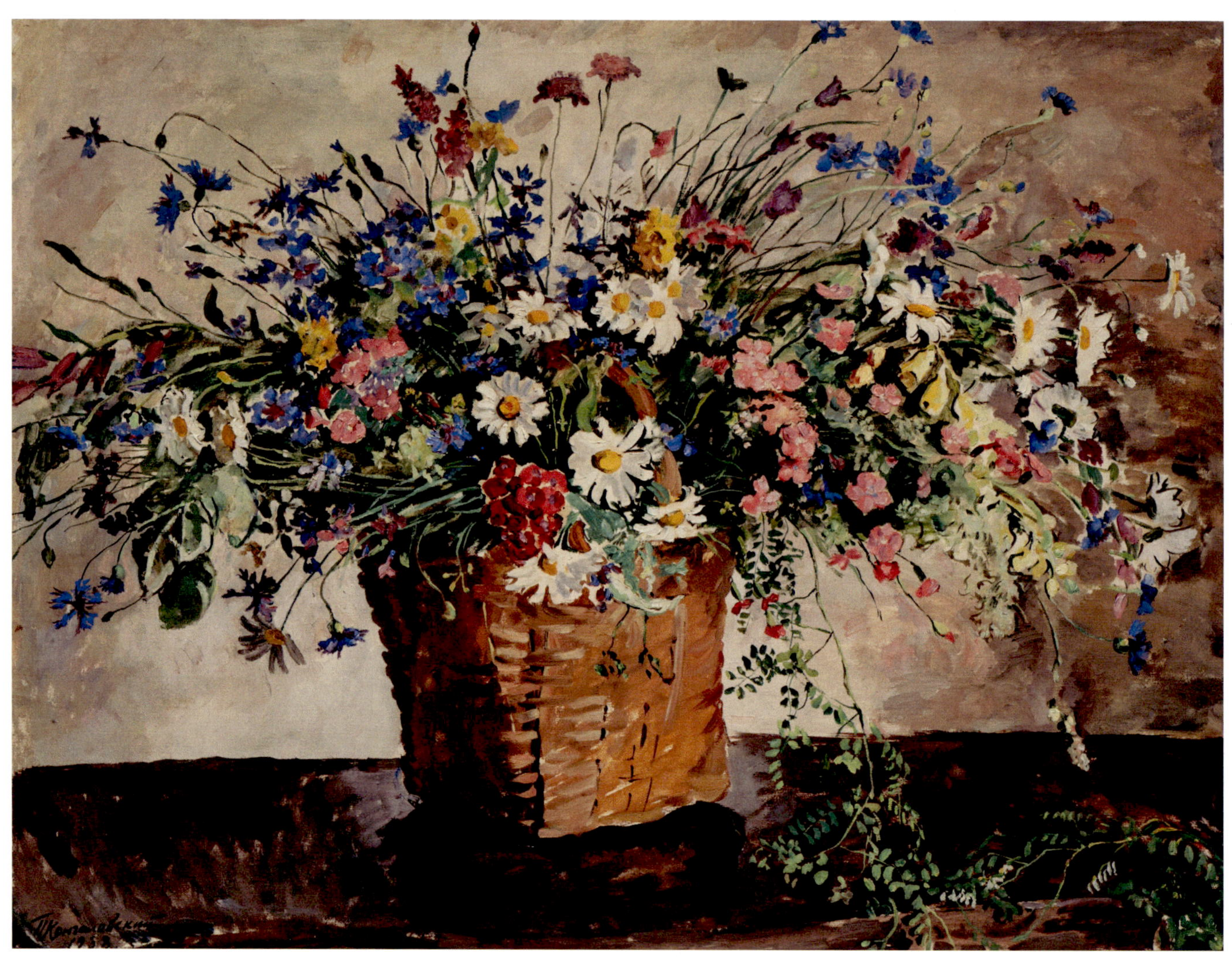

KONCHALOVSKY Petr Petrovich | *Still Life, Field Flowers*
1938
Oil on canvas, 103 × 132.5 cm
The State Russian Museum, St Petersburg

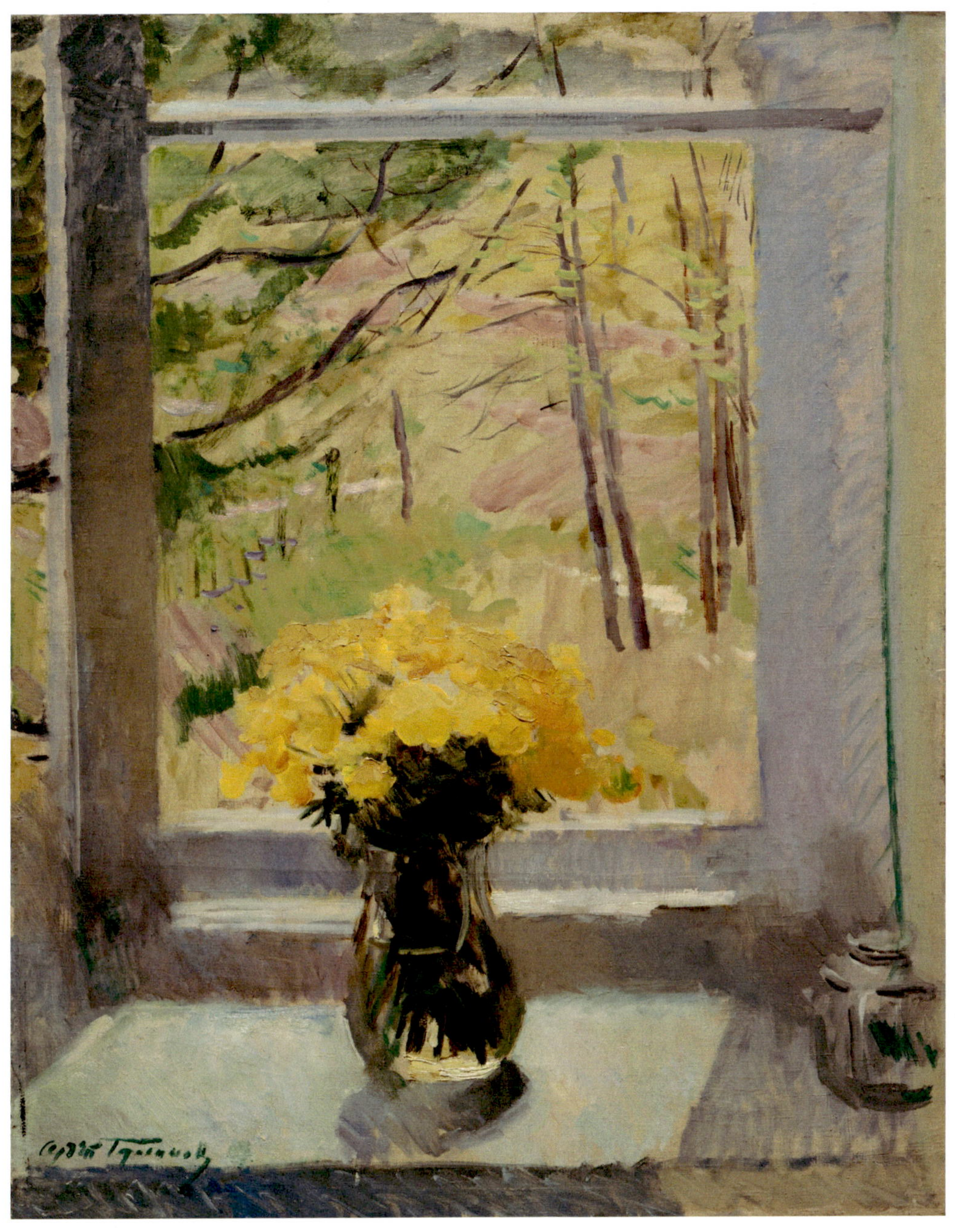

GERASIMOV Sergey Vasilyevich | *Bouquet of Globe Flowers*
1938
Oil on canvas, 100 × 75.5 cm
The State Russian Museum, St Petersburg

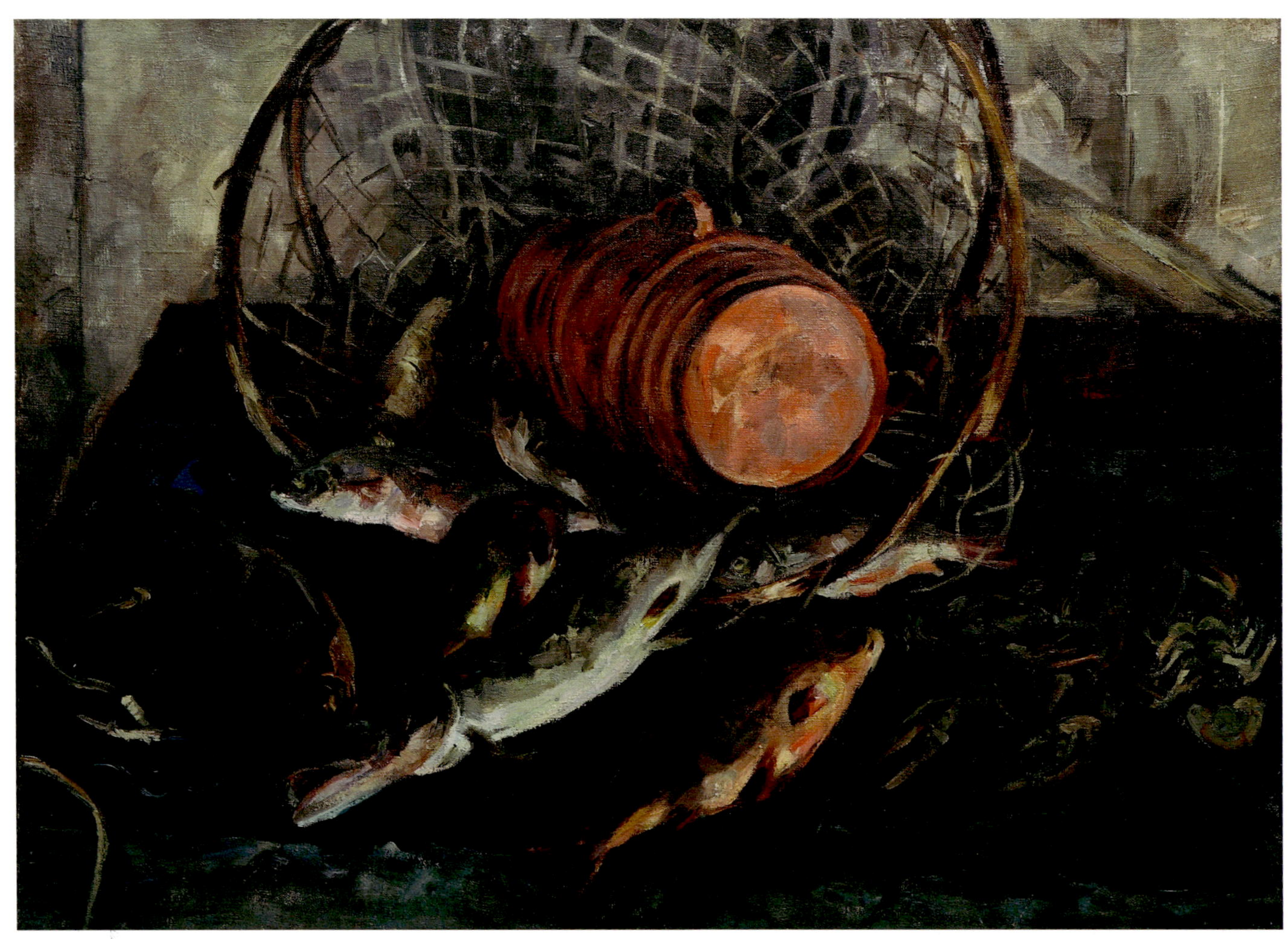

OSMERKIN Alexander Alexandrovich | *Volga, Fish*
1938
Oil on canvas, 67.7 × 91 cm
Yaroslavl Art Museum

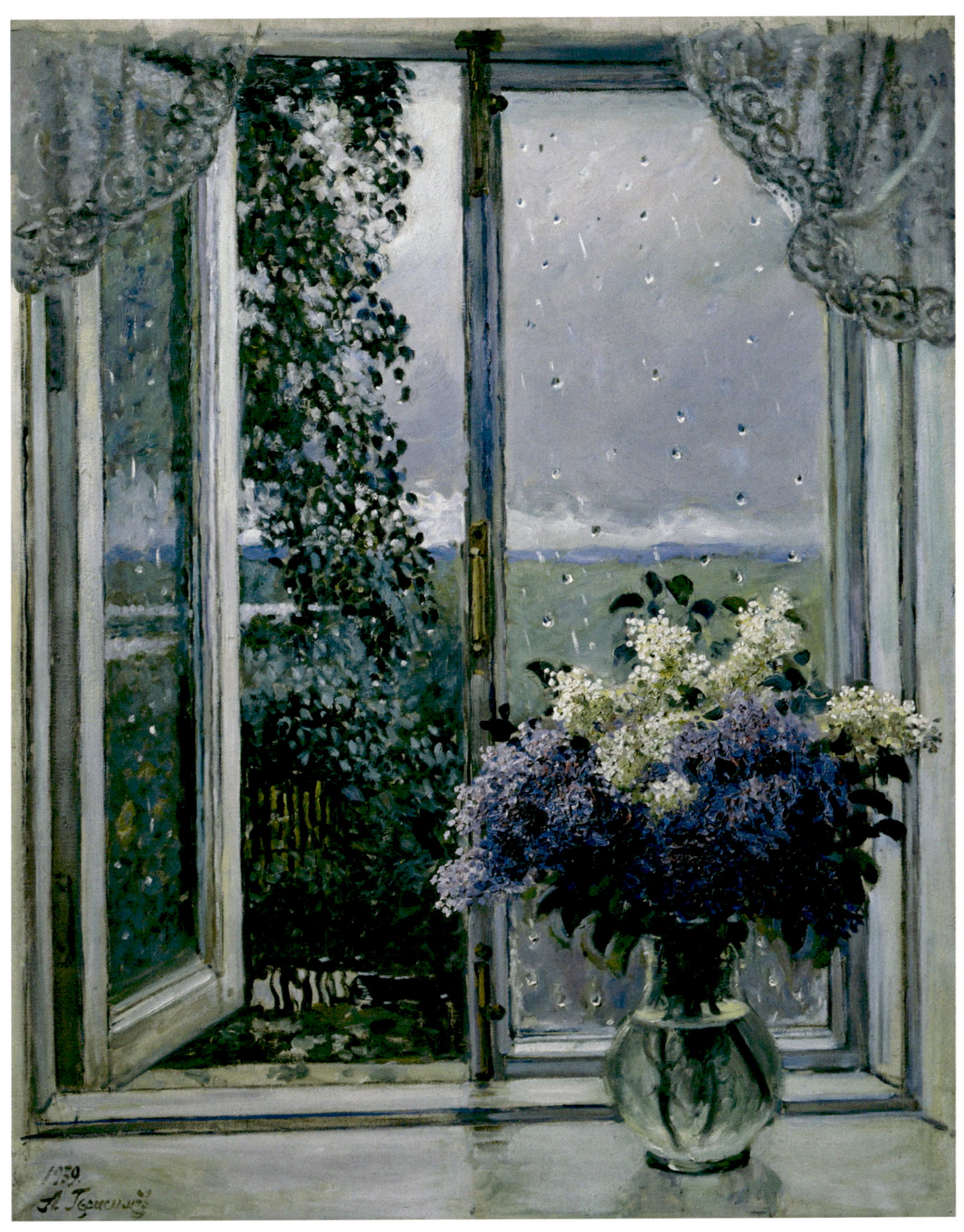

GERASIMOV Aleksandr Mikhaylovich | *Midday, Warm Rain*
1939
Oil on canvas, 126 × 100 cm
The State Russian Museum, St Petersburg

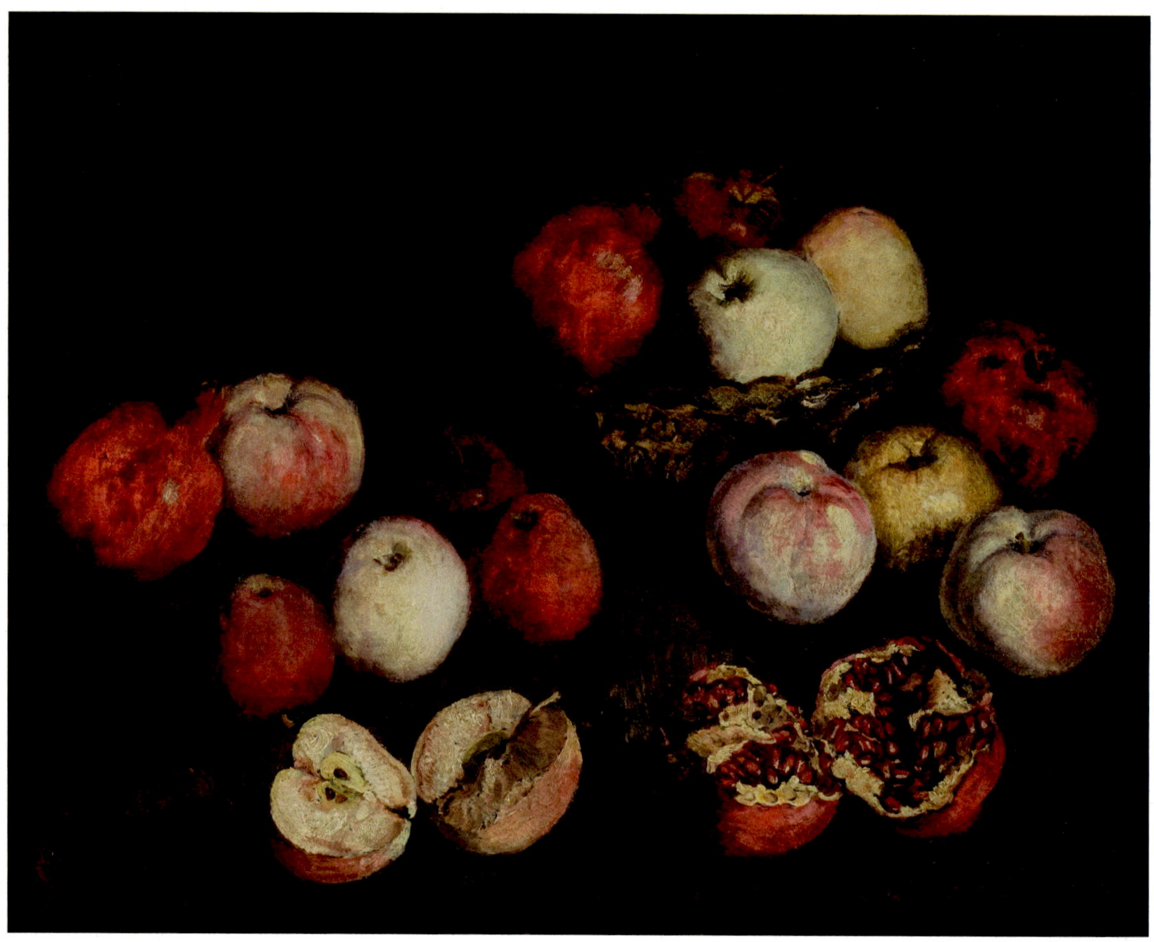

MASHKOV Ilya Ivanovich | *Still Life with Apples and Pomegranate*
1939
Oil on canvas, 62.4 × 76 cm
Samara Regional Art Museum

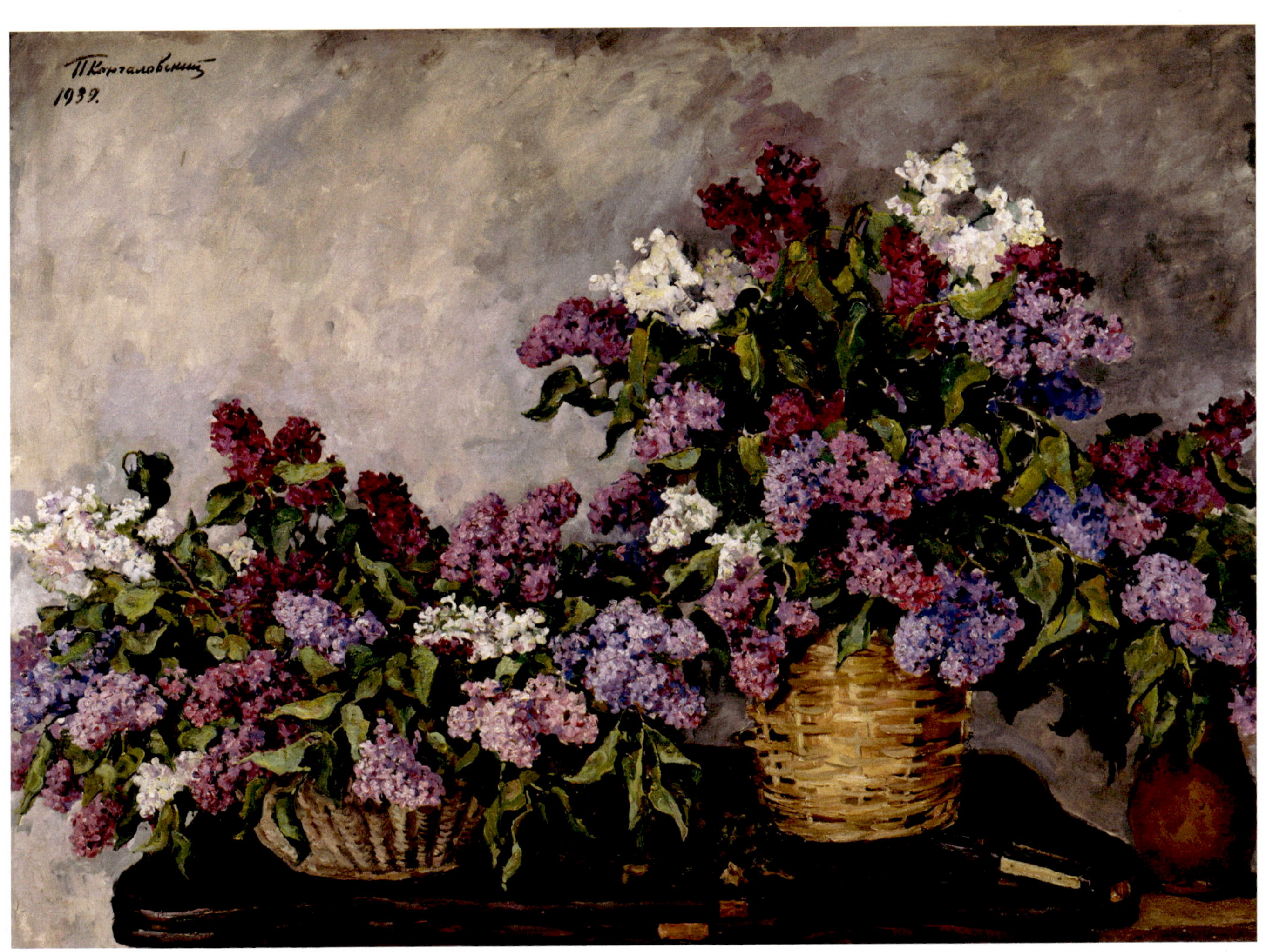

KONCHALOVSKY Petr Petrovich | *Lilacs in Two Baskets*
1939
Oil on canvas, 137 × 186 cm
The State Russian Museum, St Petersburg

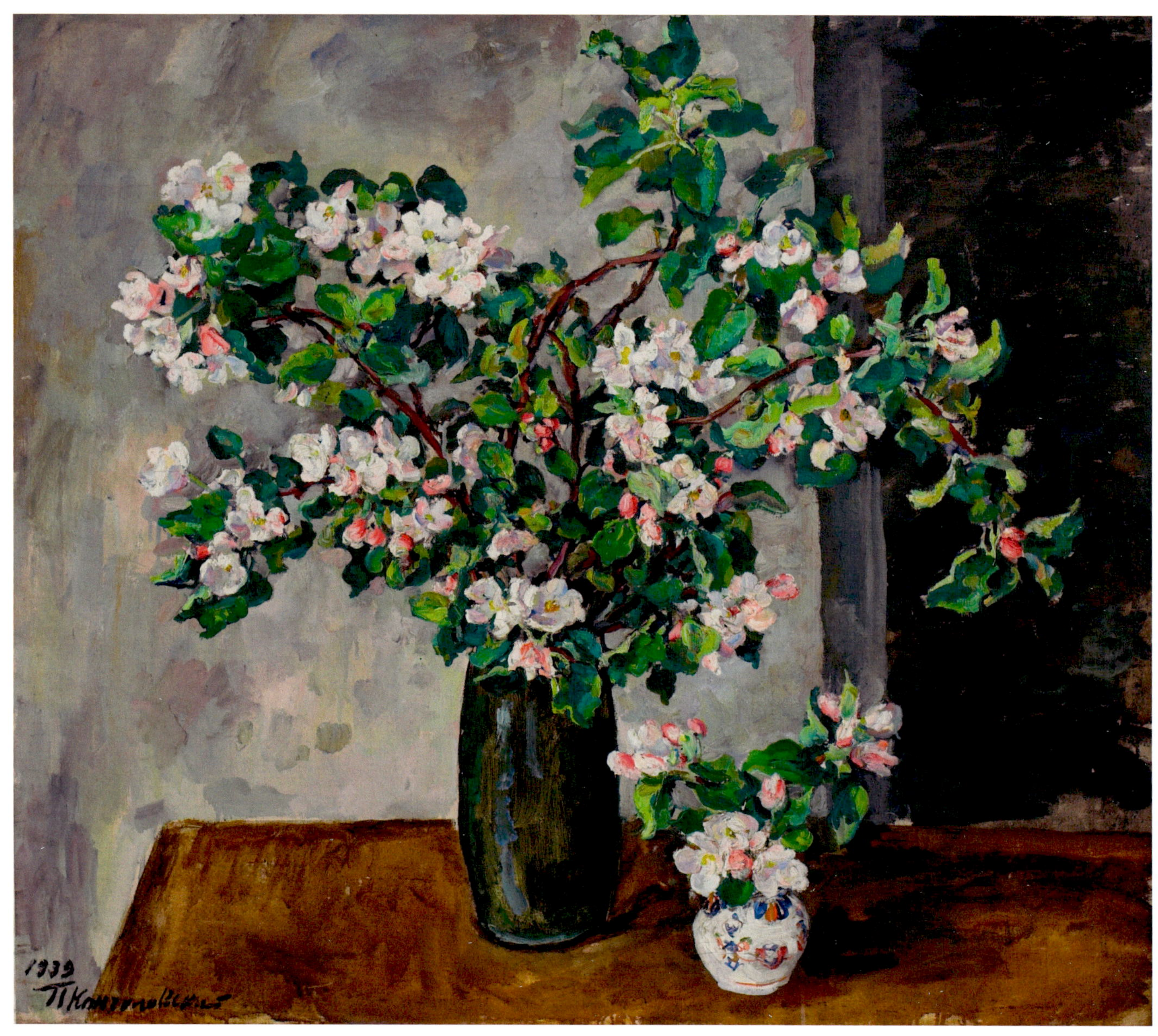

KONCHALOVSKY Petr Petrovich | *Branch of Apple Tree*
1939
Oil on canvas, 92 × 103 cm
Krasnoyarsk Art Museum named after V. I. Surikov

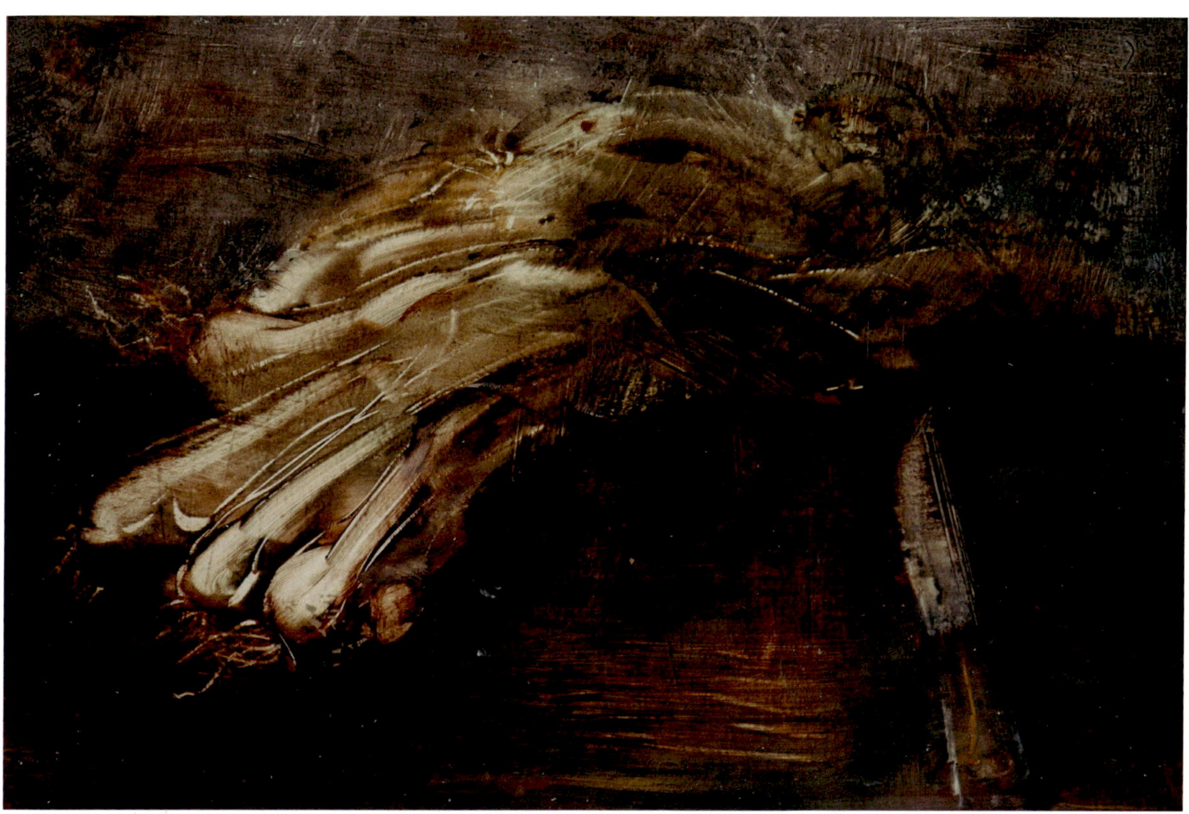

TATLIN Vladimir Yevgraphovich | *Onion*
1940
Oil on cardboard, 33 × 46 cm
The State Russian Museum, St Petersburg

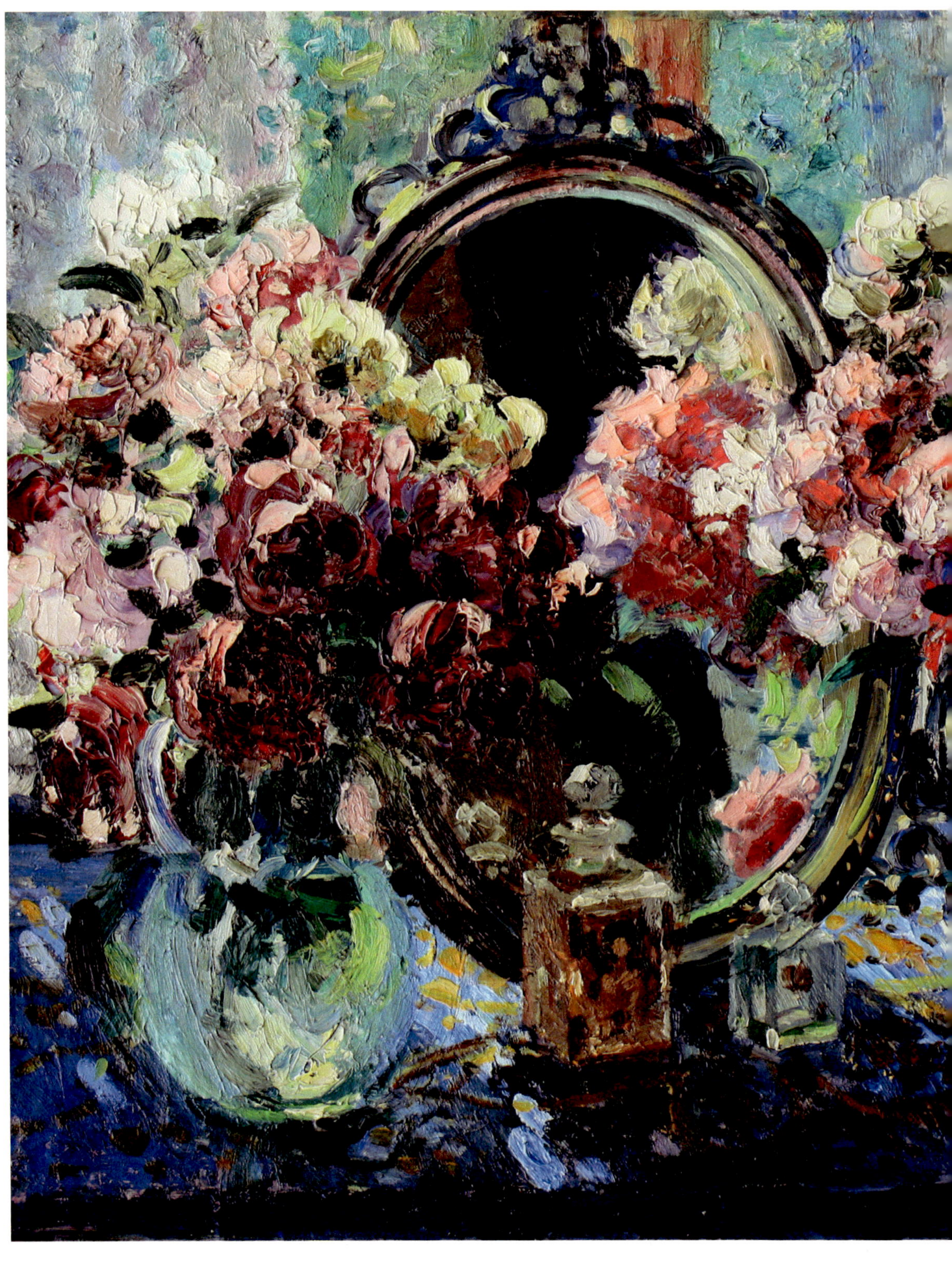

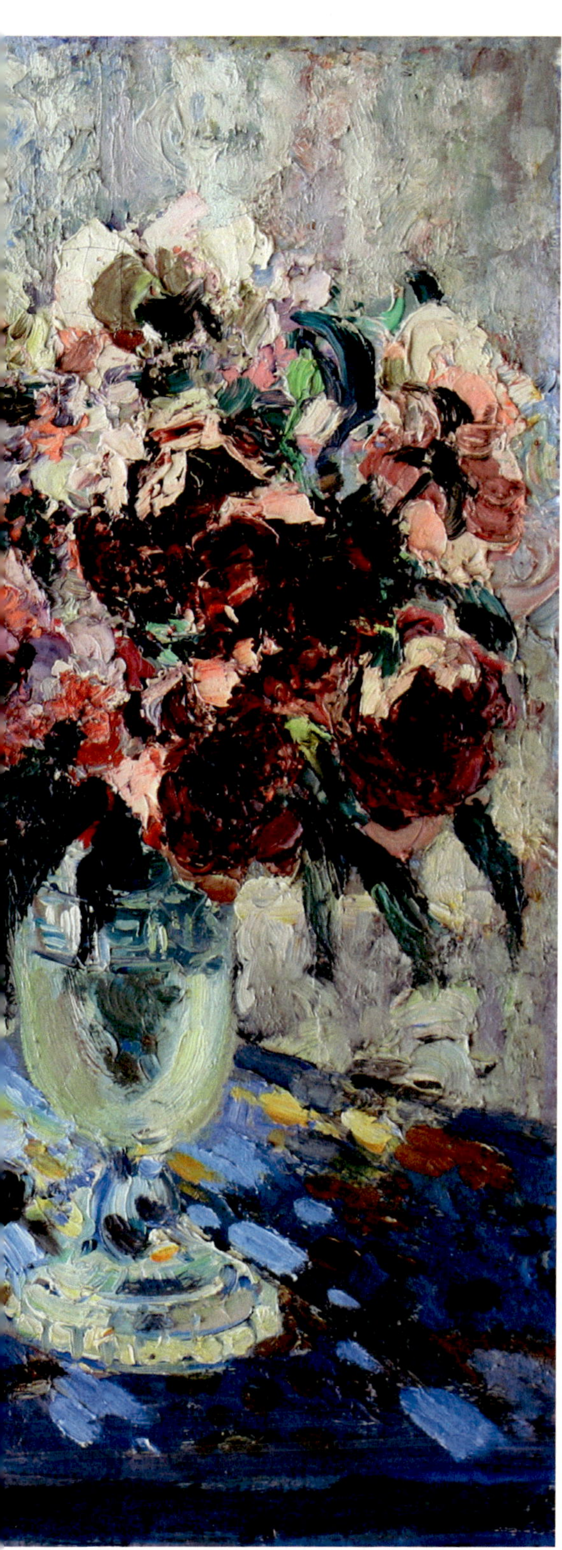

GERASIMOV Aleksandr Mikhaylovich

Roses
1940s
Oil on canvas, 85.5 × 105.5 cm
Kursk State Picture Gallery named after
A. A. Deineka

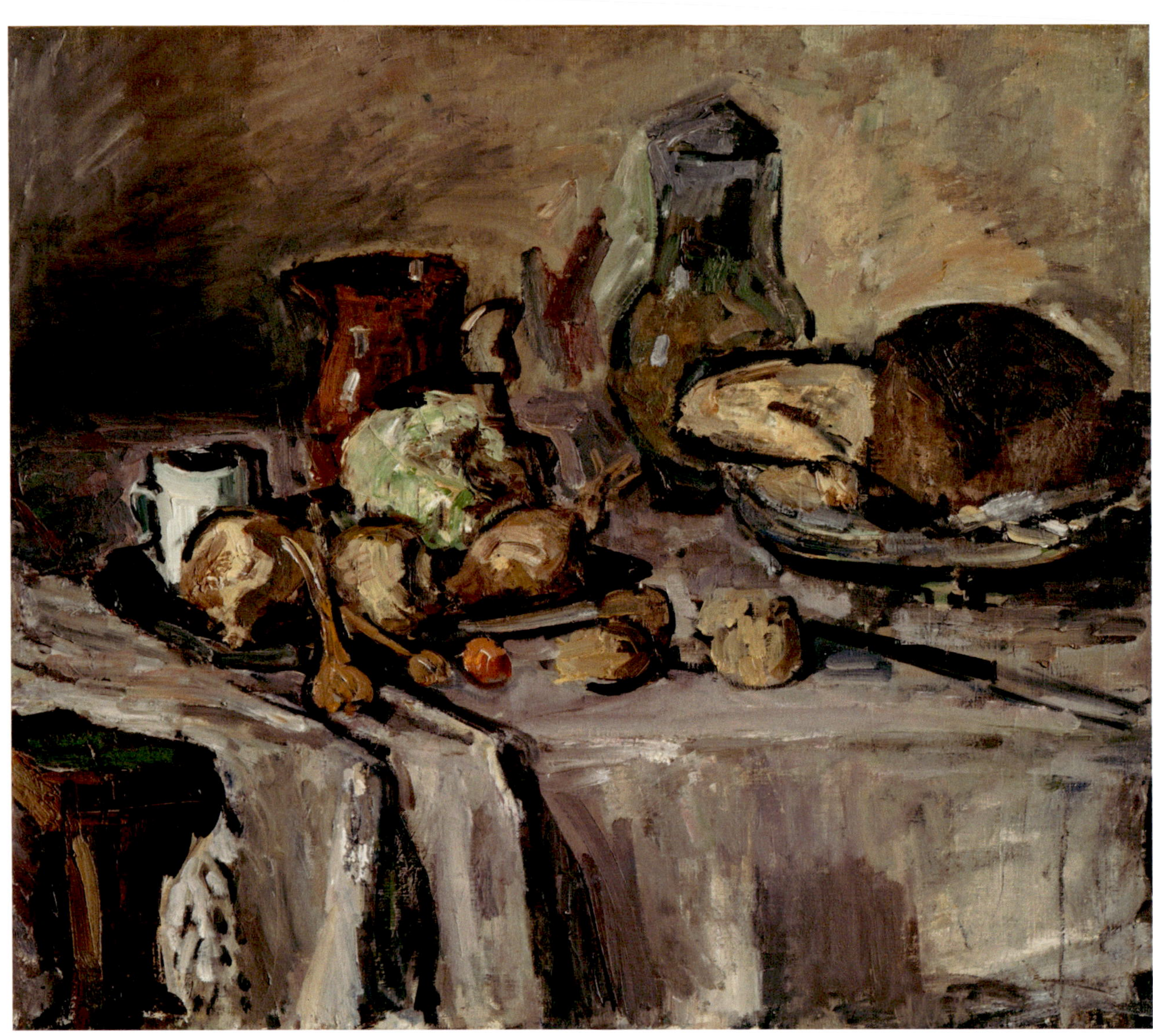

UDALTSOVA Nadezhda Andreevna | *War Bread*
1942
Oil on canvas, 69 × 80 cm
The State Russian Museum, St Petersburg

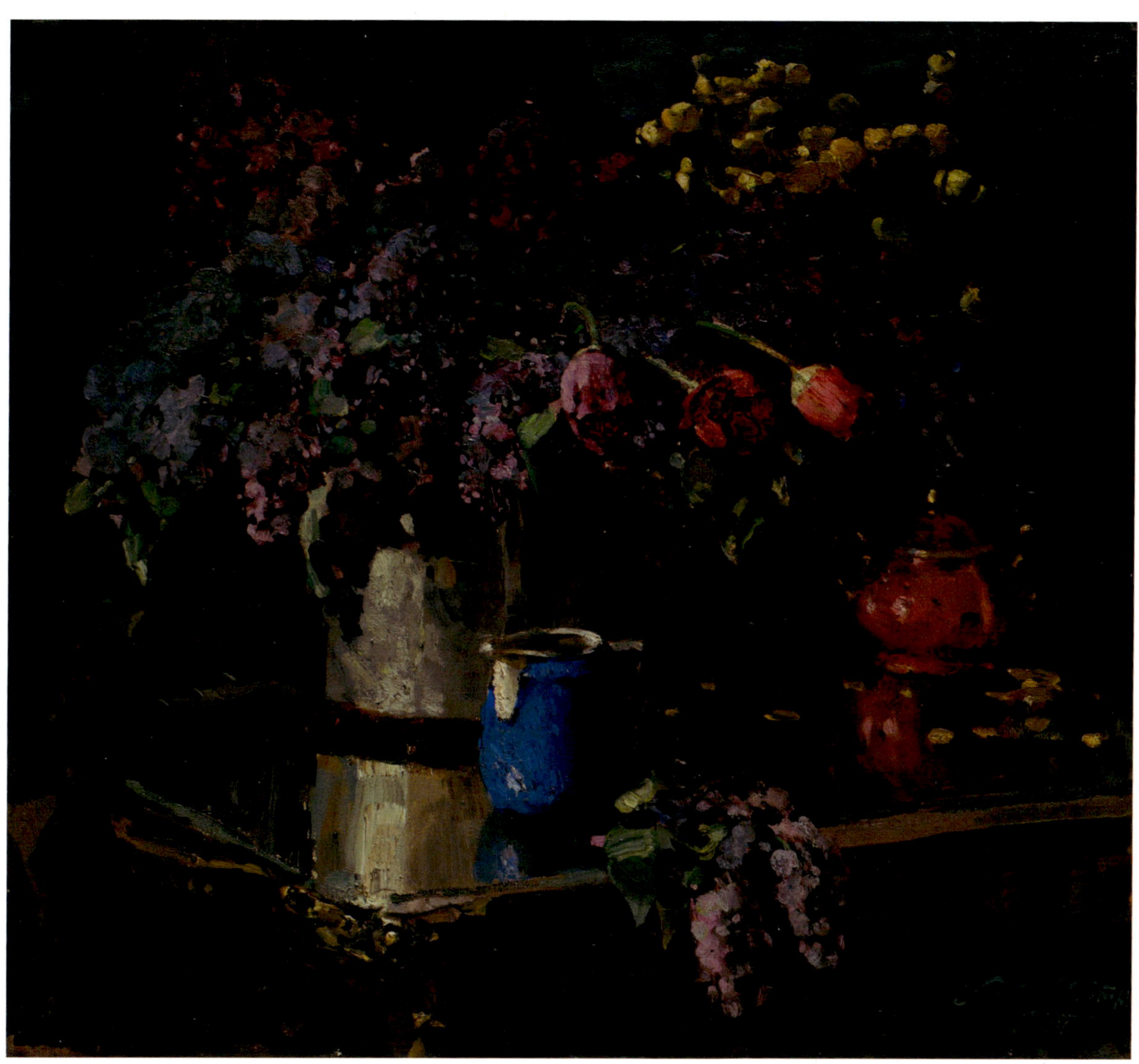

KOTOV Pyotr Ivanovich | *Lilac*
1944
Oil on canvas, 65 × 60 cm
Irkutsk Regional Art Museum named after
V. P. Sukachov

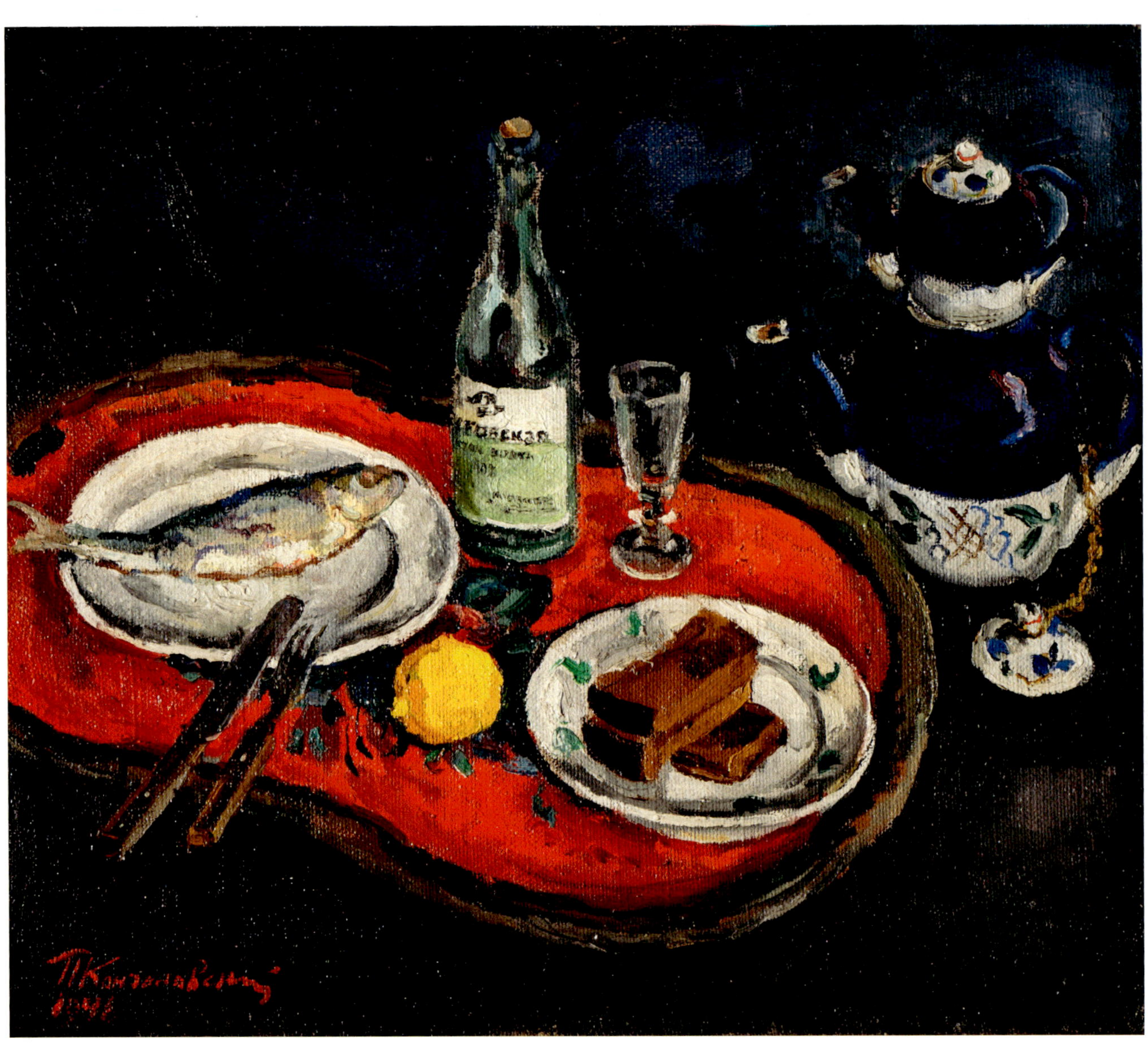

KONCHALOVSKY Petr Petrovich | *Still Life, Tea Set*
1946
Oil on canvas, 78.5 × 89.3 cm
The State Russian Museum, St Petersburg

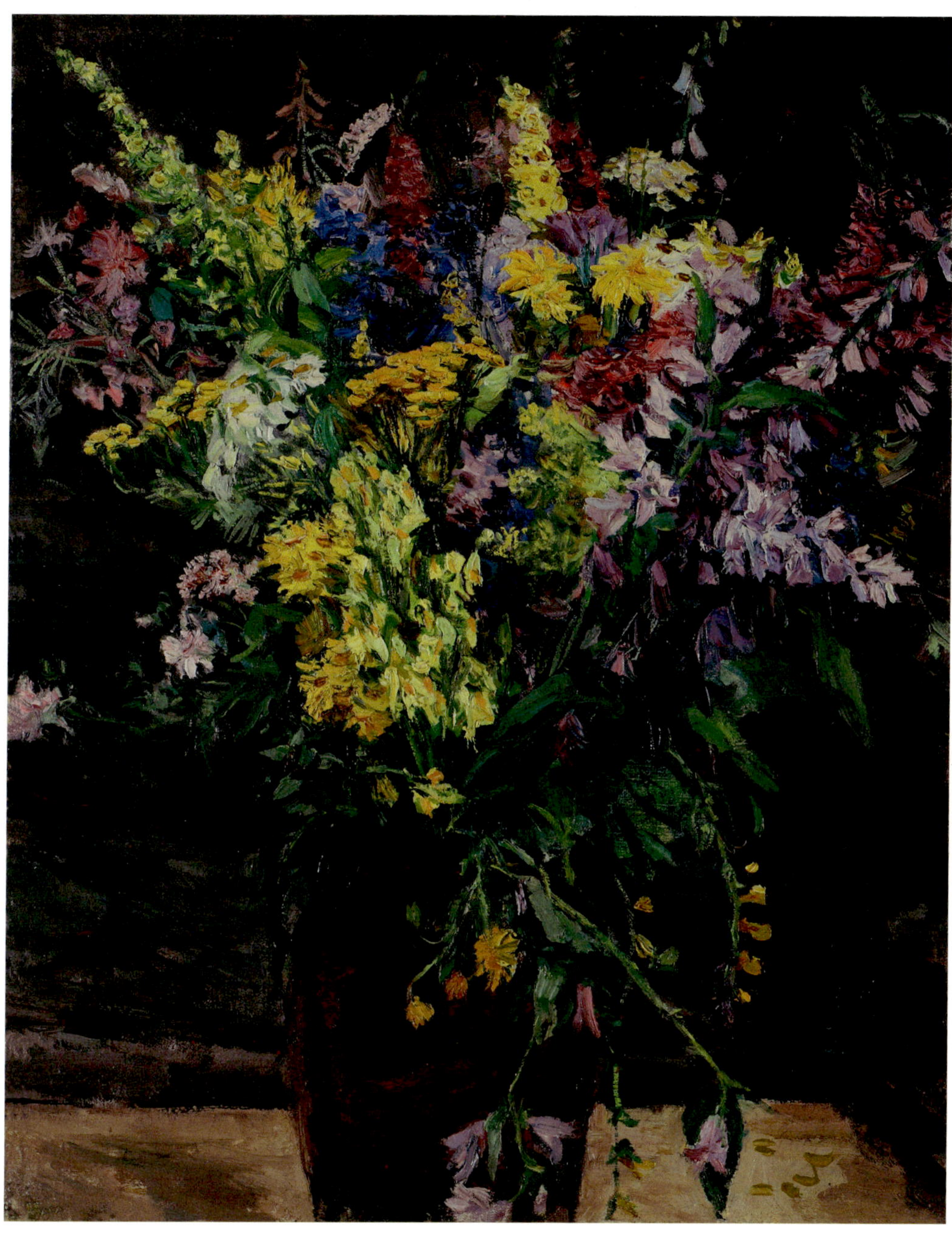

PLASTOV Arkady Alexandrovich | *Forest Flowers*
1946–47
Oil on canvas, 73.5 × 57.5 cm
Private collection

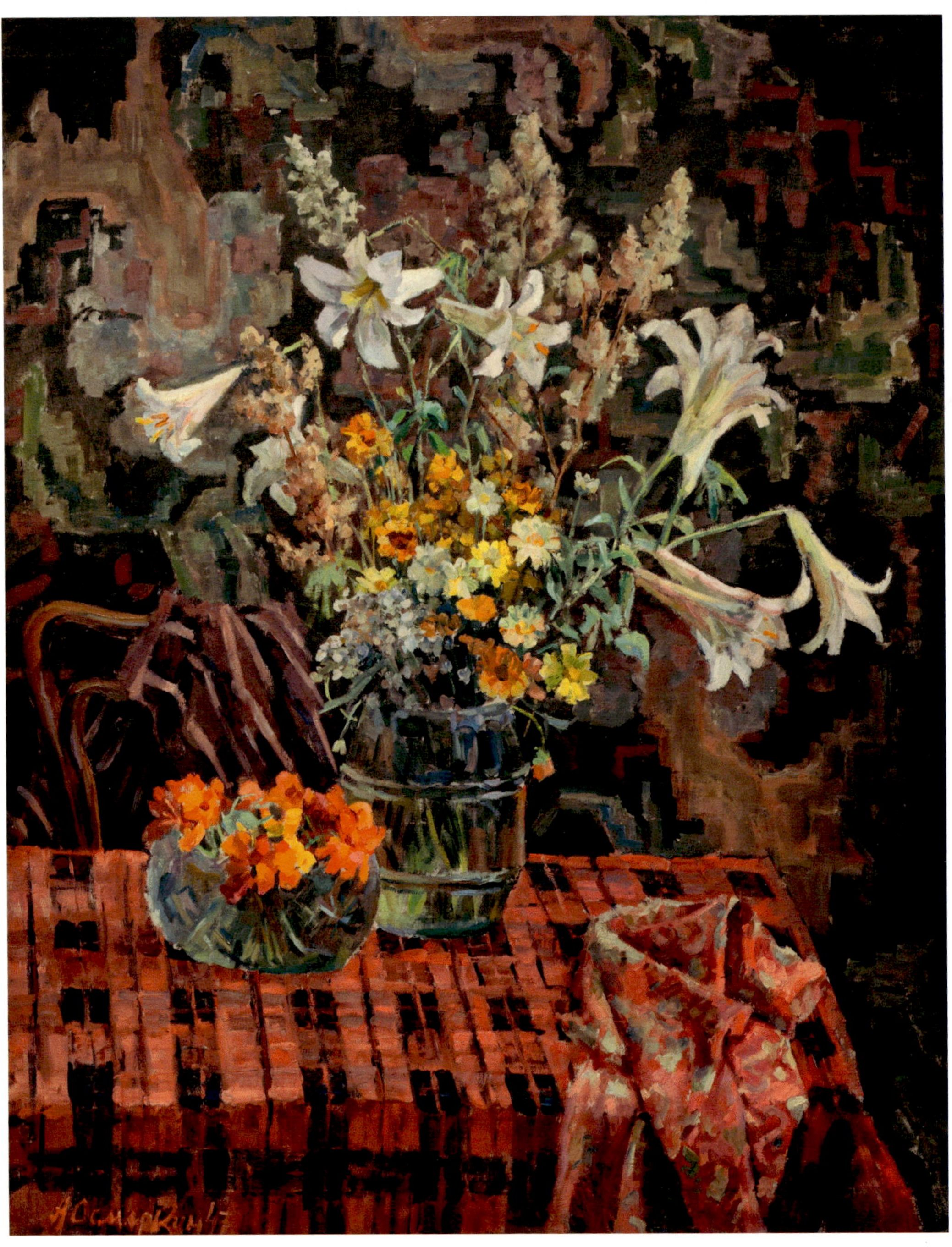

OSMERKIN Alexander Alexandrovich | *Lilies and Nasturtiums*
1947
Oil on canvas, 130 × 100 cm
The State Russian Museum, St Petersburg

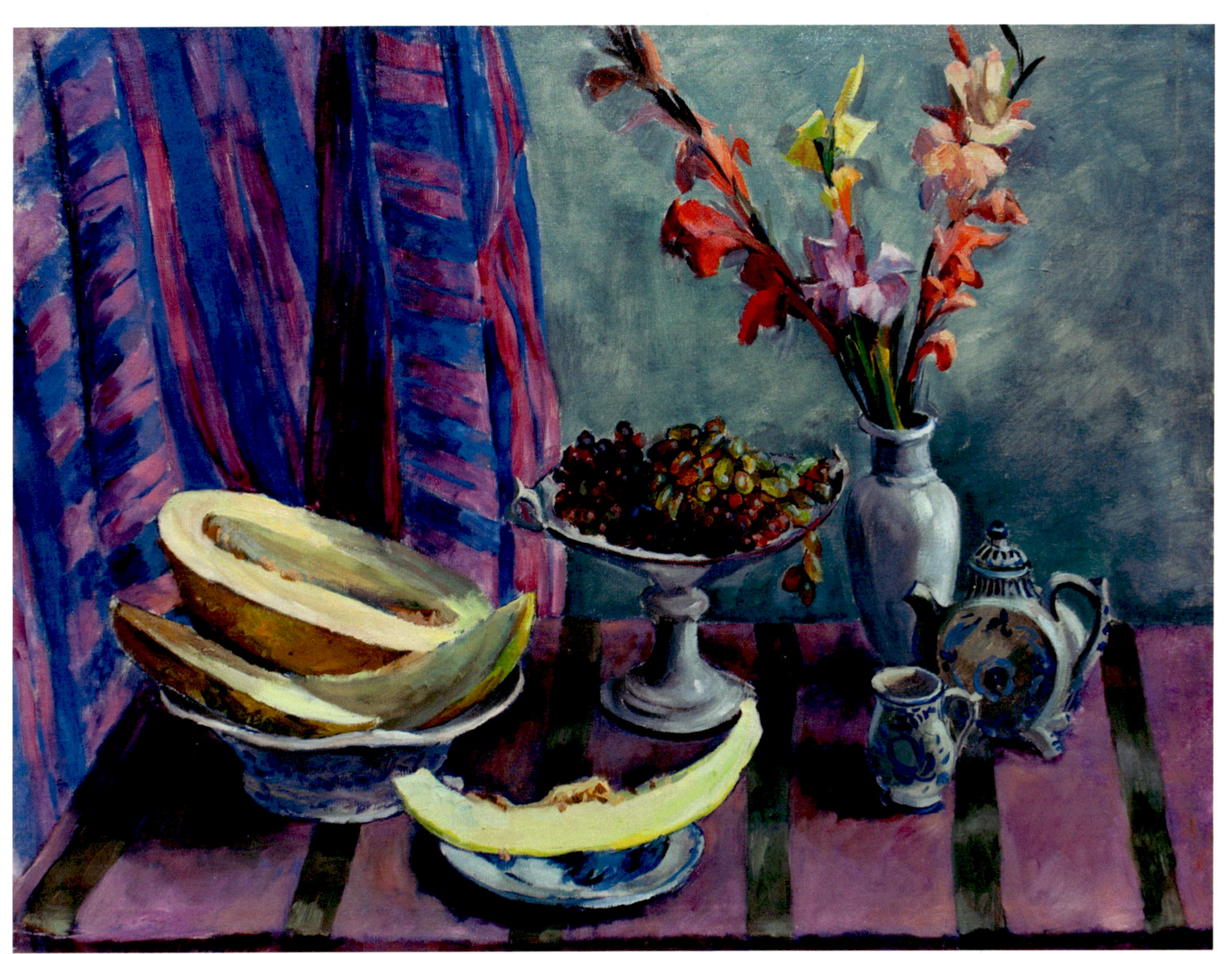

OSMERKIN Alexander Alexandrovich | *Still Life with Melon*
1948
Oil on canvas, 92.3 × 117 cm
Kursk State Picture Gallery named after A. A. Deineka

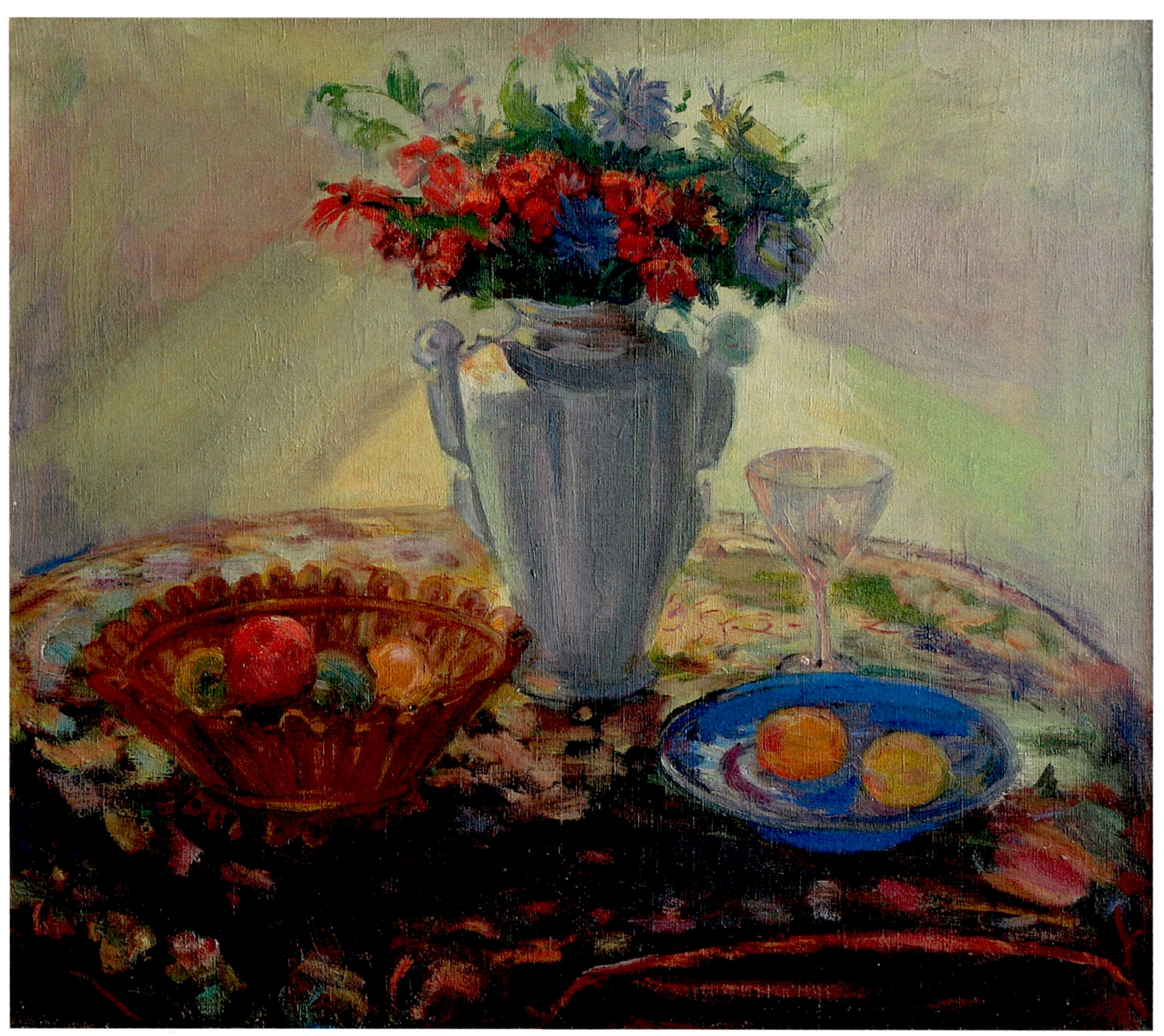

KUZNETZOV Pavel Varfolomevich | *Still Life*
1950
Oil on canvas, 70.5 × 80 cm
Yaroslavl Art Museum

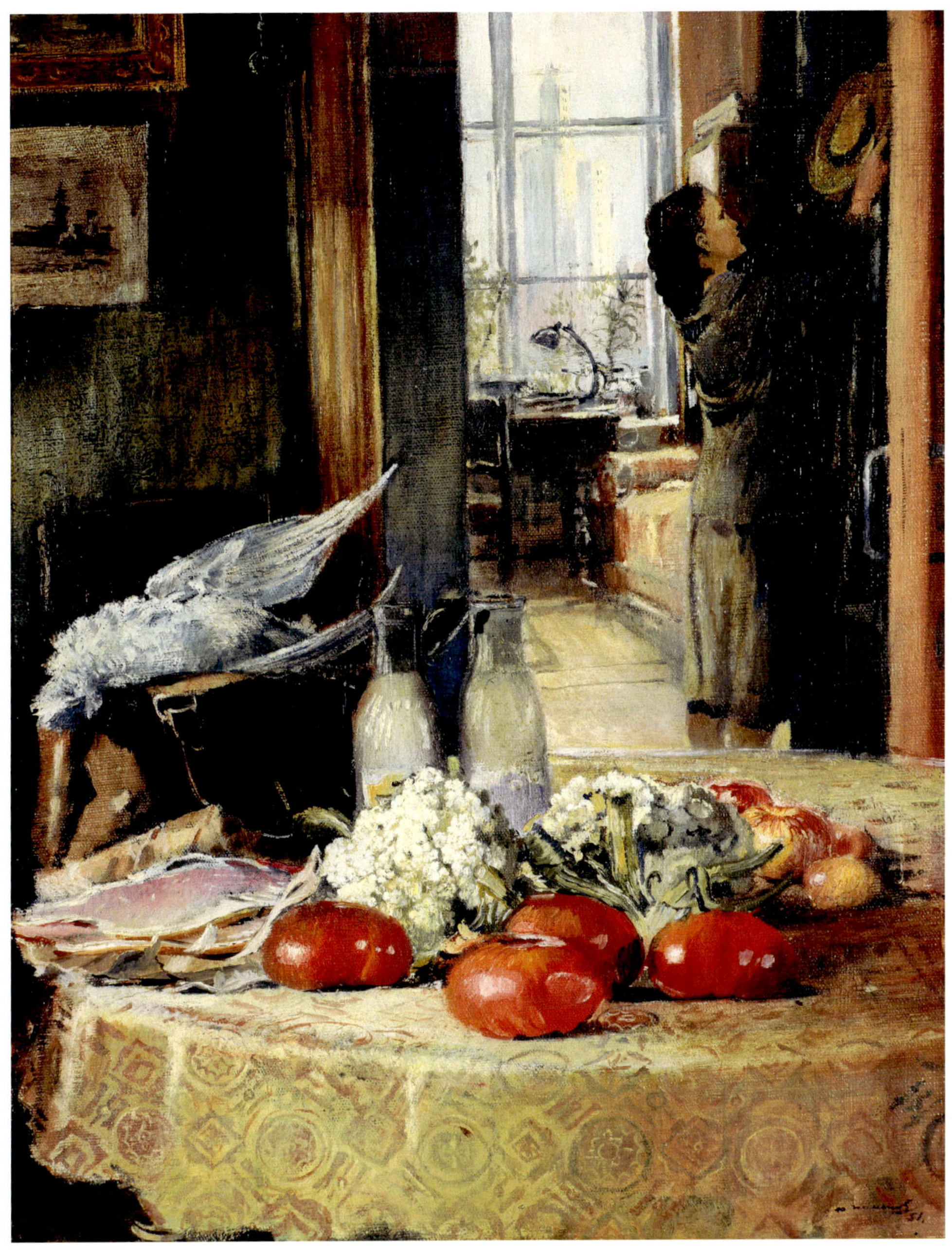

PIMENOV Yury Ivanovich | *Morning Shopping*
1951
Oil on canvas, 64 × 48 cm
The State Tretyakov Gallery, Moscow

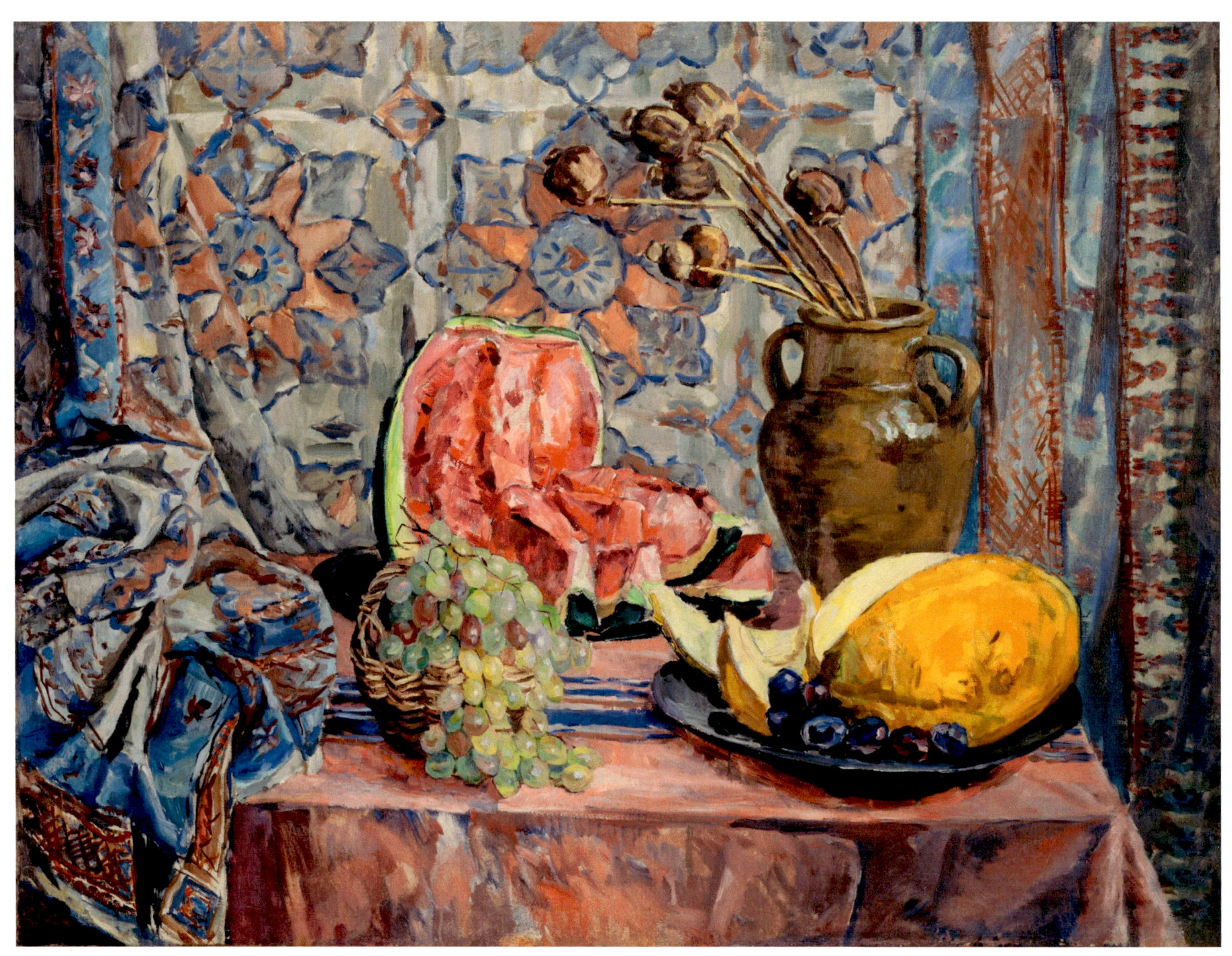

OSMERKIN Alexander Alexandrovich | *Still Life Against Persian Fabric*
1952
Oil on canvas, 97.5 × 126 cm
The State Russian Museum, St Petersburg

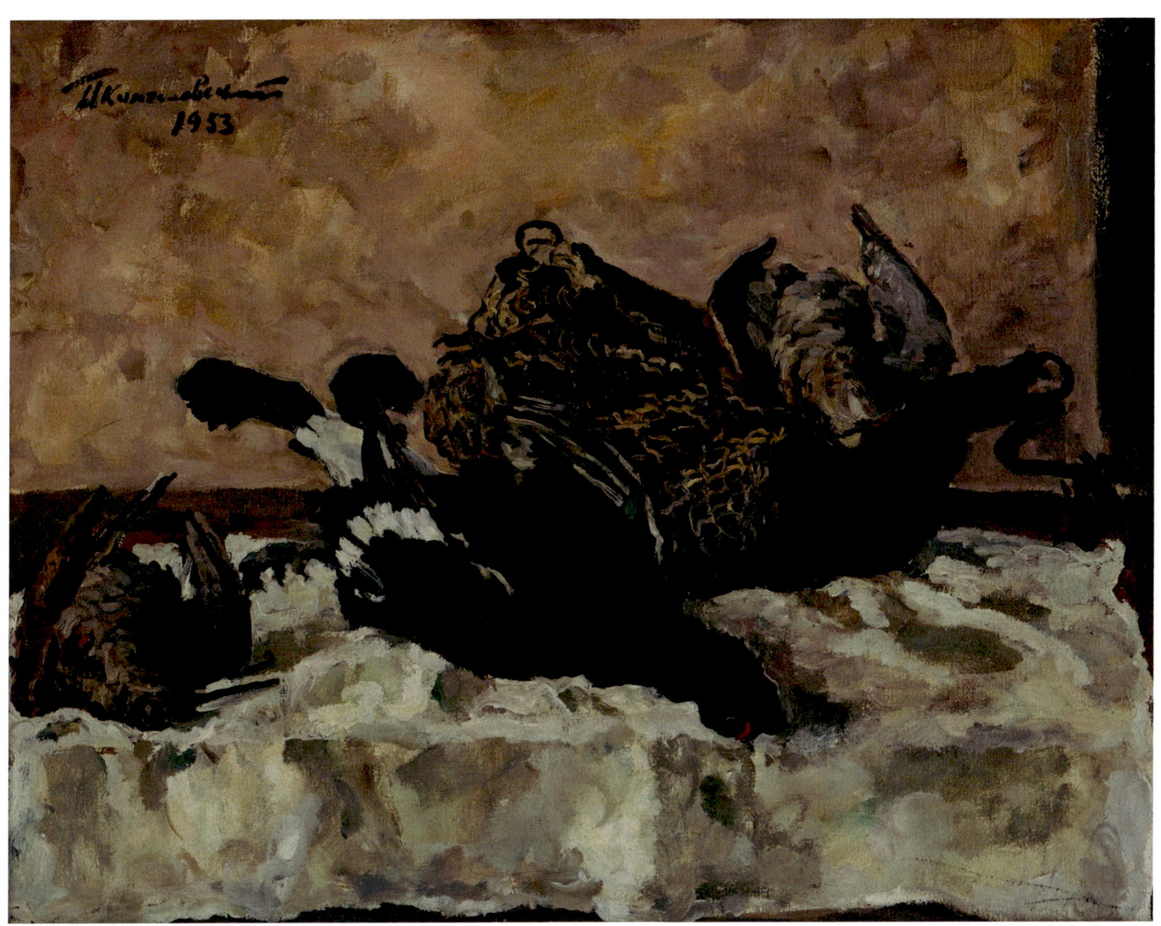

KONCHALOVSKY Petr Petrovich | *Black Grouse and Woodcock*
1953
Oil on canvas, 77 × 96 cm
Samara Regional Art Museum

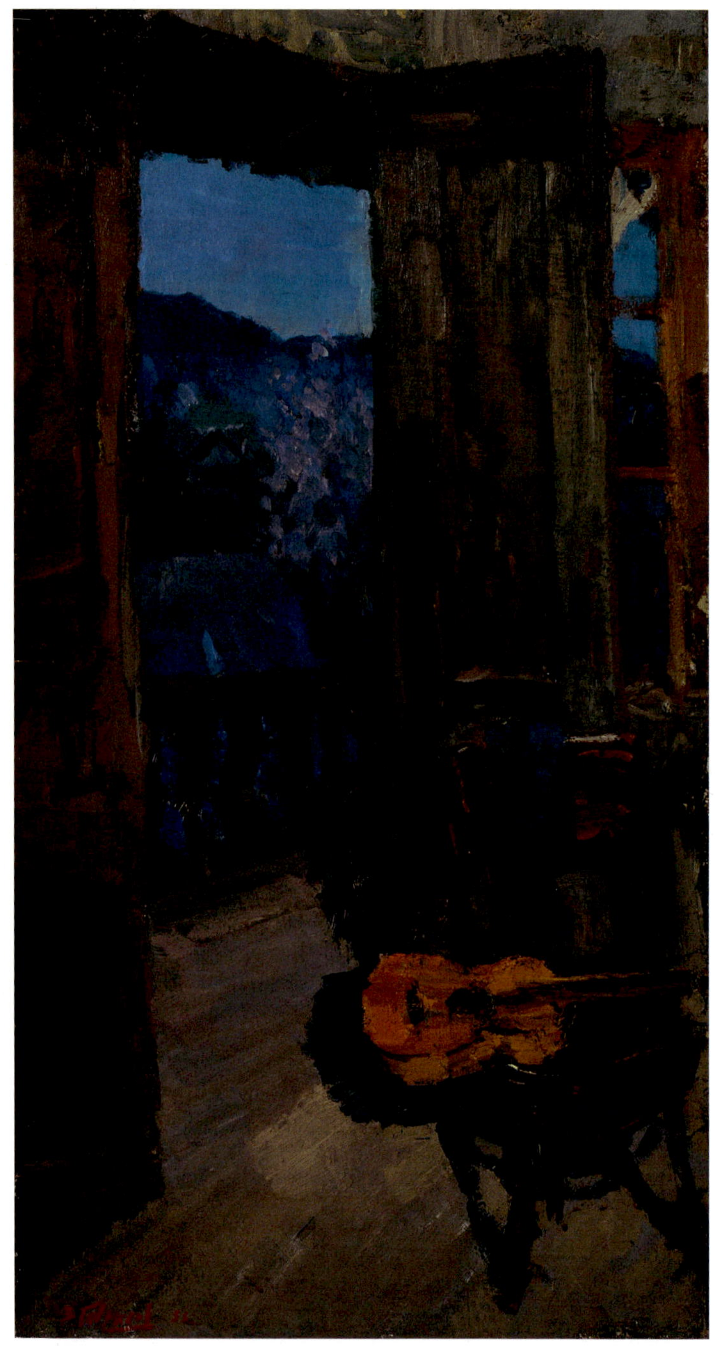

GAVRILOV Vladimir Nikolaevich | *In Jvari*
1958
Oil on canvas, 100 × 52 cm
Private collection

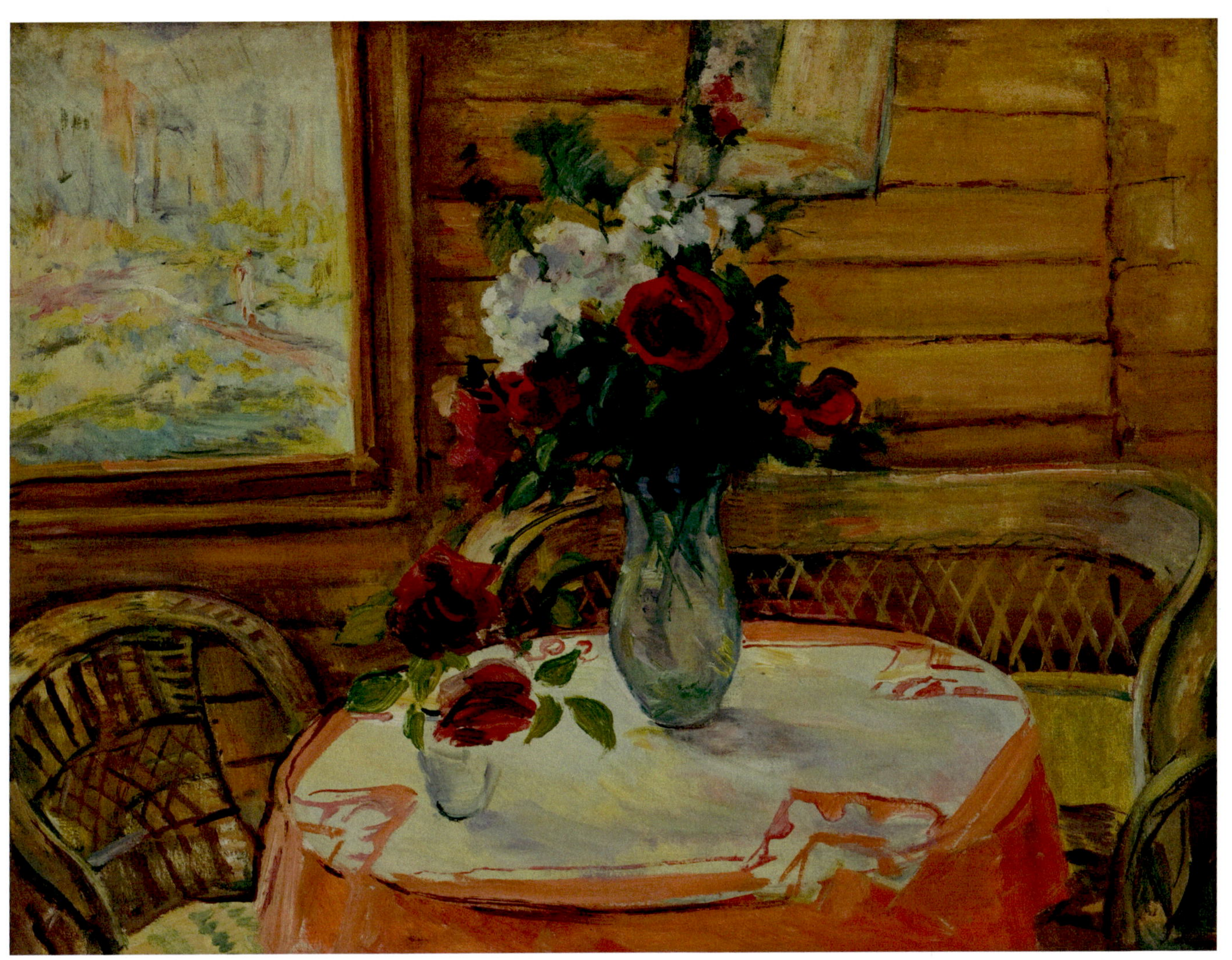

KUZNETSOV Pavel Varfolomevich | *Summer*
Before 1960
Oil on canvas, 78.3 × 100.3 cm
Samara Regional Art Museum

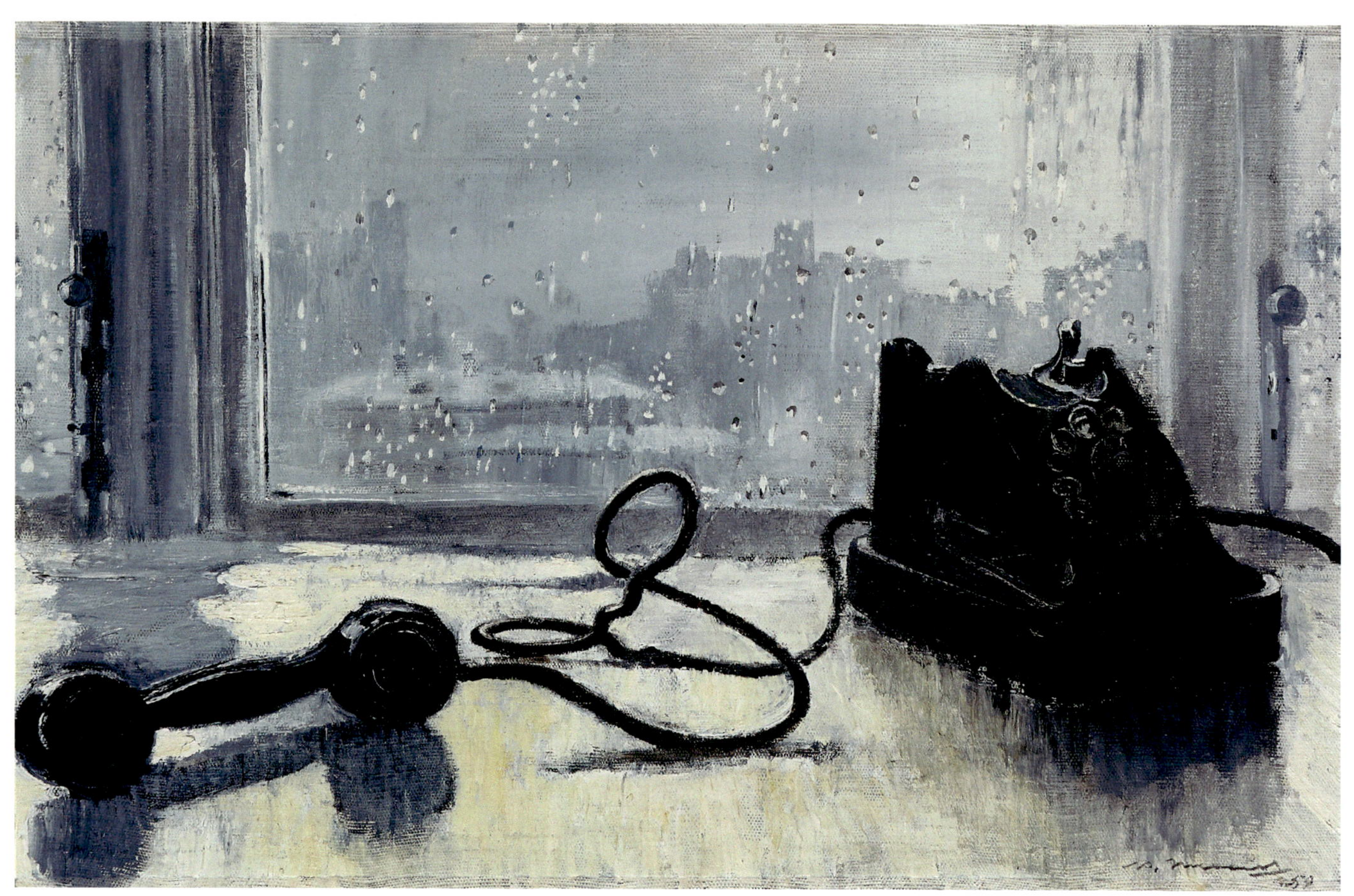

PIMENOV Yury Ivanovich | *Waiting*
1959
Oil on canvas on cardboard, 40 × 60 cm
The State Tretyakov Gallery, Moscow

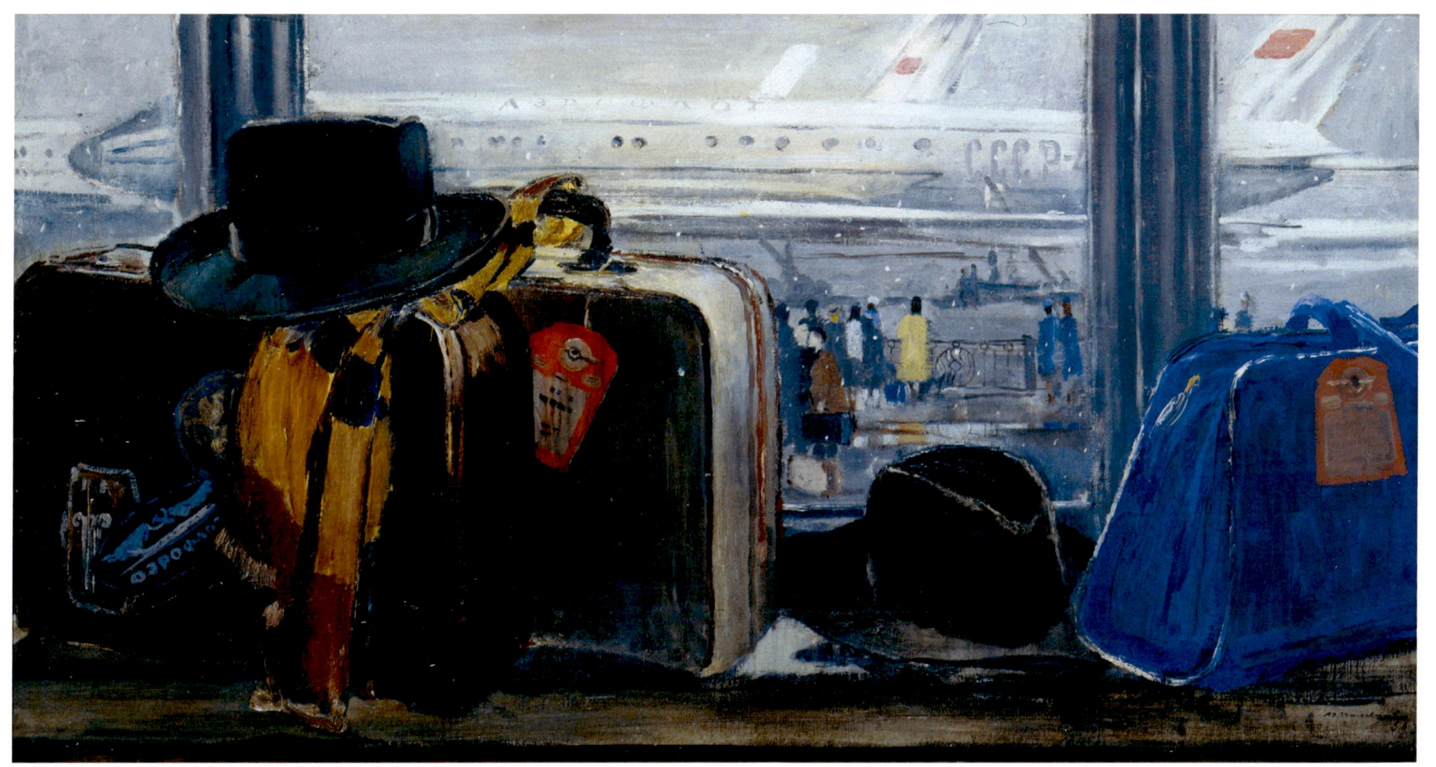

PIMENOV Yury Ivanovich | *Faraway Road*
1959
Oil on canvas, 50 × 90 cm
Kiev National Picture Gallery

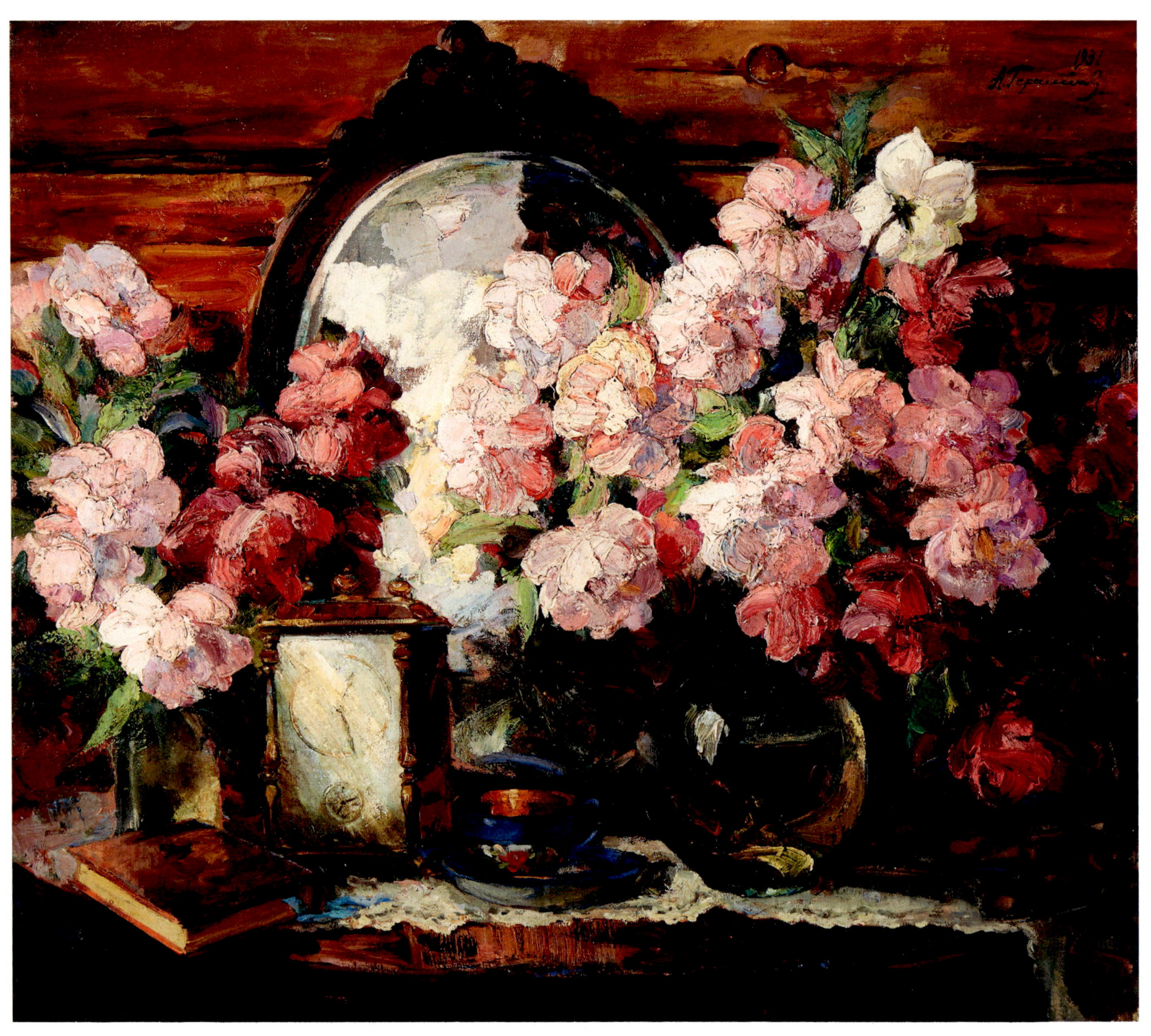

GERASIMOV Aleksandr Mikhaylovich | *Still Life with Peonies*
1960
Oil on canvas, 88 × 95 cm
Kiev National Picture Gallery

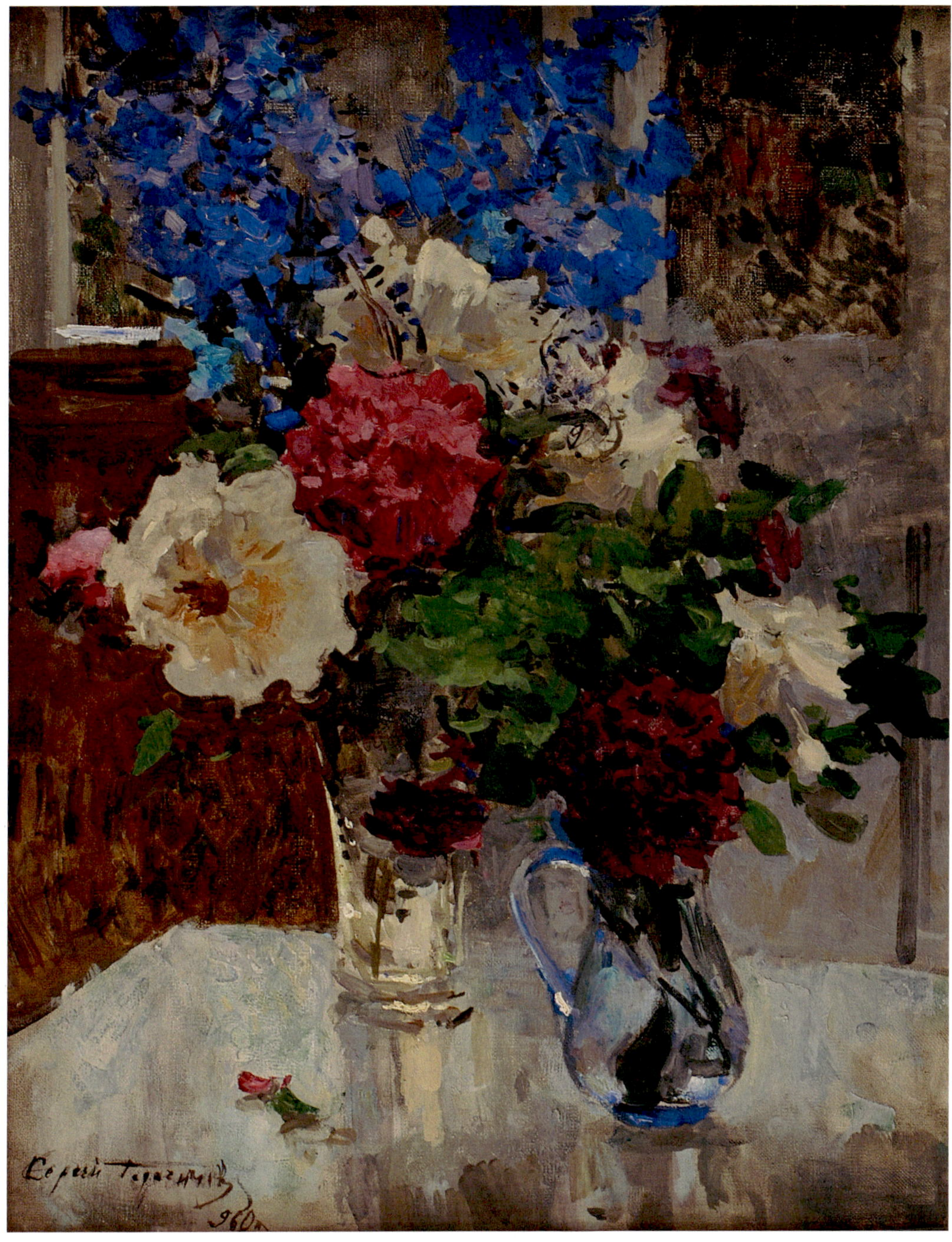

GERASIMOV Sergey Vasilyevich | *Still Life, Bouquet*
1960
Oil on canvas, 90.2 × 71 cm
The State Regional Art Museum named after
I. P. Pojalostin, Ryazan

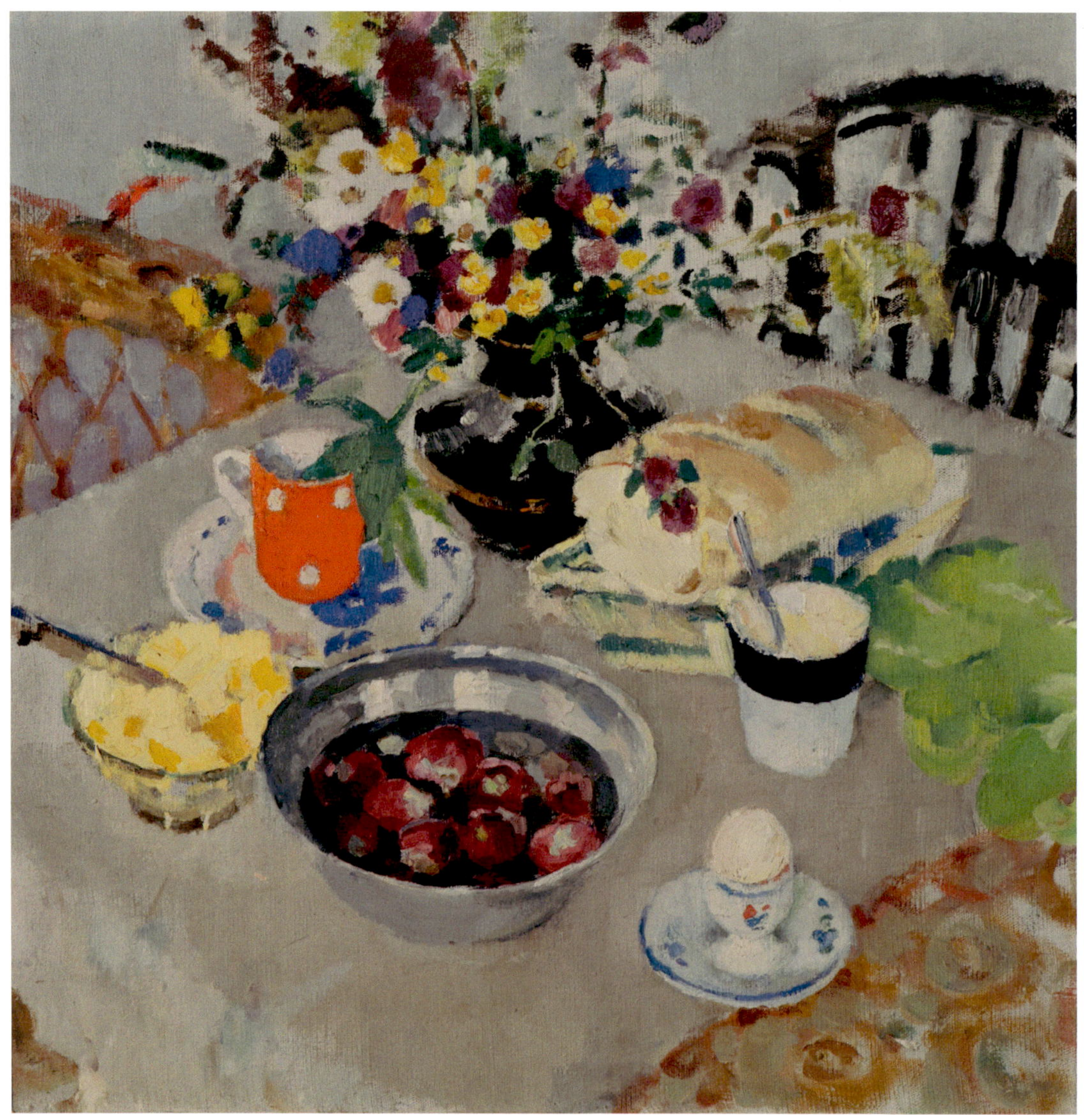

BOGAEVSKAYA Olga Borisovna | *Still Life*
1960
Oil on canvas, 65 × 65 cm
The State Russian Museum, St Petersburg

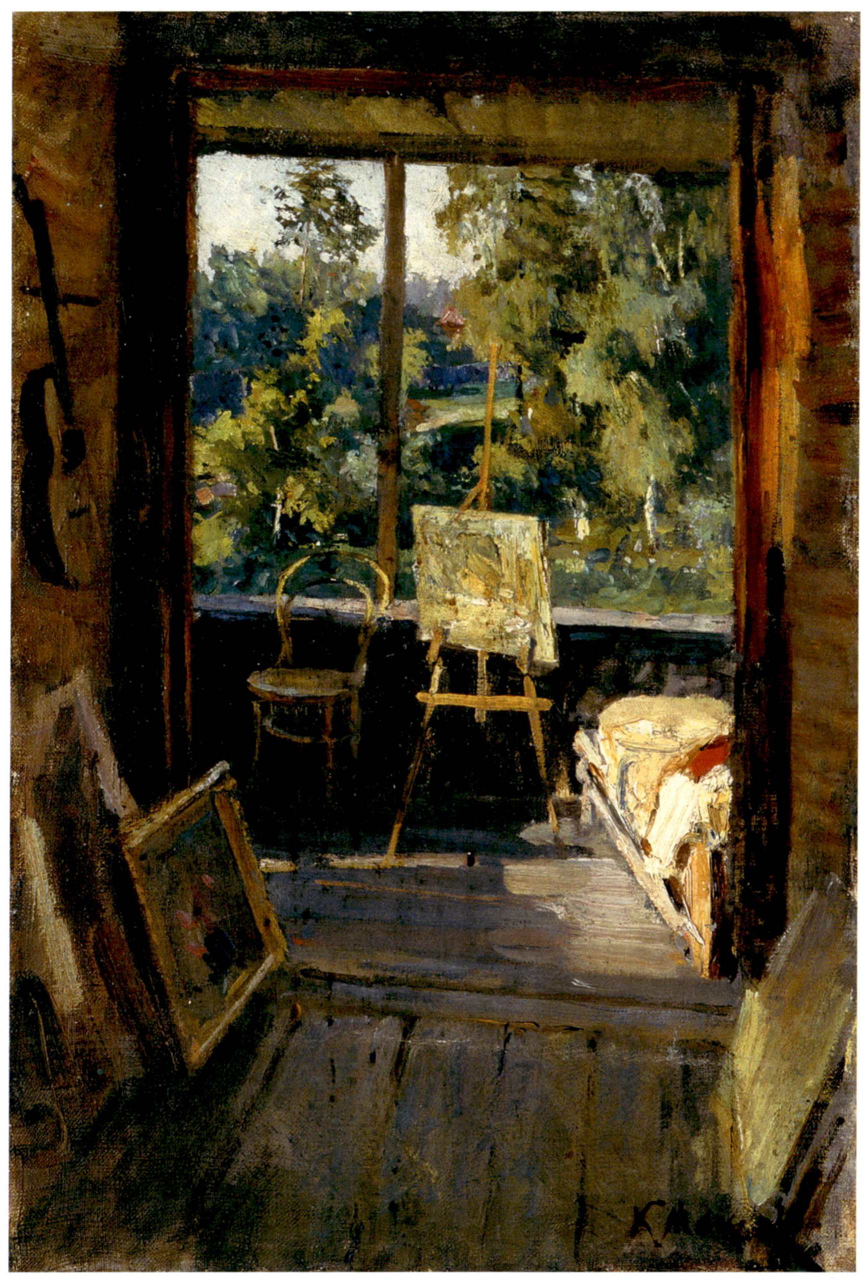

MAKSIMOV Konstantin Mefodovich | *Studio and a Window View*
1963
Oil on canvas, 60 × 40 cm
Private collection

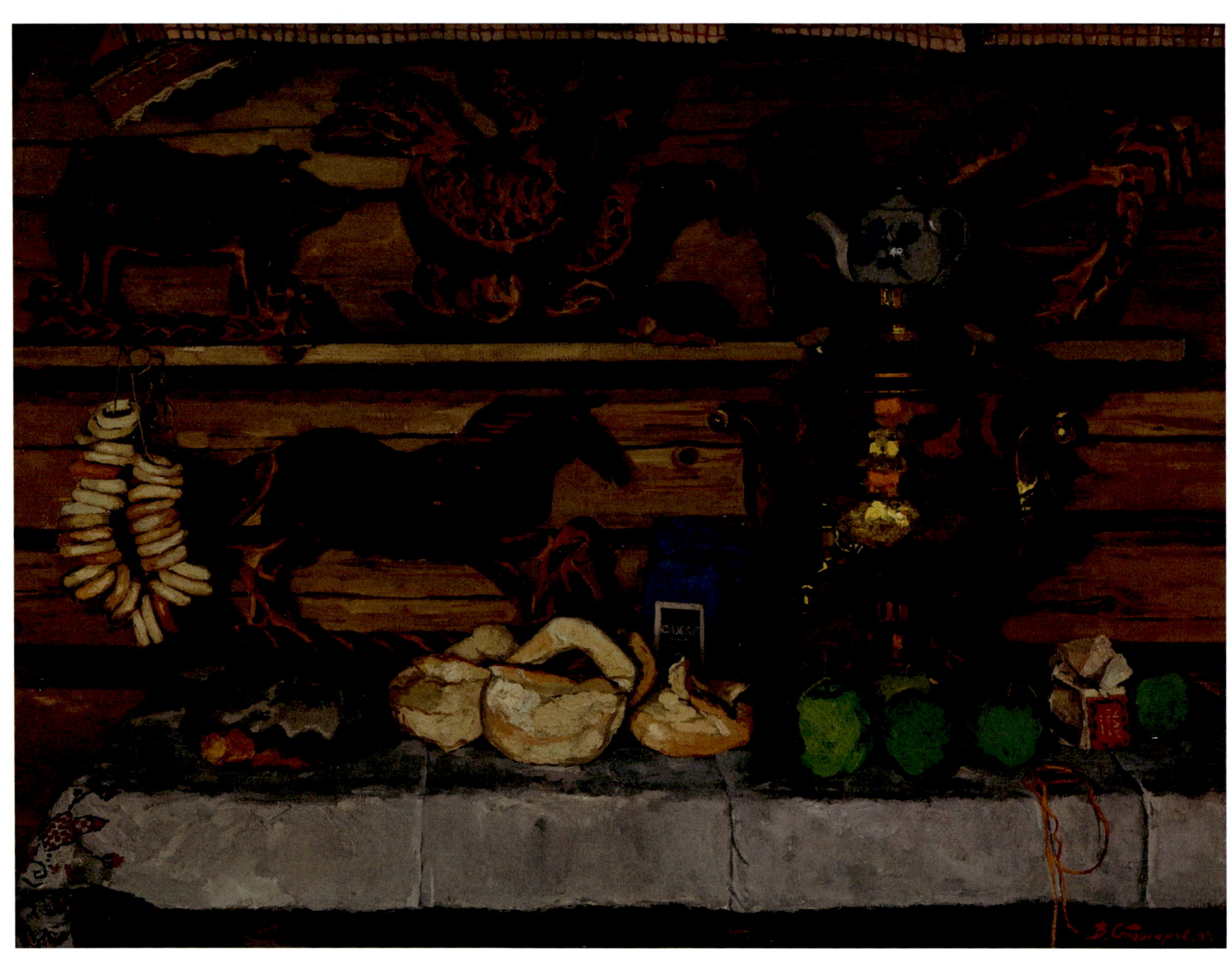

STOZHAROV Vladimir Fedorovich | *Moscow Bread*
1964
Oil on canvas, 99 × 139.5 cm
Samara Regional Art Museum

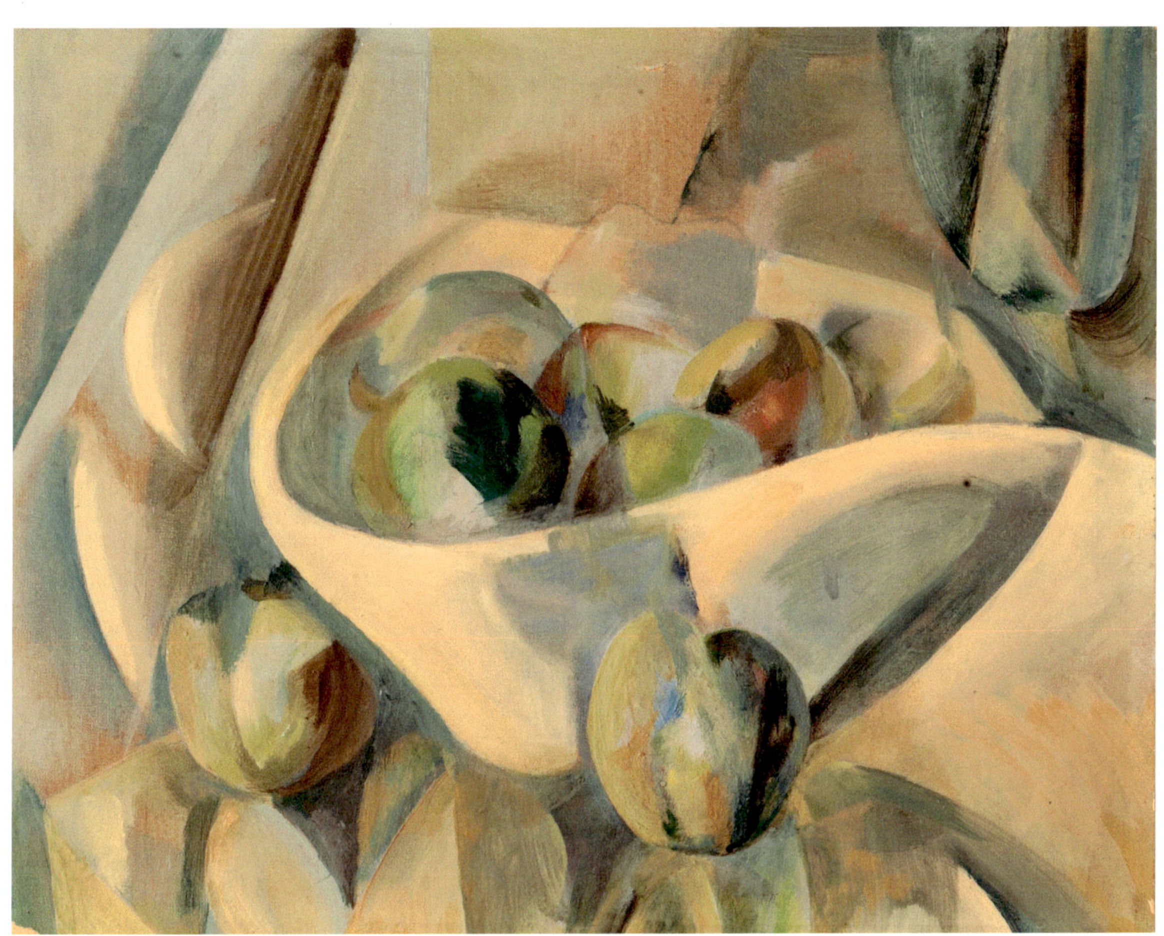

KONDRATIEV Pavel Mikhailovich | *Apples in a Vase*
1964
Oil on cardboard, 22.5 × 29 cm
The State Russian Museum, St Petersburg

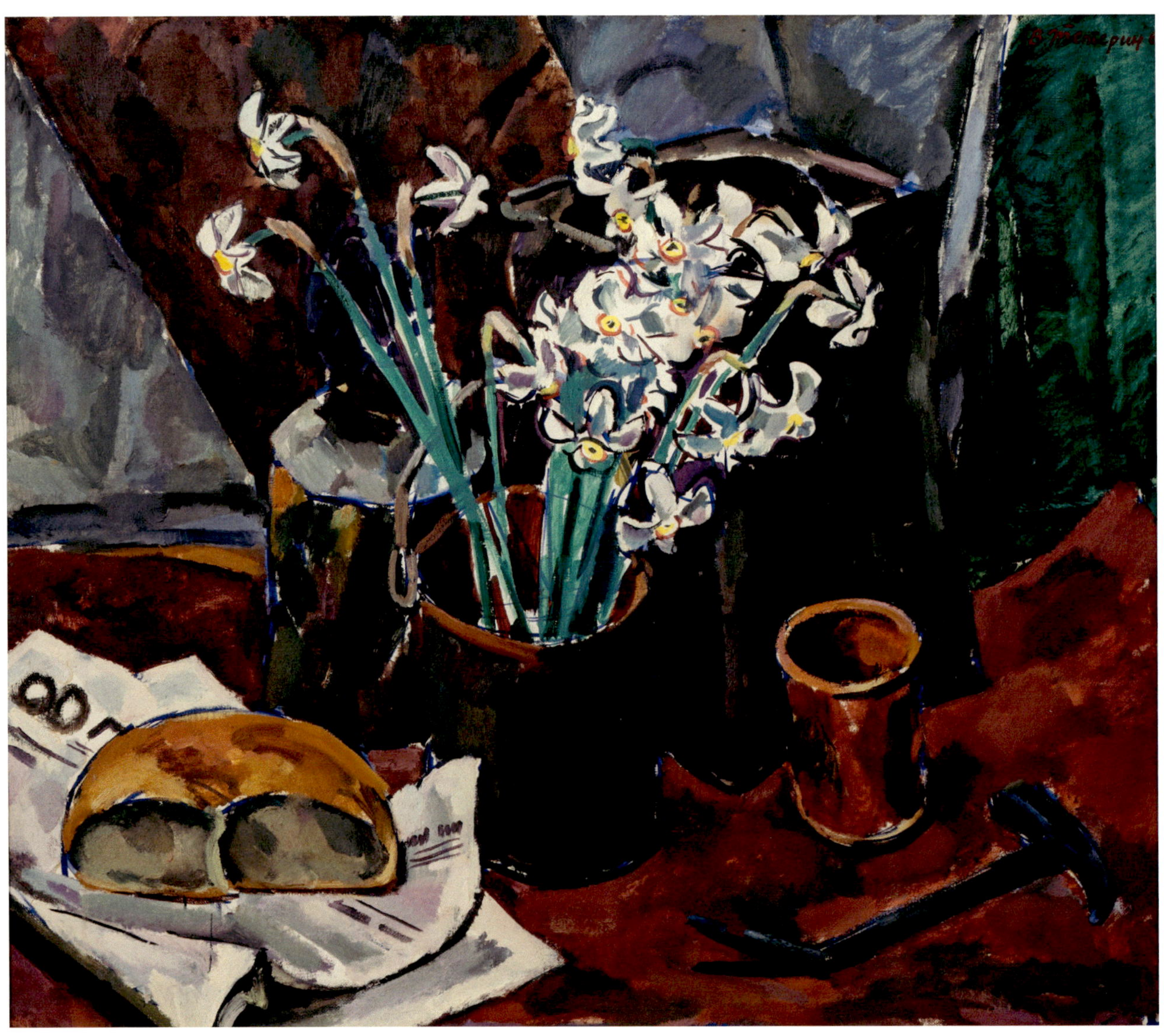

TETERIN Victor Kuzmich | *Still Life with Daffodils, Black and White*
1964
Oil on canvas, 100 × 115 cm
The State Russian Museum, St Petersburg

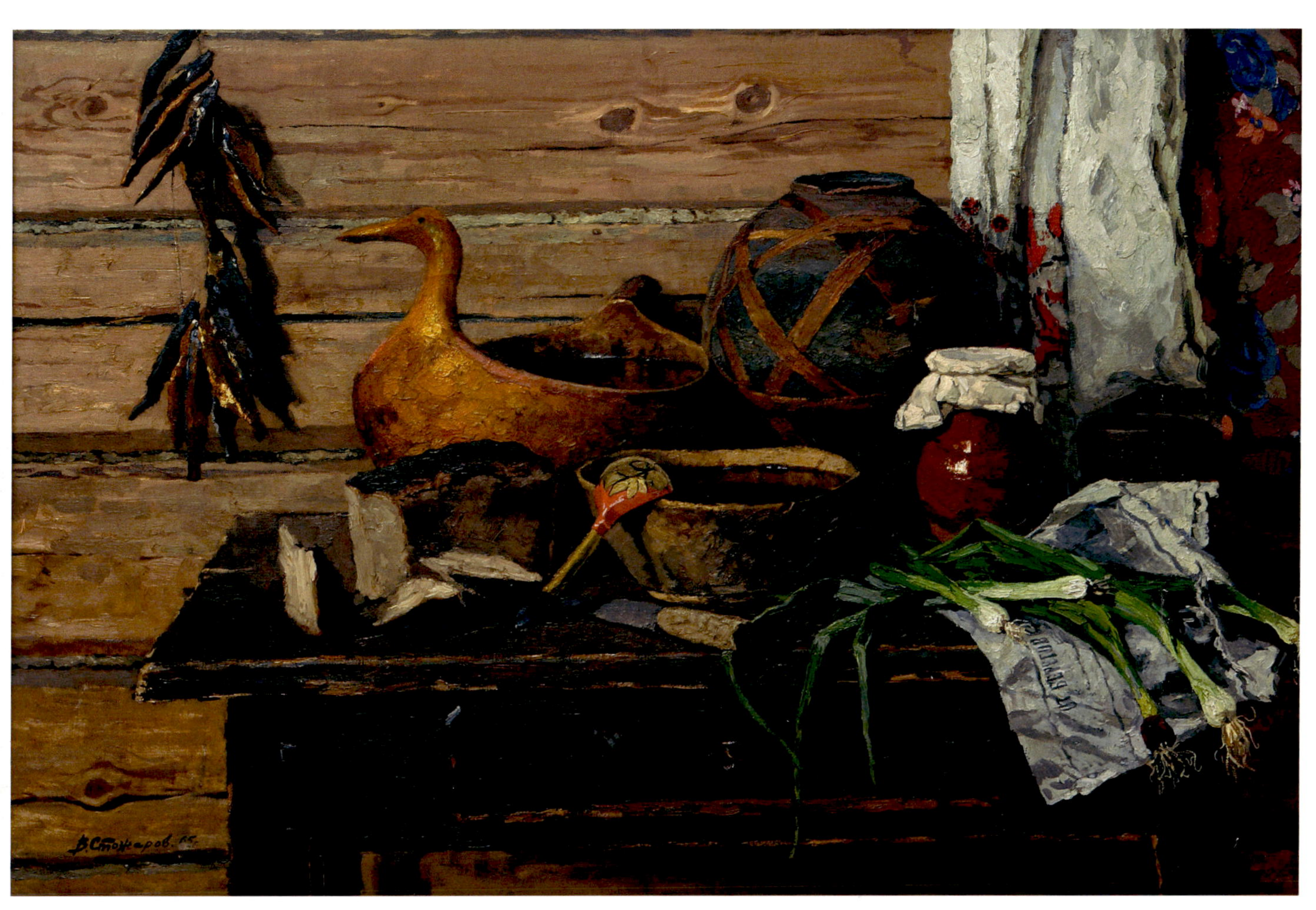

STOZHAROV Vladimir Fedorovich | *Goblet with Kvas, Still Life*
1965
Oil on canvas, 90 × 130 cm
Yaroslavl Art Museum

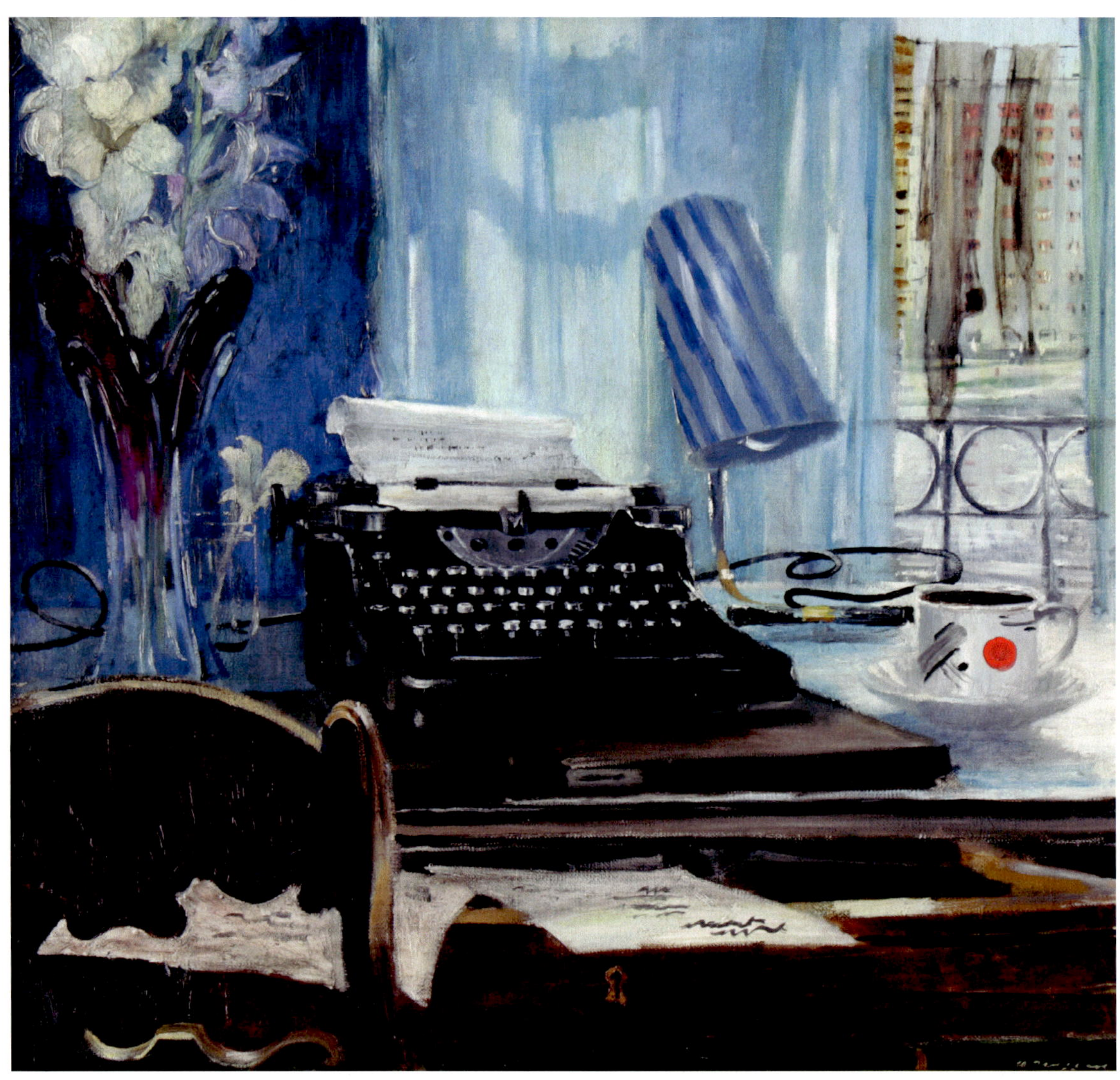

PIMENOV Yury Ivanovich | *Lyrical Poems*
1965
Oil on canvas, 73.5 × 78 cm
Kursk State Picture Gallery named after A. A. Deineka

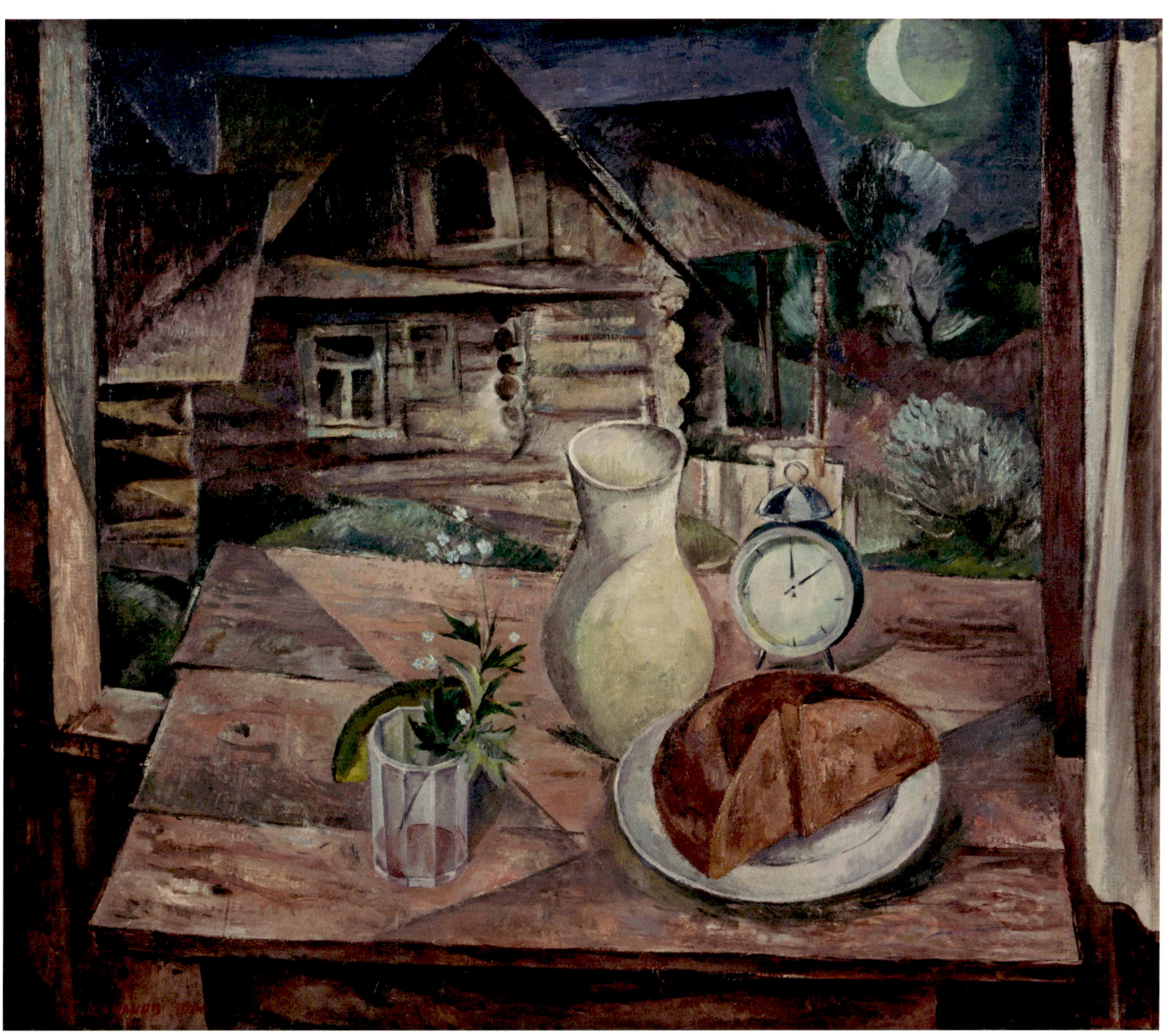

SHAMANOV Boris Ivanovich | *Still Life with Alarm Clock*
1966
Oil on canvas, 97 × 109.5 cm
The State Russian Museum, St Petersburg

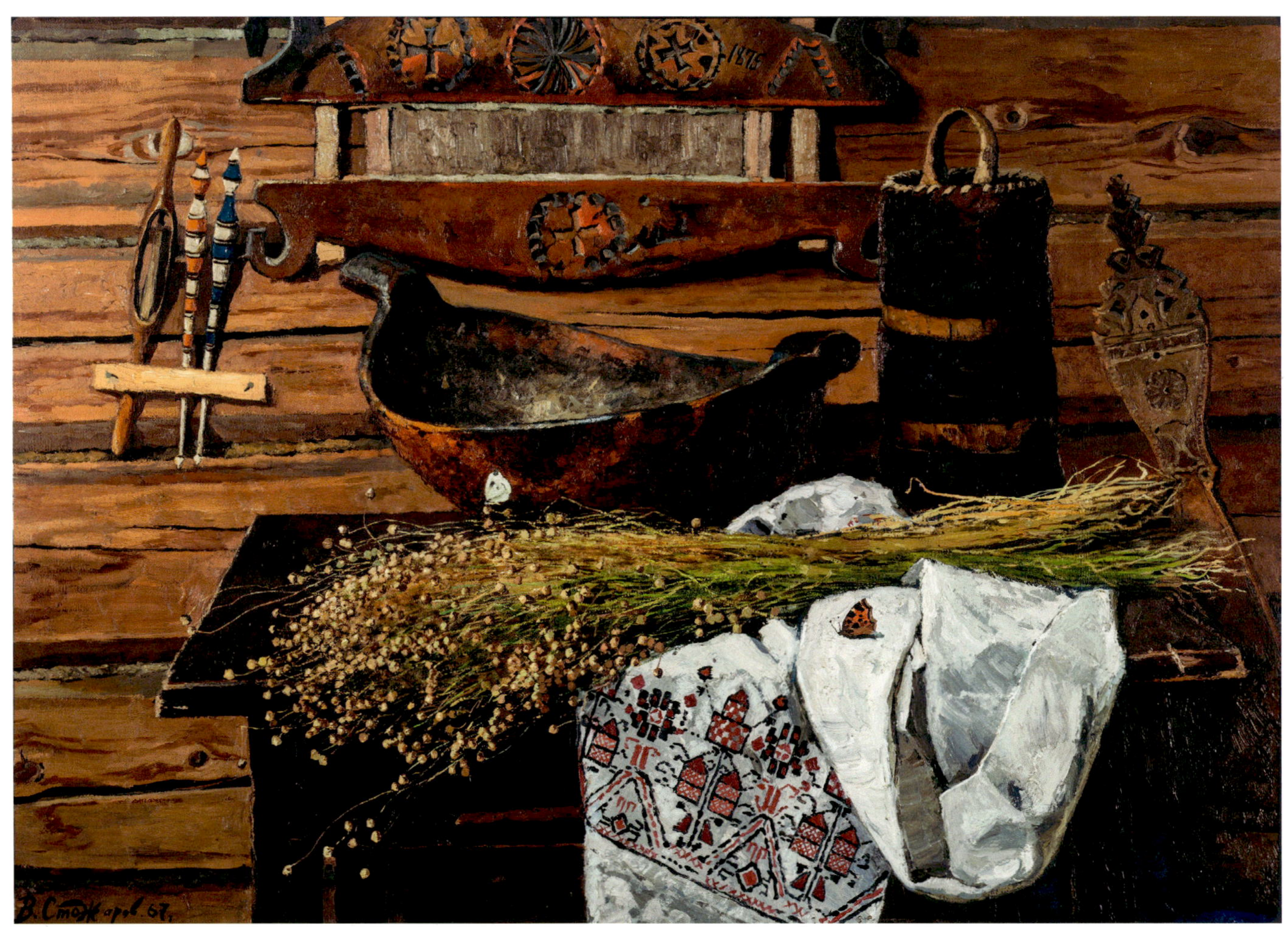

STOZHAROV Vladimir Fedorovich | *Linen*
1967
Oil on canvas, 89 × 124.5 cm
The State Tretyakov Gallery, Moscow

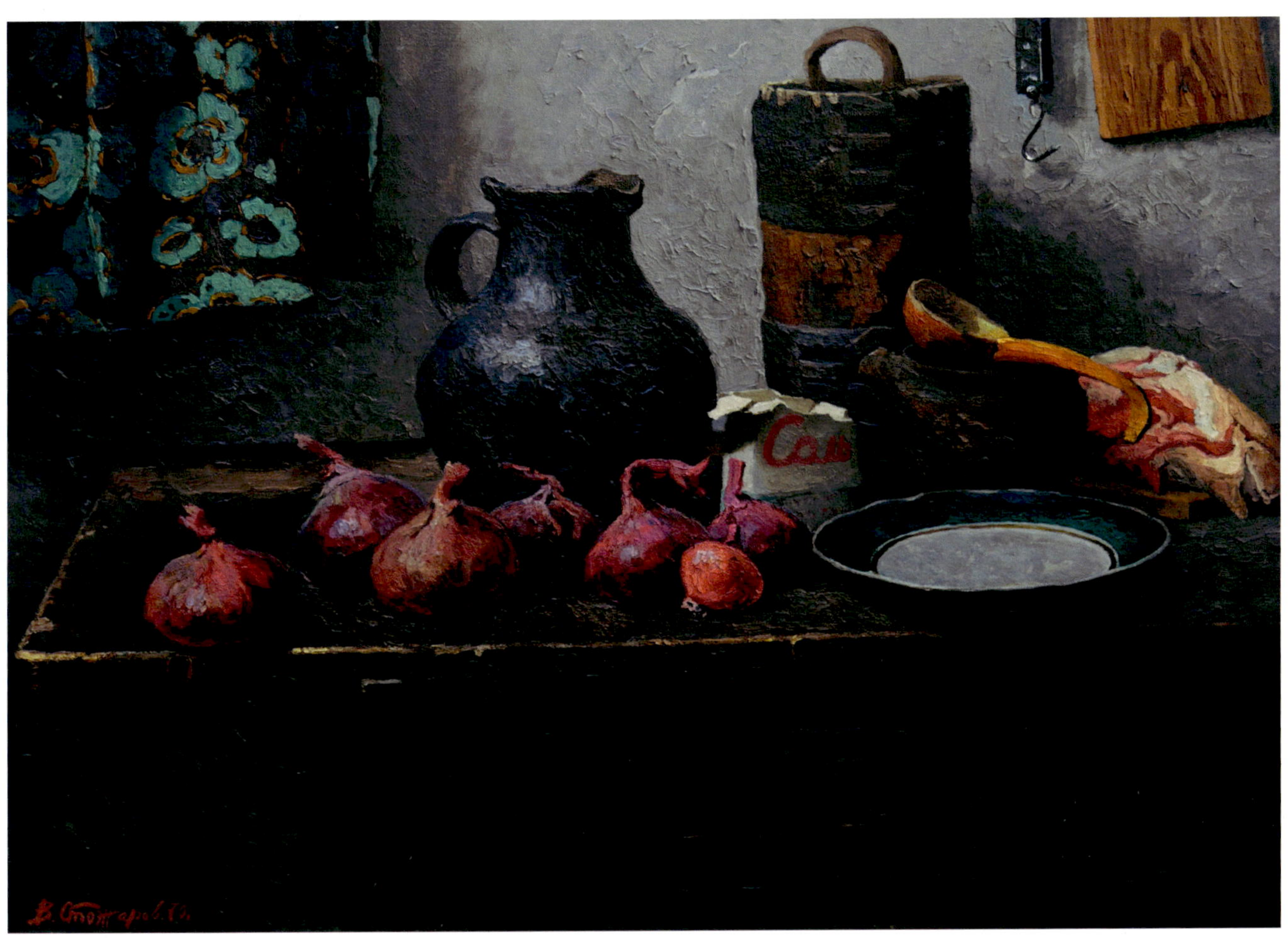

STOZHAROV Vladimir Fedorovich | *Romanov's Onion*
1970
Oil on canvas, 80 × 110 cm
Kursk State Picture Gallery named after A. A. Deineka

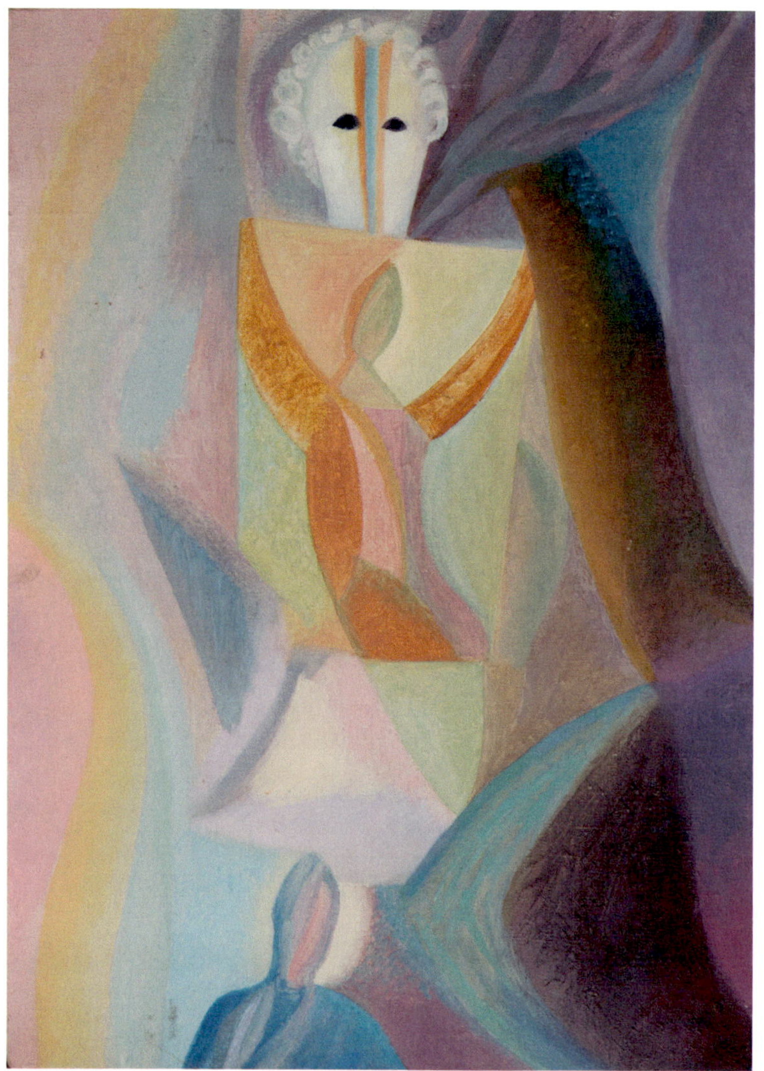

GLEBOVA Tatyana Nikolaevna | *Still Life with Artwork*
1970
Oil on canvas, 57.5 × 40.5 cm
The State Russian Museum, St Petersburg

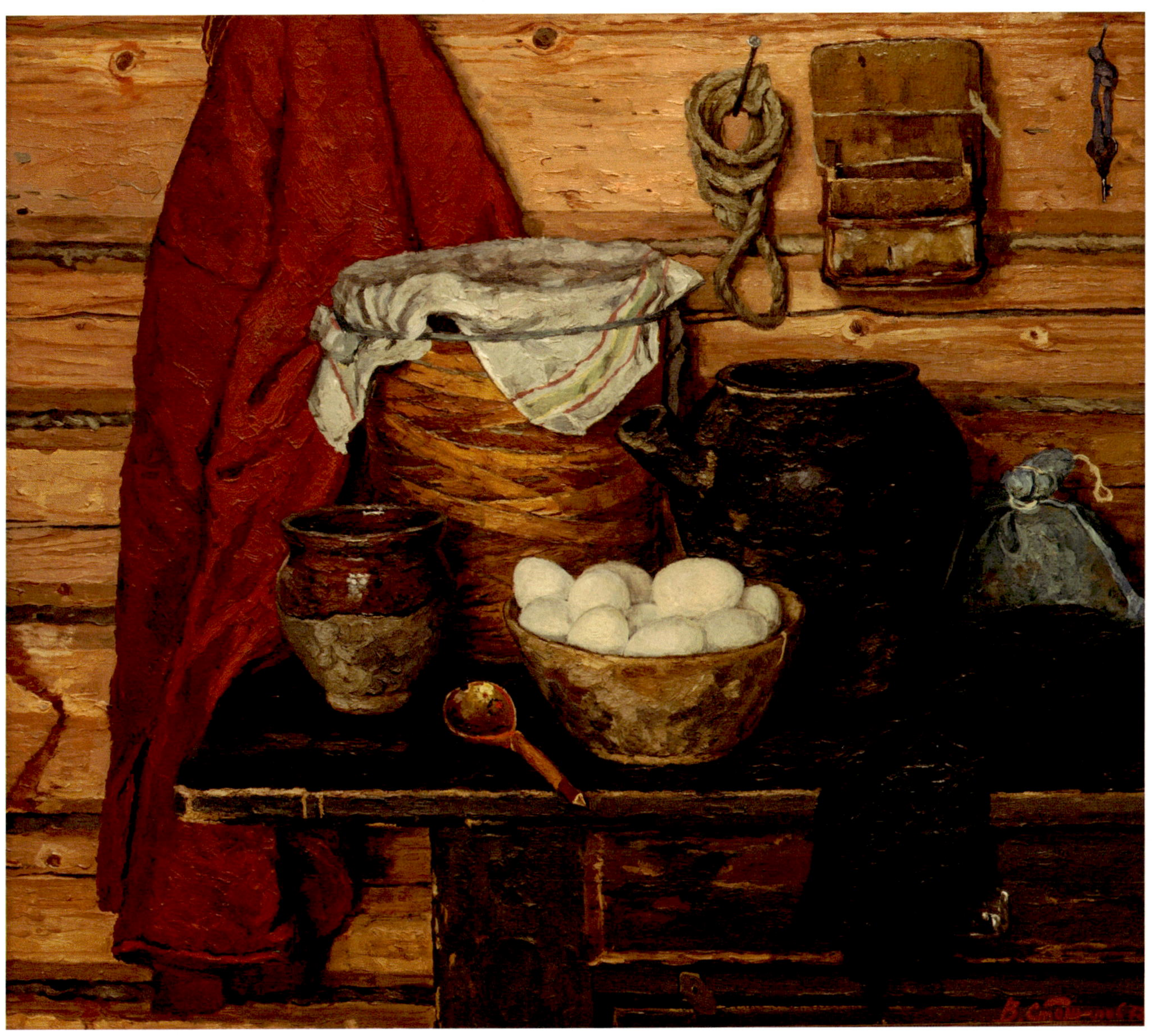

STOZHAROV Vladimir Fedorovich | *Still Life with Soured Milk*
1972
Oil on canvas, 90 × 115 cm
The State Russian Museum, St Petersburg

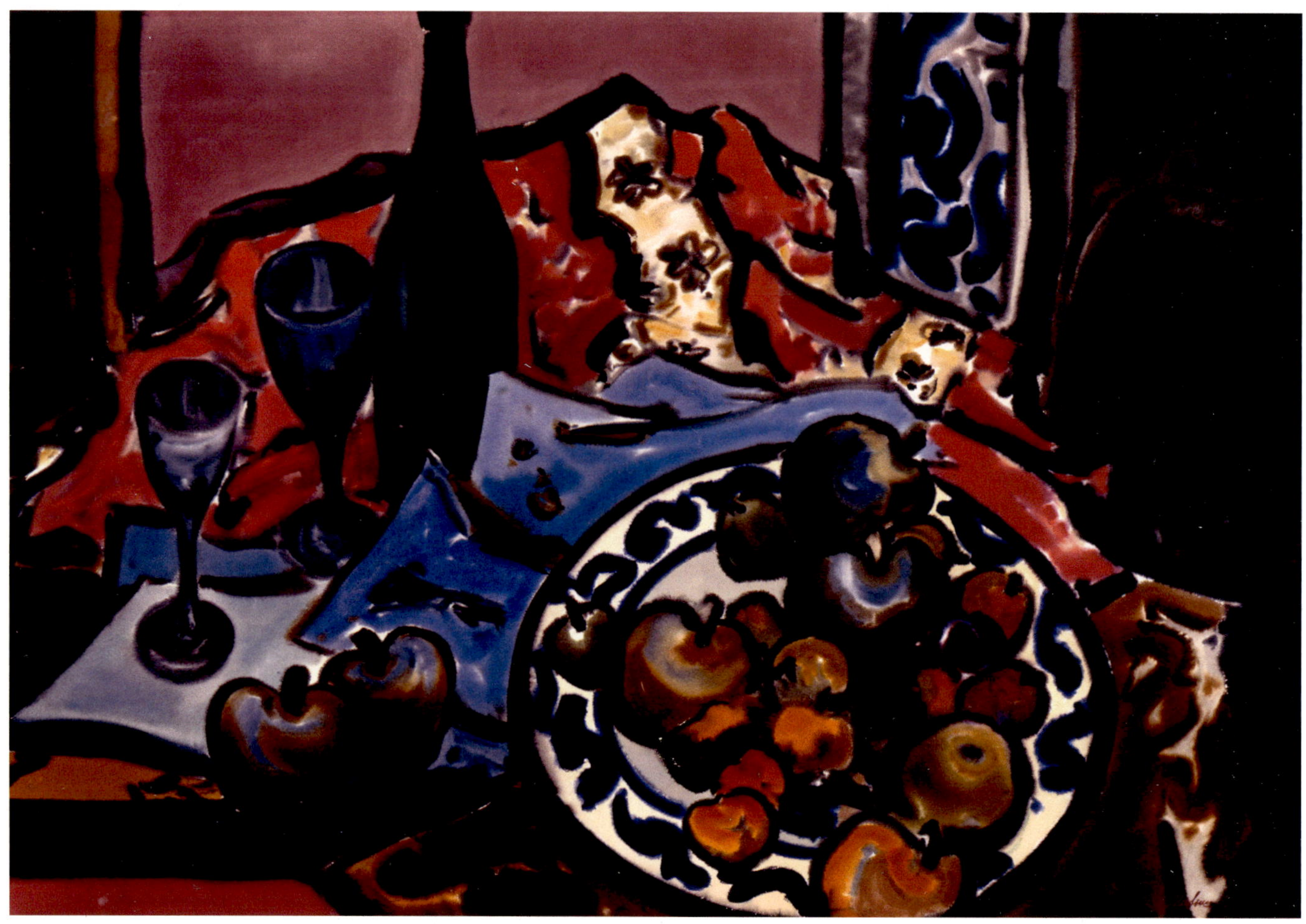

MALYSH Gavriil Kondratyevich | *Still Life*
1973
Oil on canvas, 72 × 102 cm
Private collection

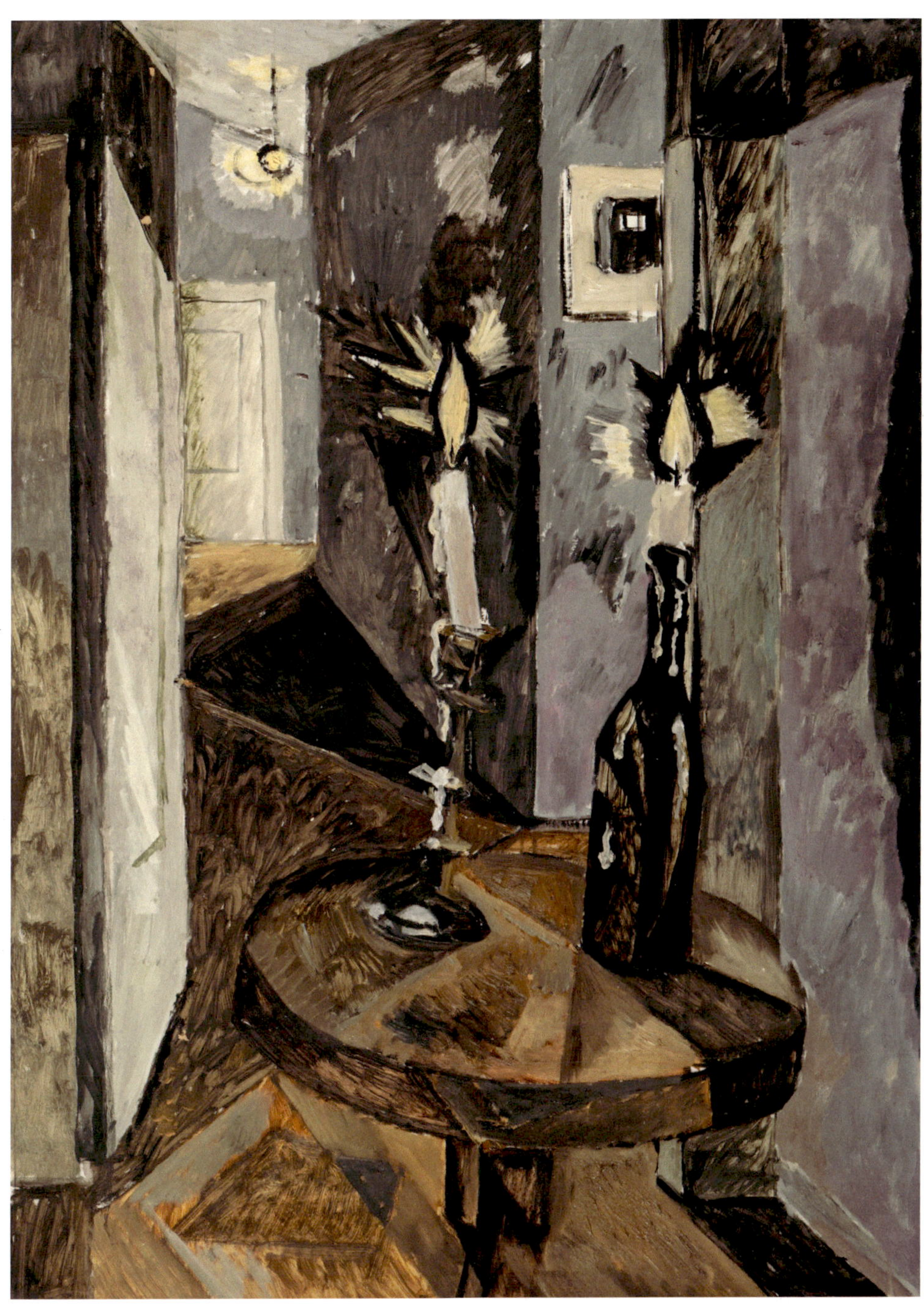

ELKONIN Victor Borisovich | *Lighted Candles with Hallway in Background*
1973
Oil on fibreglass, 122 × 86 cm
The State Russian Museum, St Petersburg

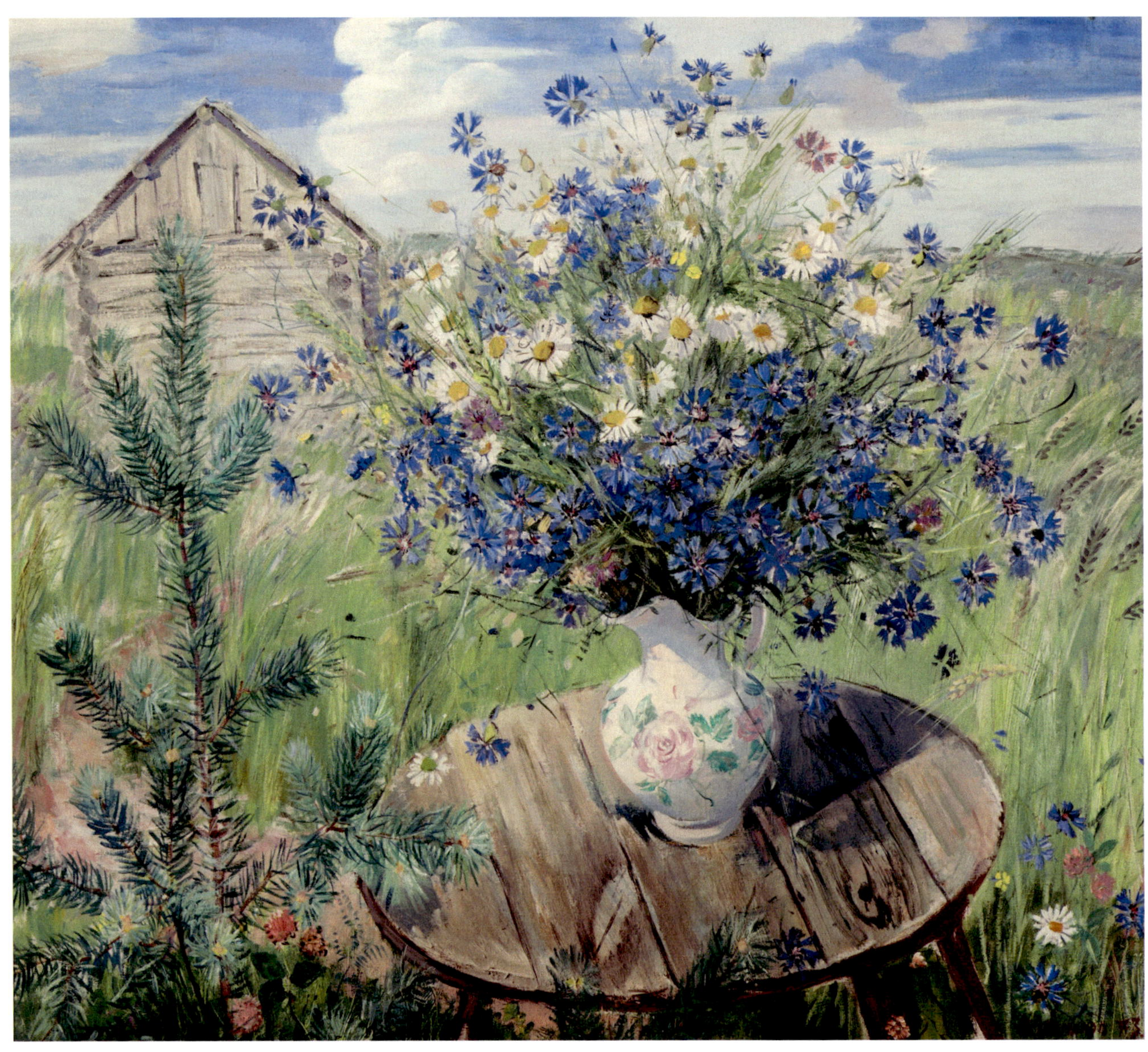

SHAMANOV Boris Ivanovich | *Green Rye, Bluebells*
1973
Oil on canvas, 95 × 105 cm
The State Russian Museum, St Petersburg

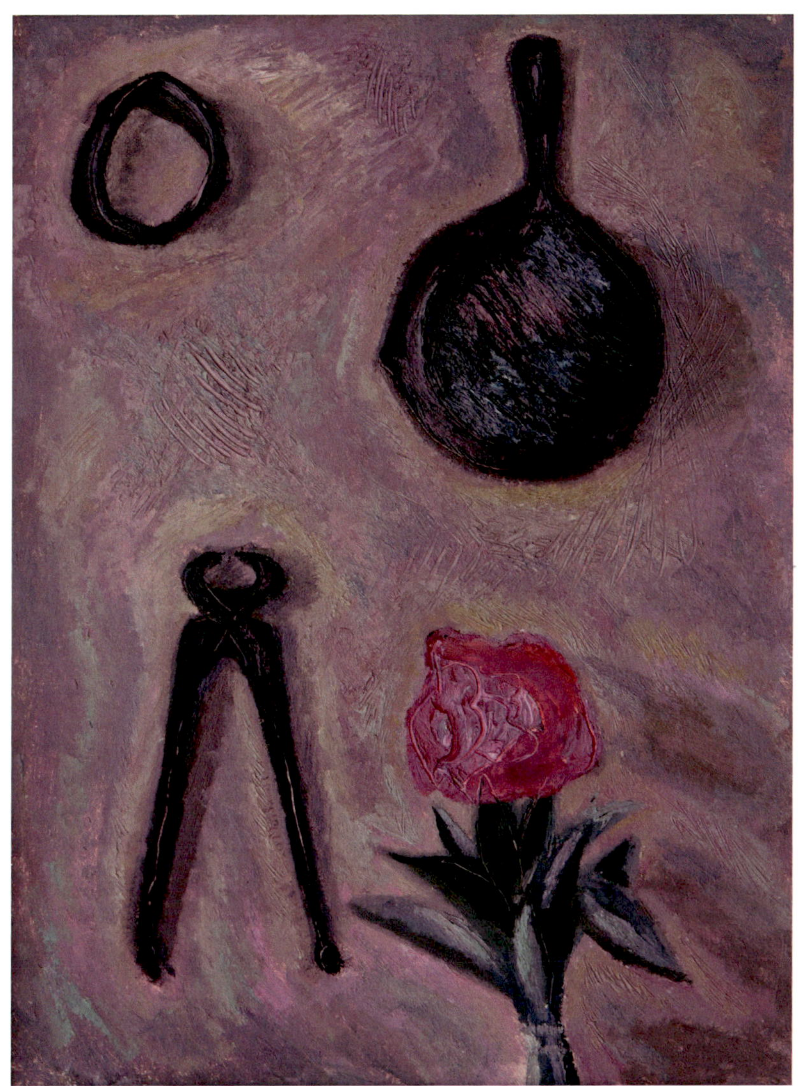

POPKOV Viktor Efimovich | *Still Life with Flower*
1973
Oil on cardboard, 69.8 × 50.7 cm
Kursk State Picture Gallery named after A. A. Deineka

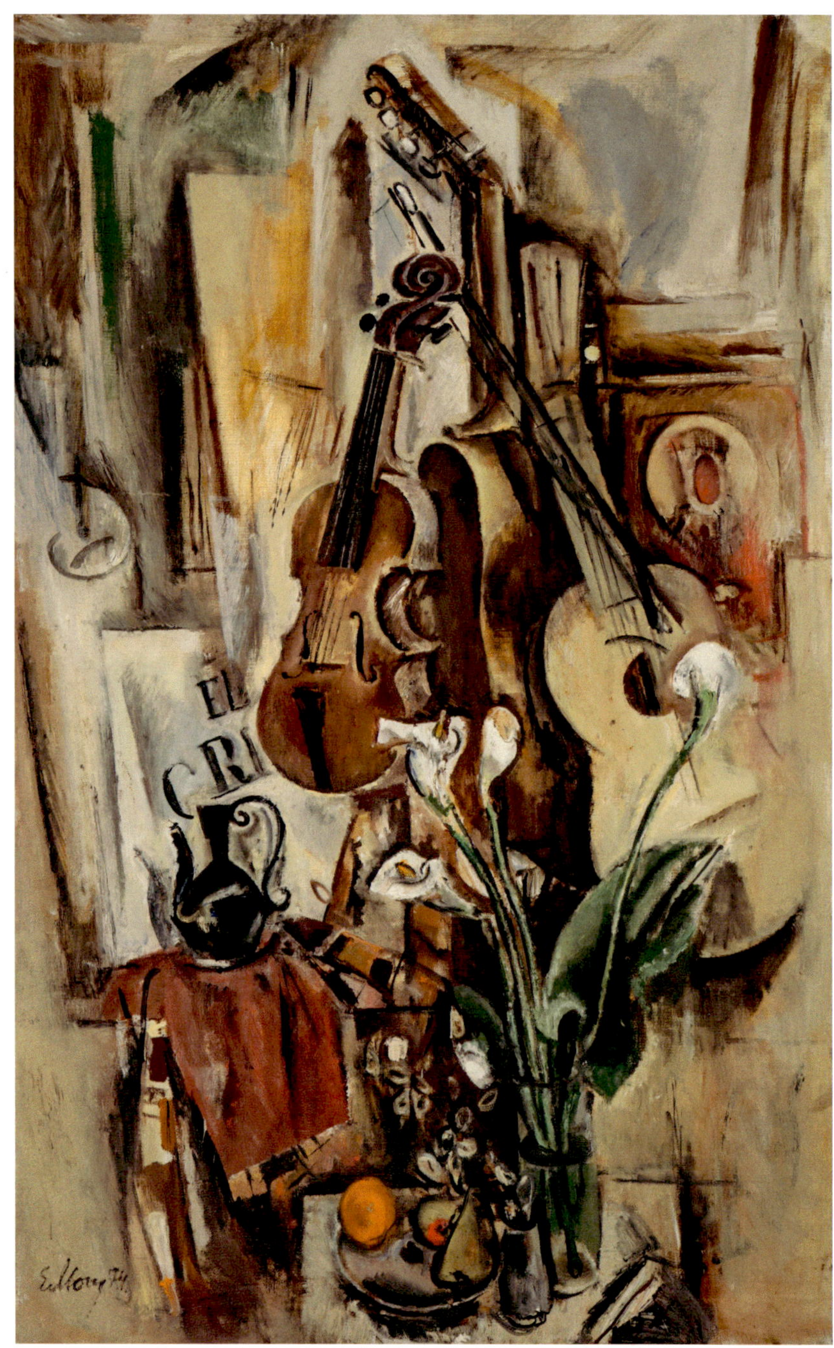

MOISEENKO Evsey Evseevich | *Vertical Still Life with String Instruments*
(Guitars, Calla Lillies)
1974
Oil on canvas, 130 × 80 cm
The State Russian Museum, St Petersburg

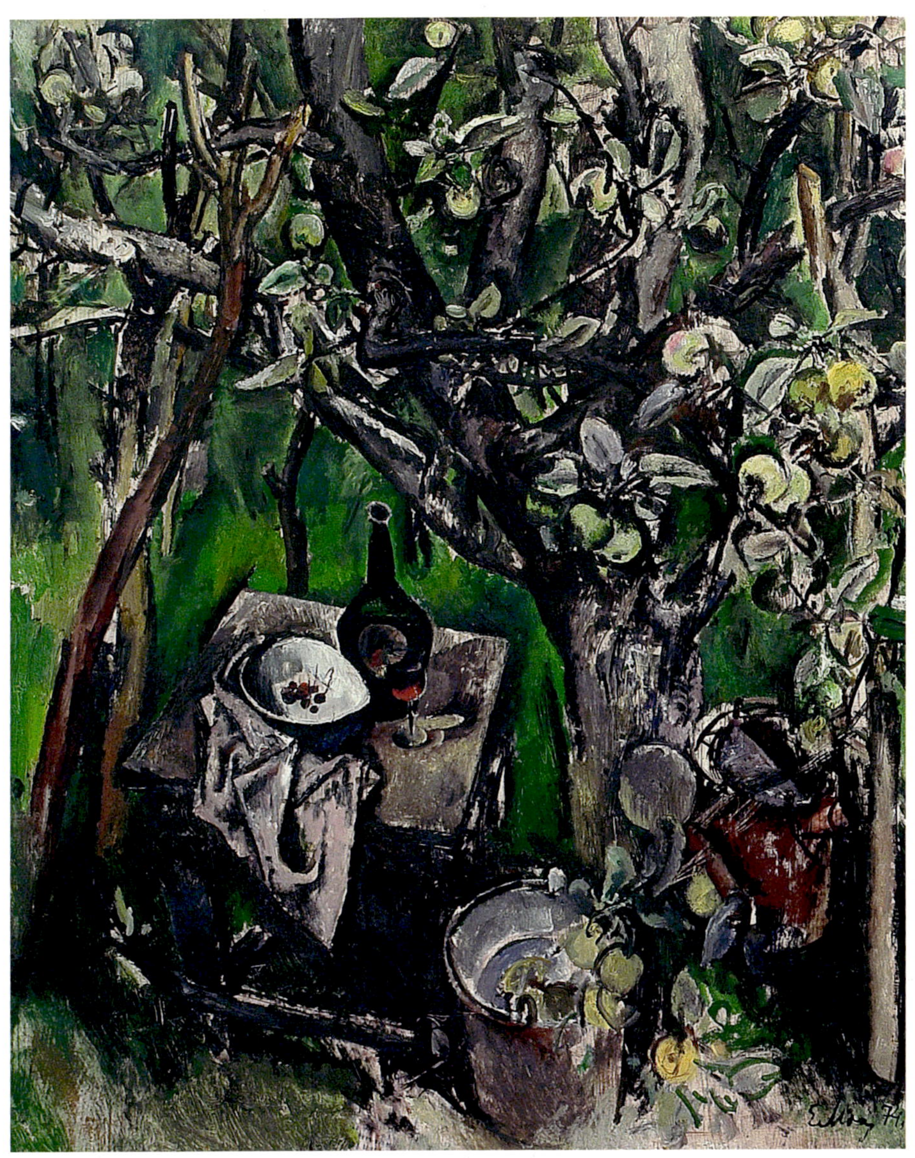

MOISEENKO Evsey Evseevich | *Still Life Under Apple Tree*
1974
Oil on canvas, 89.2 × 70.2 cm
Yaroslavl Art Museum

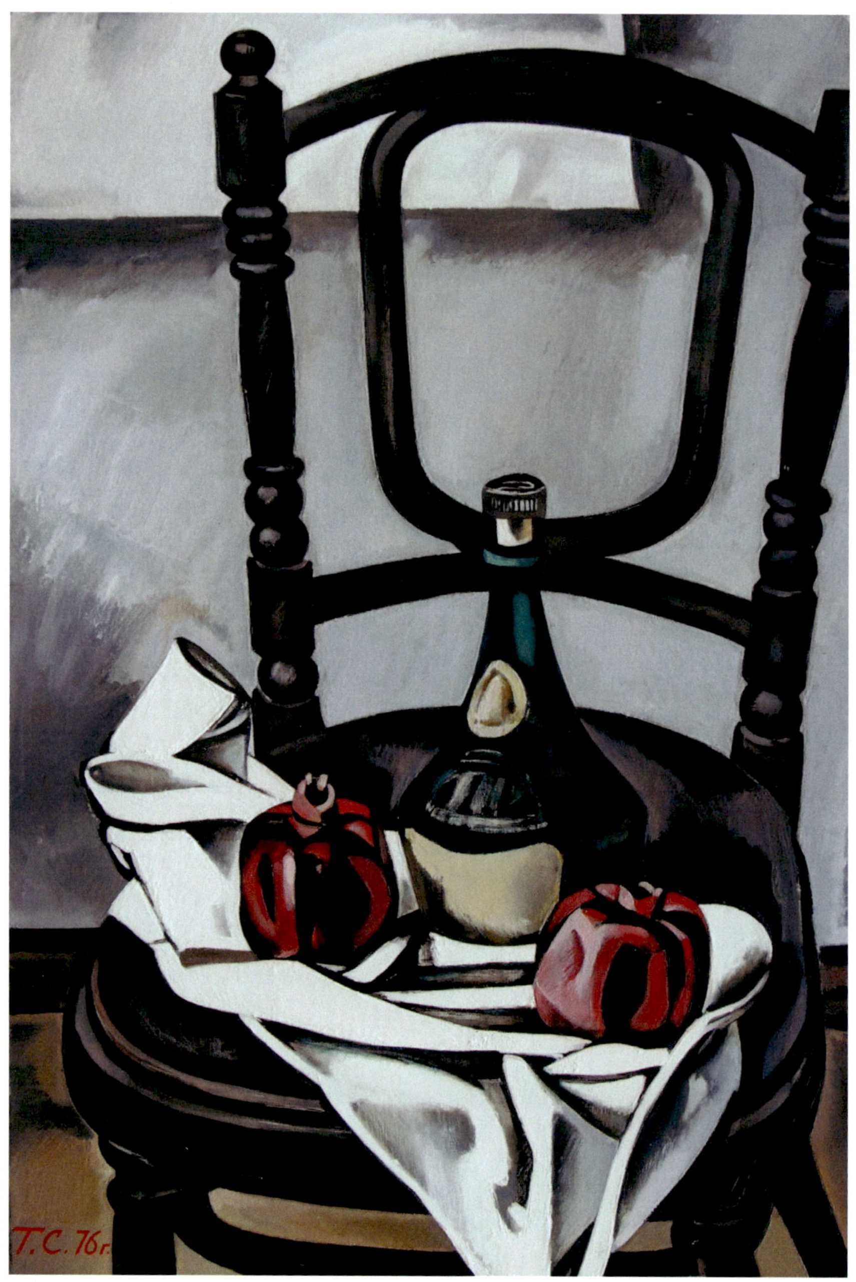

SALAHOV Tair Teymur oglu | *Still Life with Viennese Chair*
1976
Oil on canvas, 72 × 65 cm
Private Collection

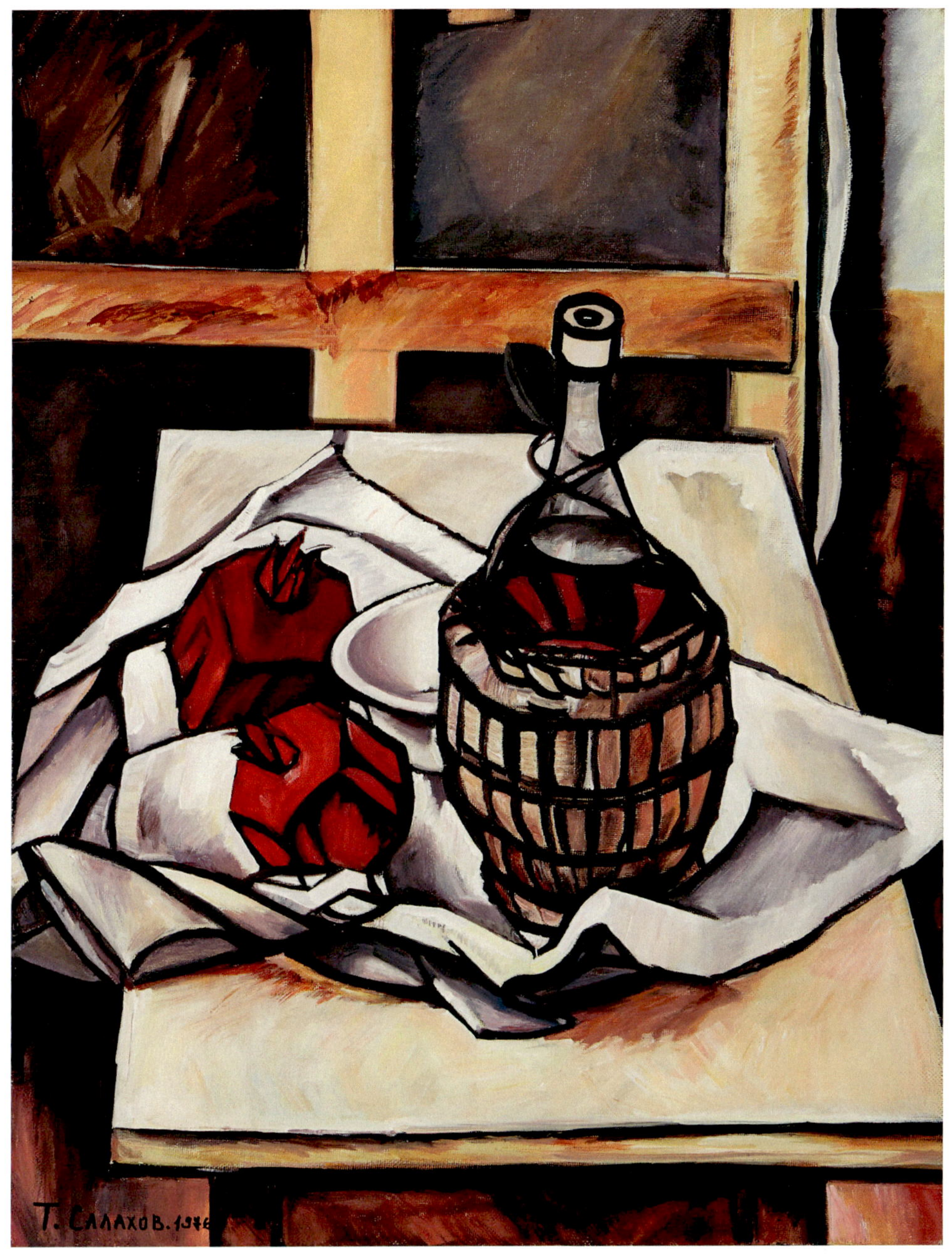

SALAHOV Tair Teymur oglu | *Still Life from a Series with Pomegranates*
1976
Oil on canvas, 80.3 × 60 cm
Private Collection

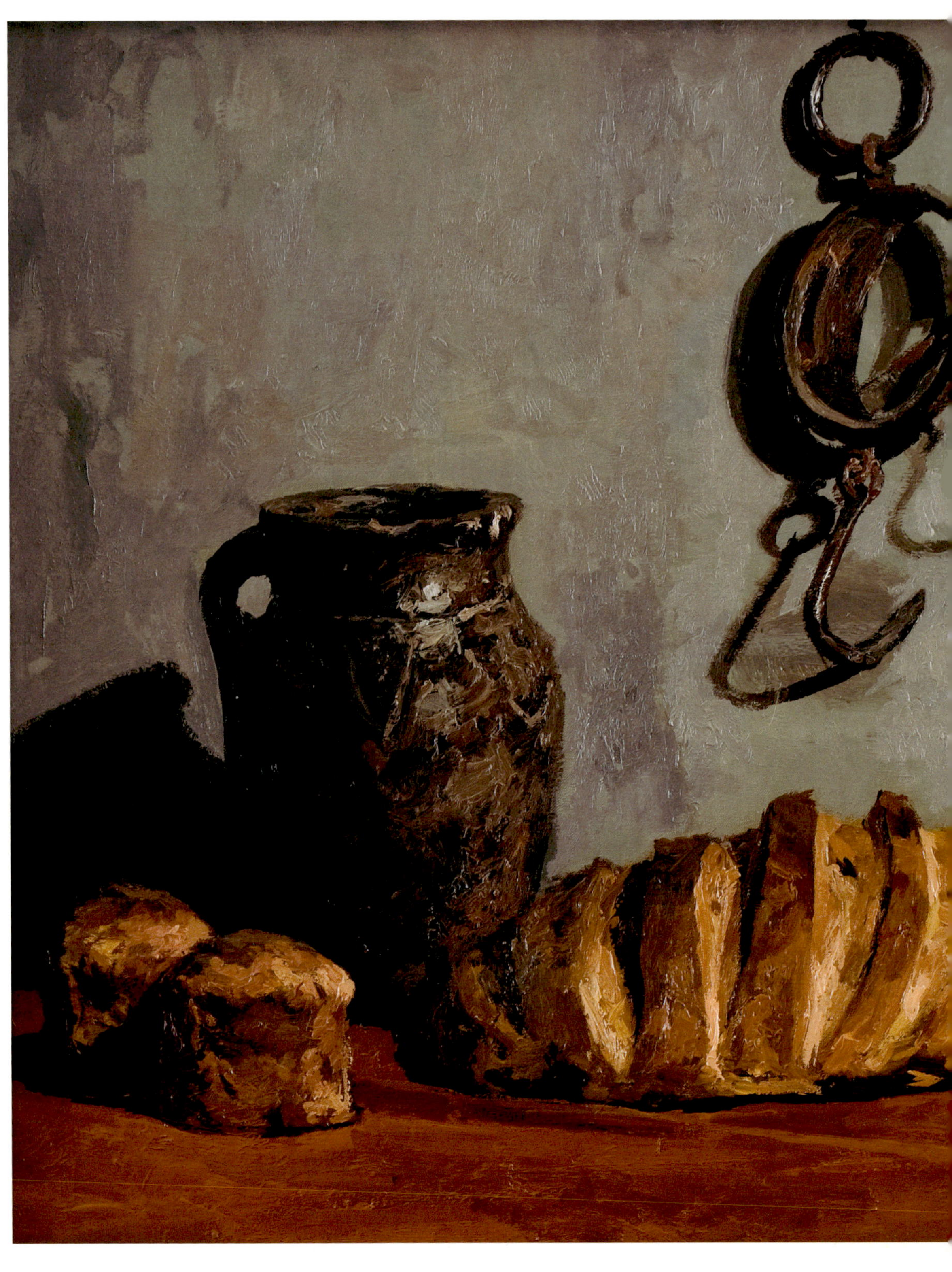

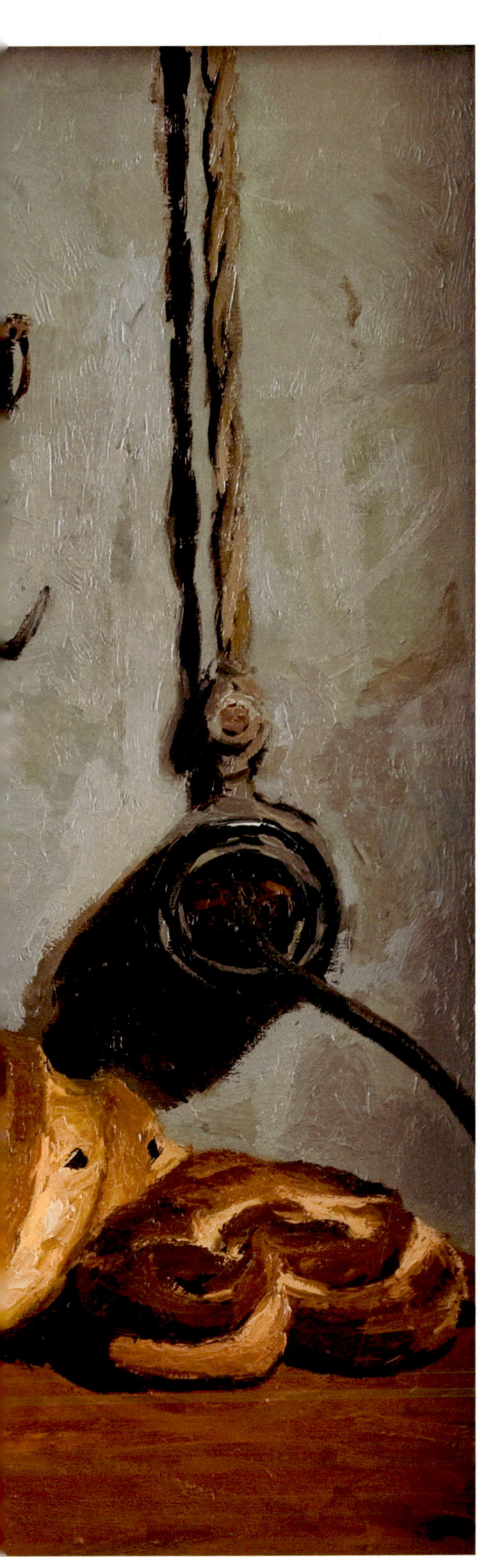

KORZHEV Geli Mikhailovich

Still Life with Bezmen
1977
Oil on canvas, 61 × 55.3 cm
The State Regional Art
Museum named after
I. P. Pojalostin, Ryazan

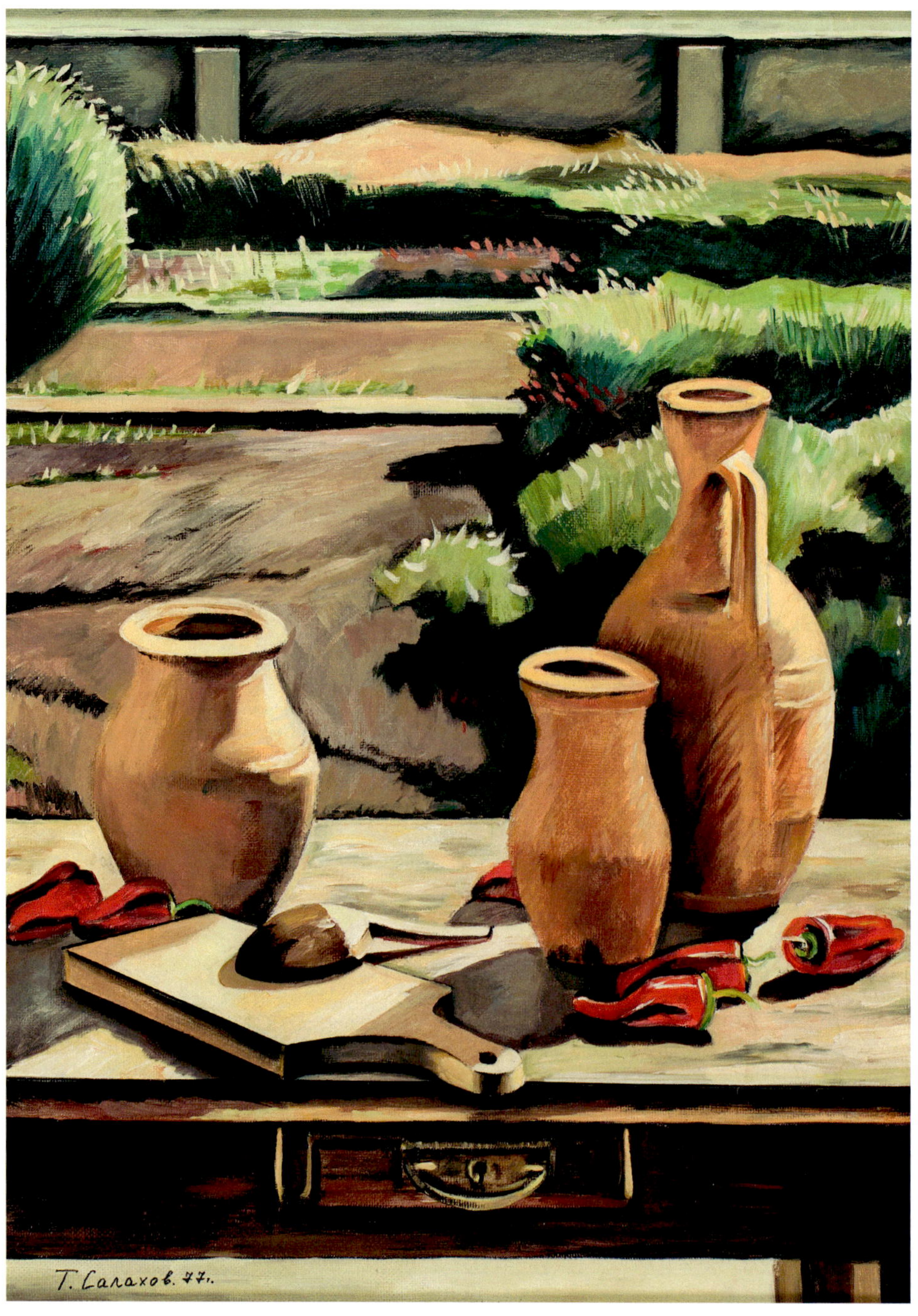

SALAHOV Tair Teymur oglu | *Still Life with Jugs*
1977
Oil on canvas, 95 × 84 cm
Private collection

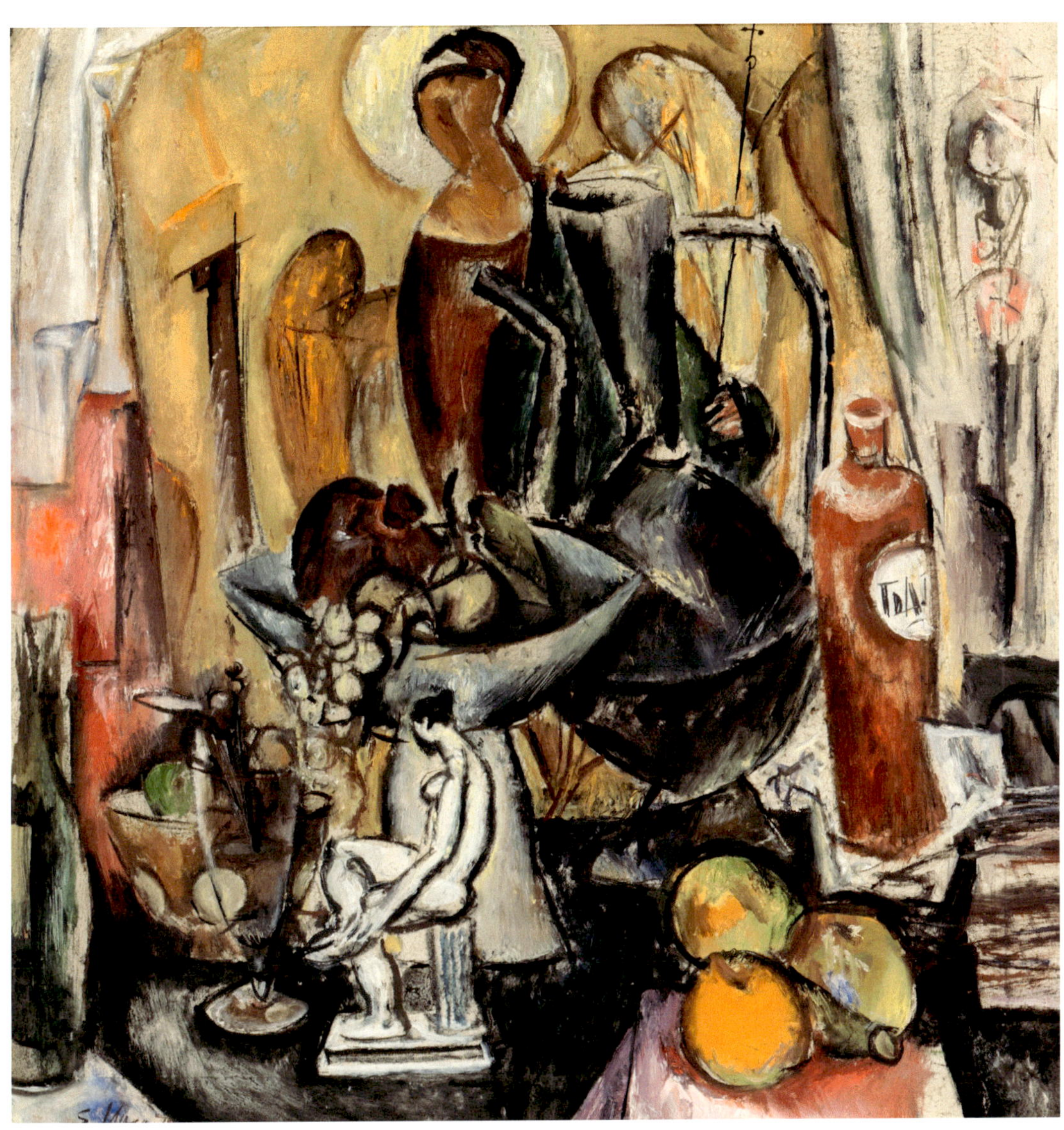

MOISEENKO Evsey Evseevich | *Still Life with an Icon*
1979
Oil on canvas, 70 × 65 cm
The State Russian Museum, St Petersburg

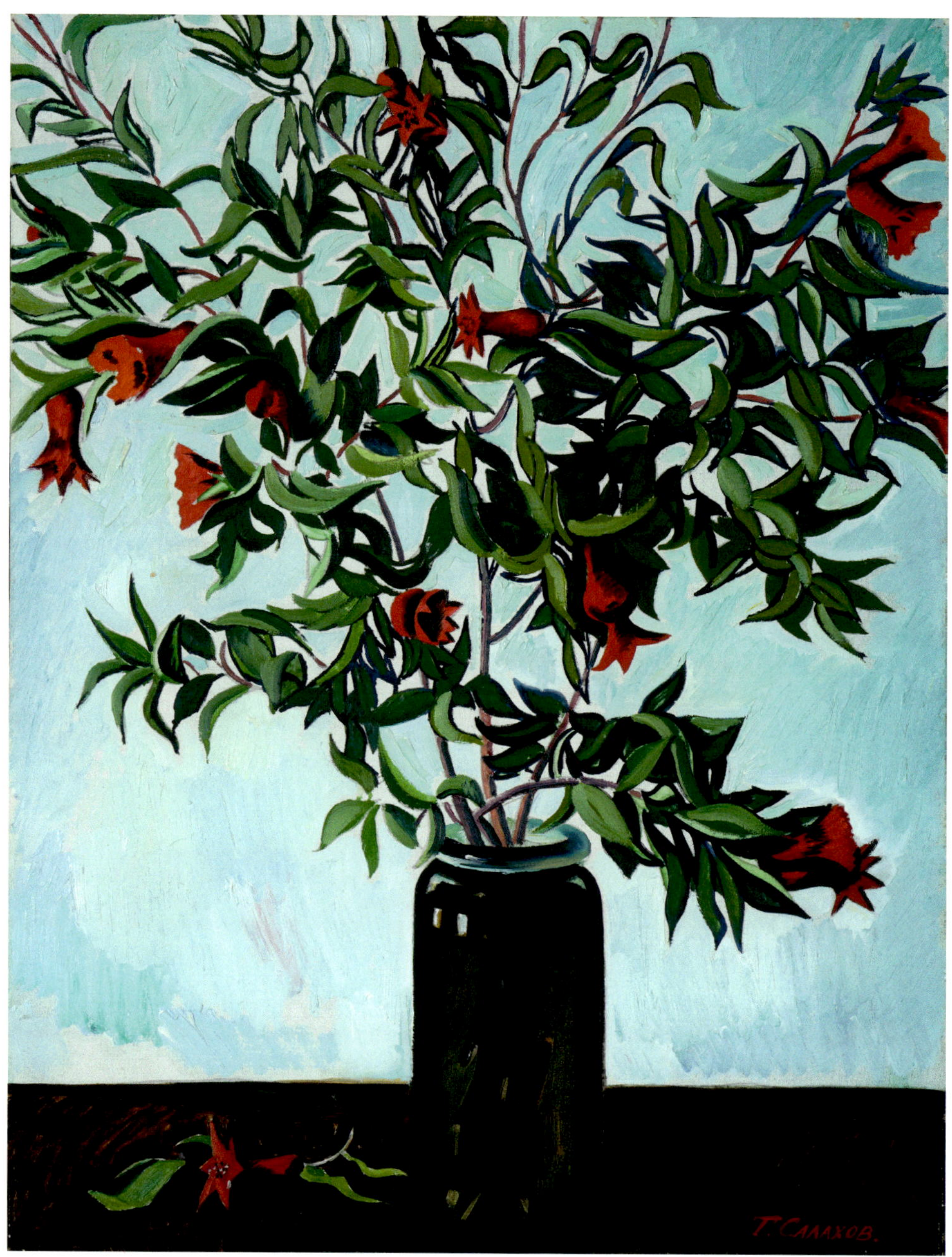

SALAHOV Tair Teymur oglu | *Blossoming Pomegranate*
1980
Oil on canvas on cardboard, 88 × 66 cm
The State Tretyakov Gallery, Moscow

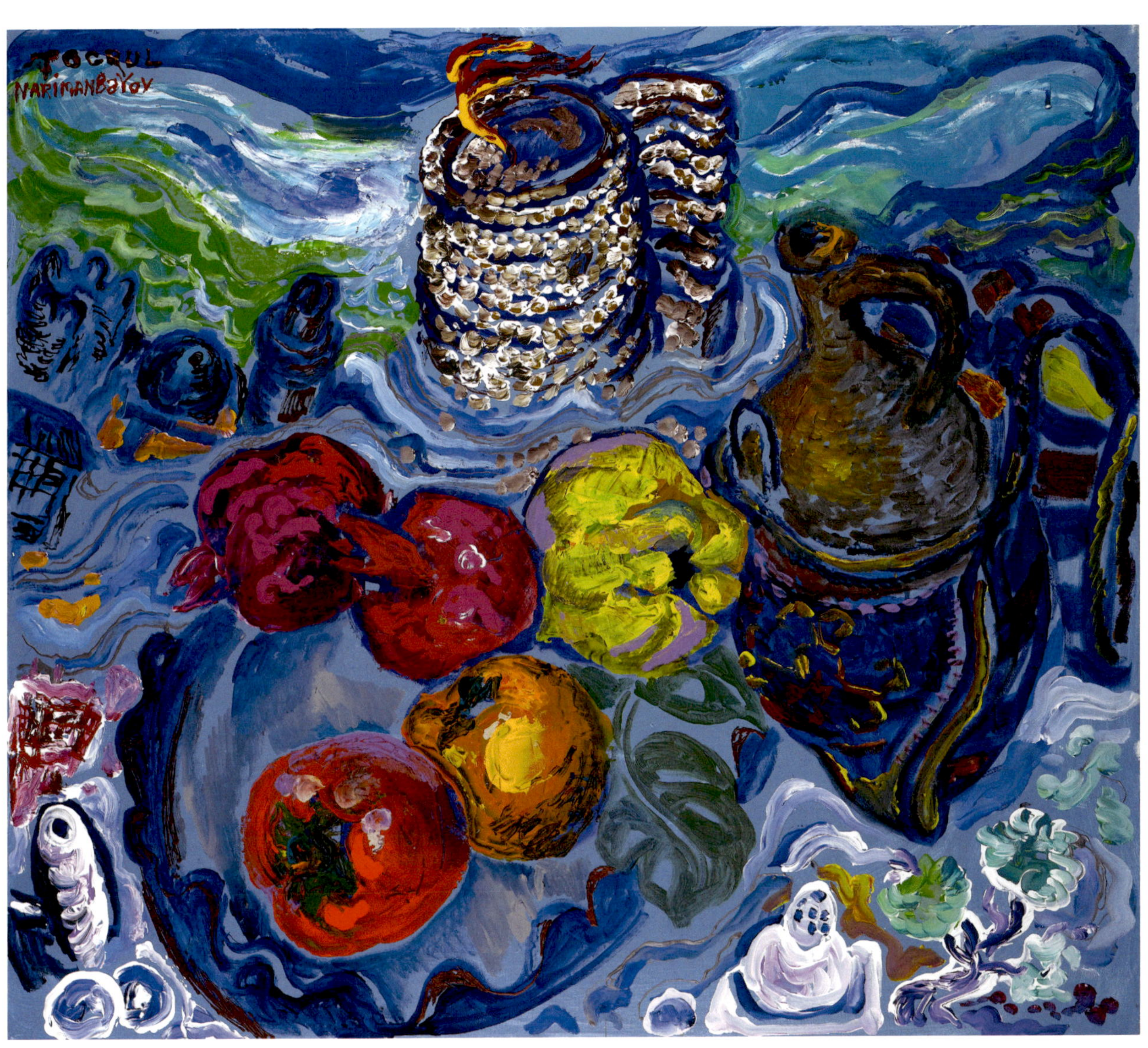

NARIMANBEKOV Togrul Farman oglu | *In Old Baku*
1980s
Oil on canvas, 90 × 99.7 cm
Private collection

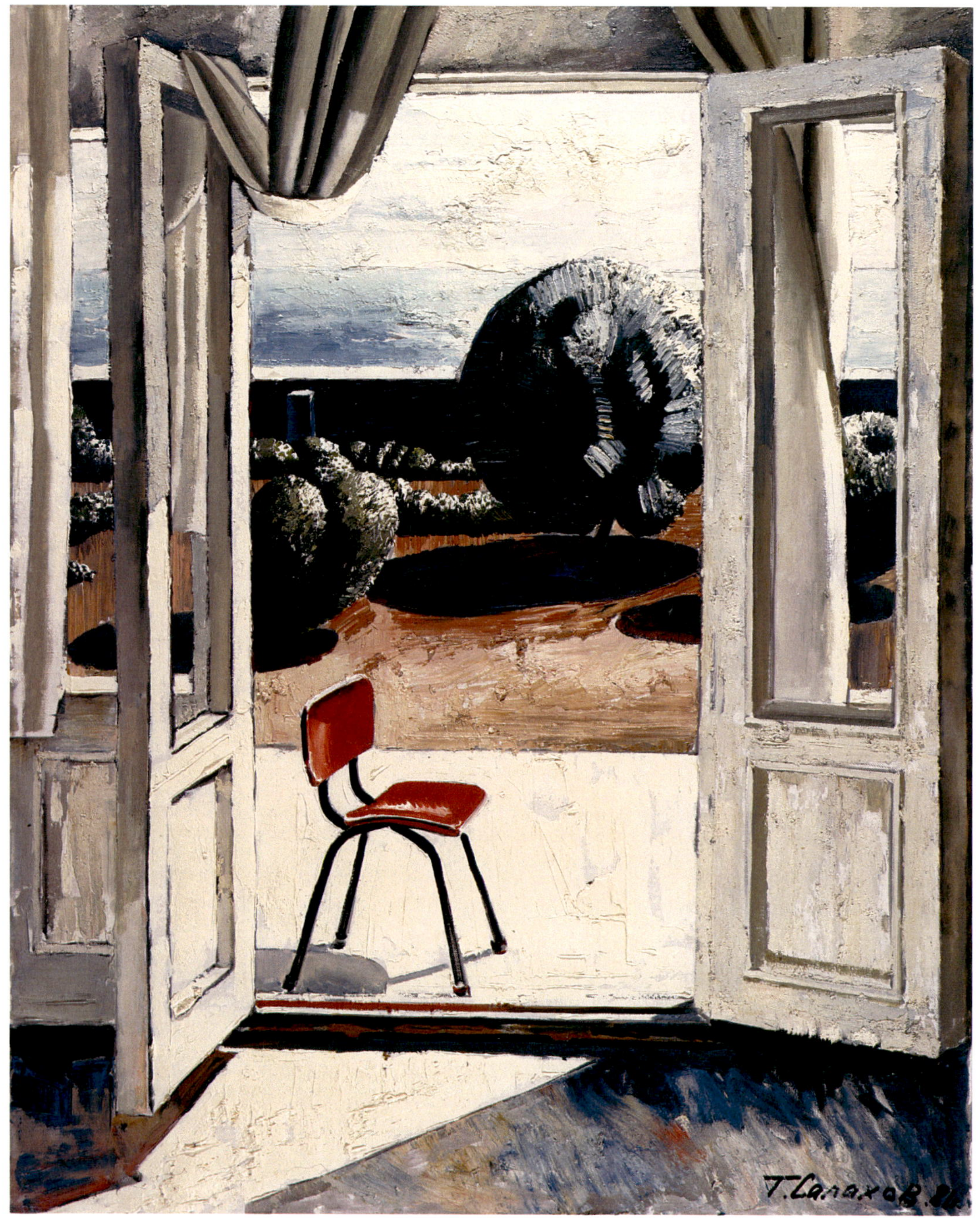

SALAHOV Tair Teymur oglu | *Red Chair*
1981
Oil on canvas, 140 × 110 cm
Private collection

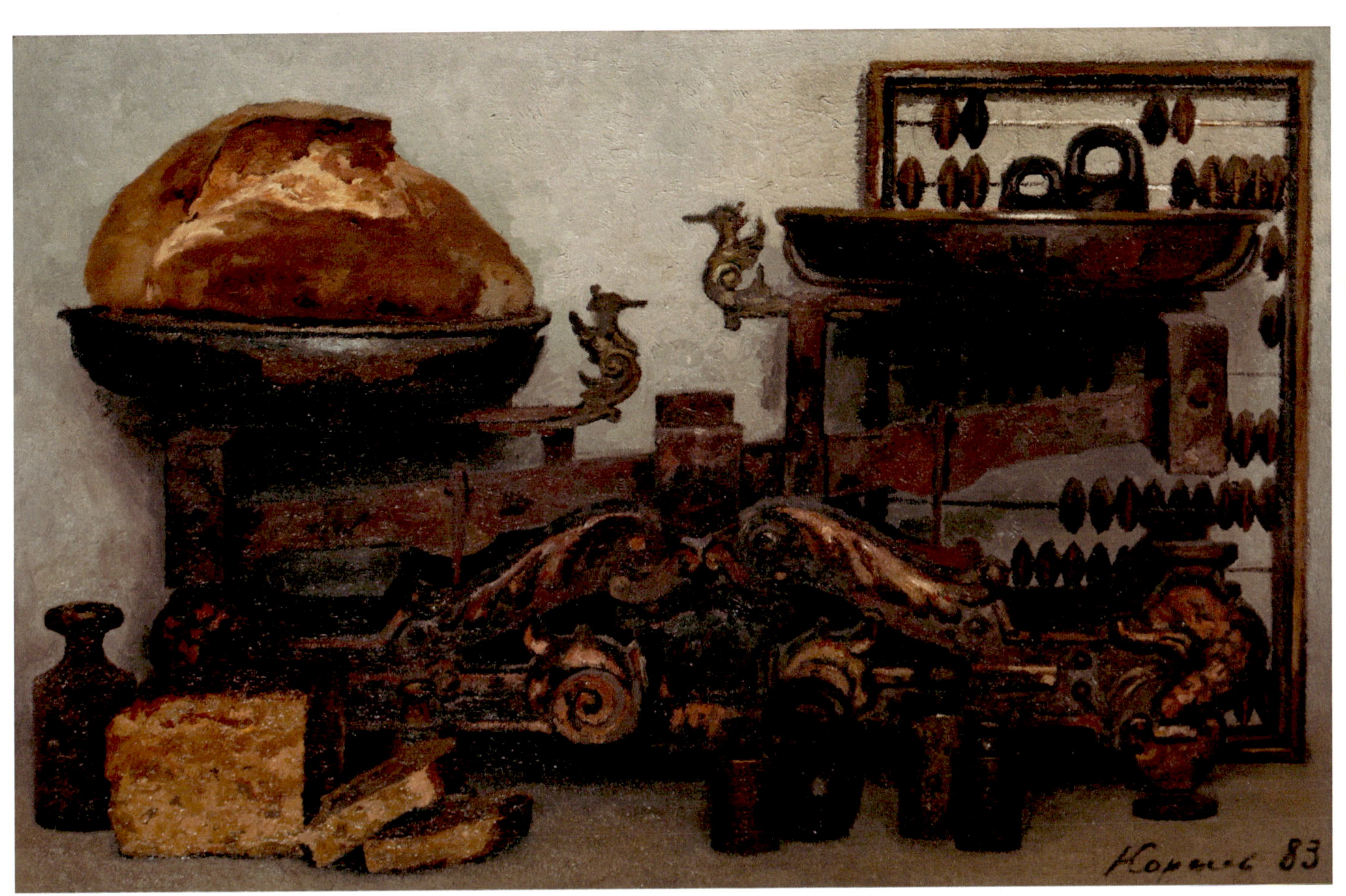

KORZHEV Geli Mikhailovich | *Still Life with Old Scales*
1983
Oil on canvas, 80 × 120 cm
The State Russian Museum, St Petersburg

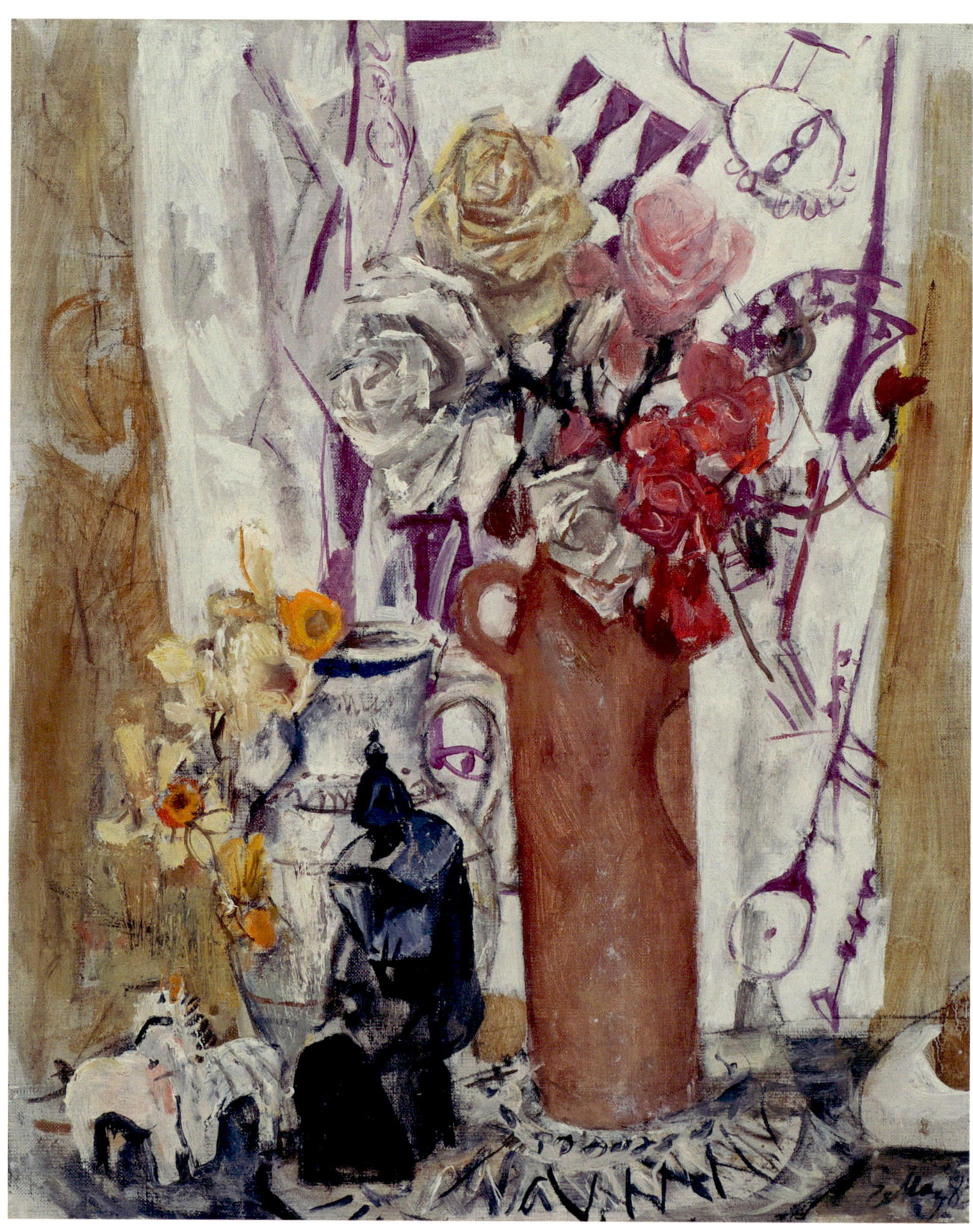

MOISEENKO Evsey Evseevich | *Still Life with a Tea Rose*
1983
Oil on canvas, 50 × 40 cm
Tver Regional Picture Gallery

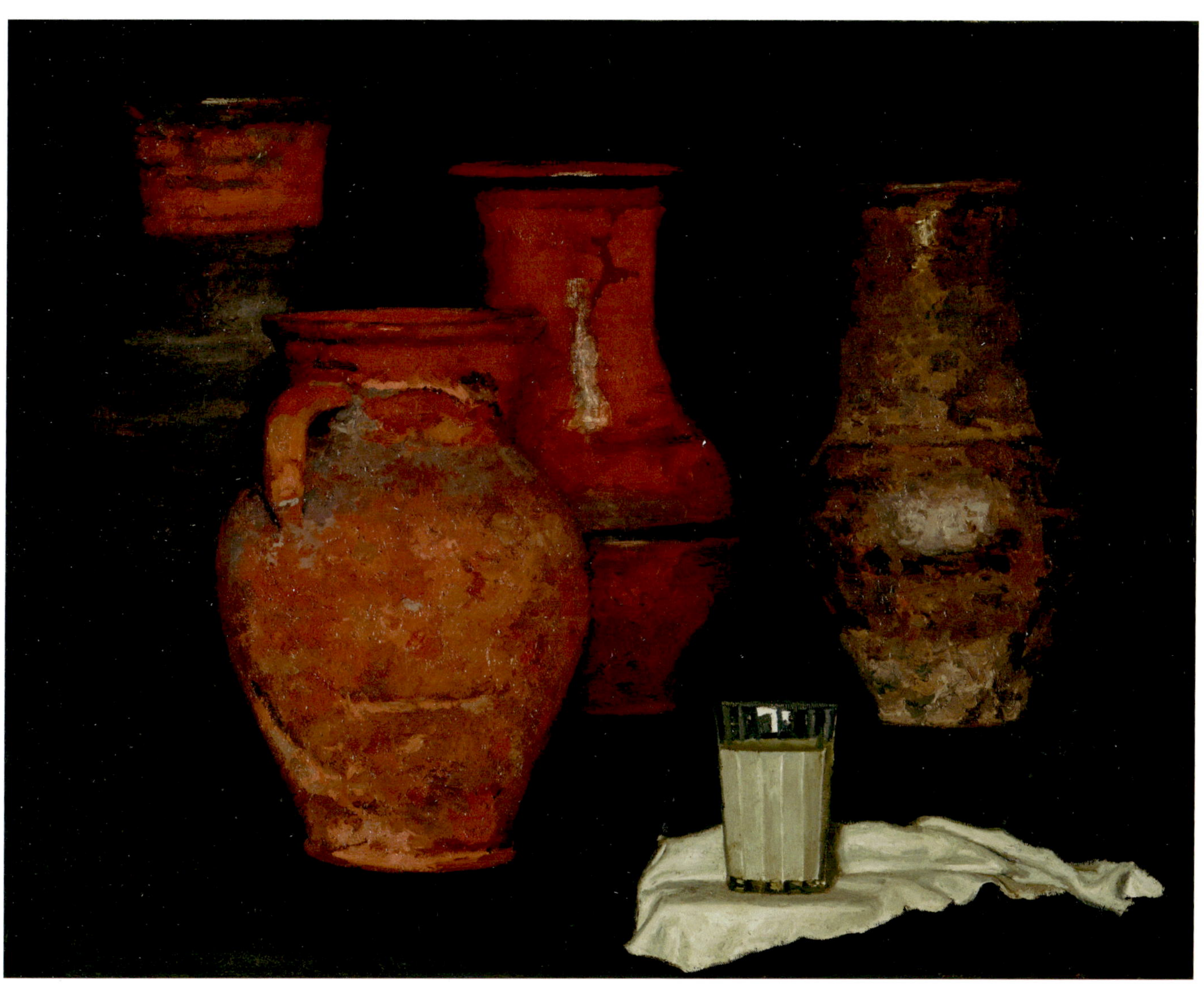

KORZHEV Geli Mikhailovich | *Glass of Milk*
1984
Oil on canvas, 73 × 90 cm
The State Tretyakov Gallery, Moscow

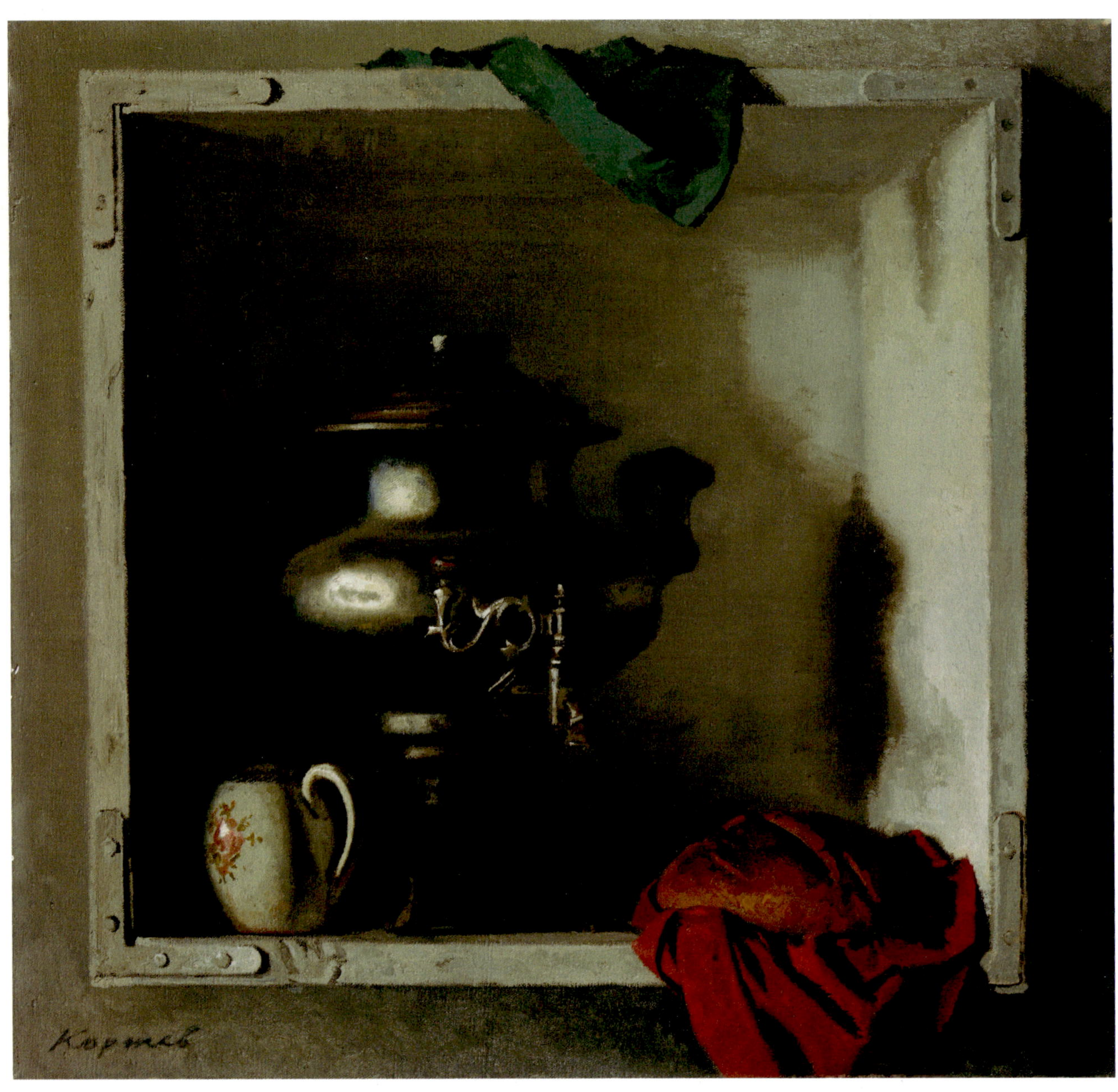

KORZHEV Geli Mikhailovich | *Samovar*
1984
Oil on canvas, 89 × 92 cm
The State Tretyakov Gallery, Moscow

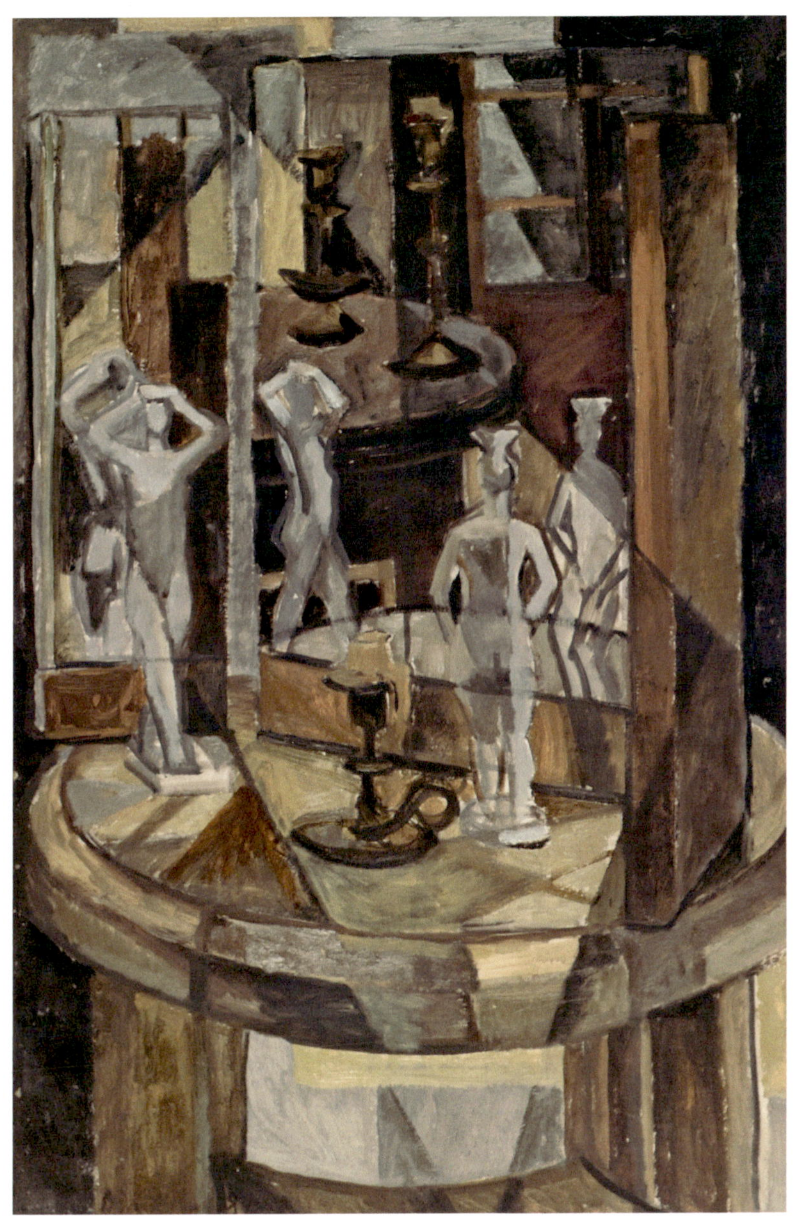

ELKONIN Victor Borisovich | *Still Life with a Mirror*
1984
Oil on cardboard, 80 × 50 cm
Tver Regional Picture Gallery

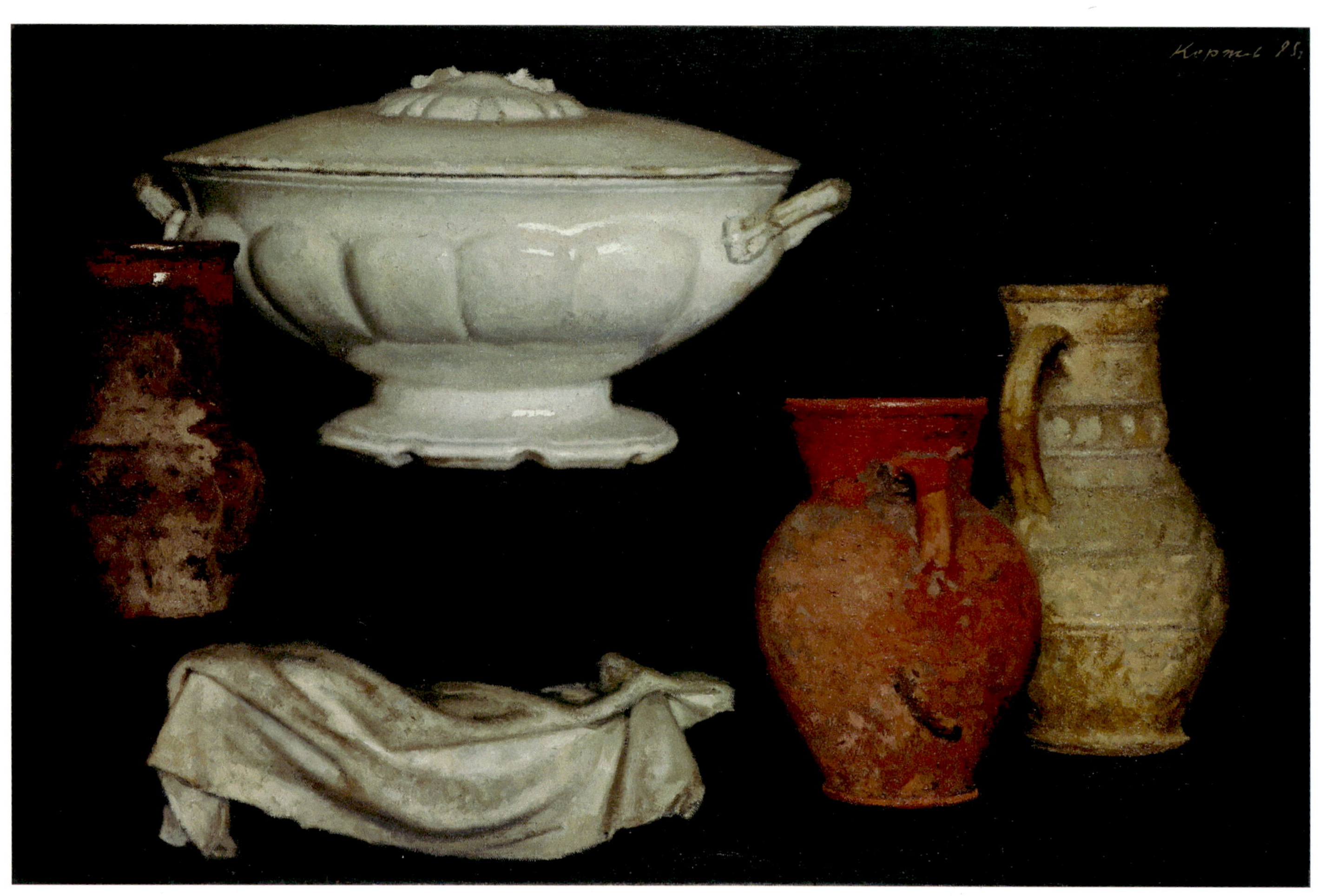

KORZHEV Geli Mikhailovich | *Soup Tureen and Clay Pots*
1985
Oil on canvas, 80.5 × 120 cm
The State Tretyakov Gallery, Moscow

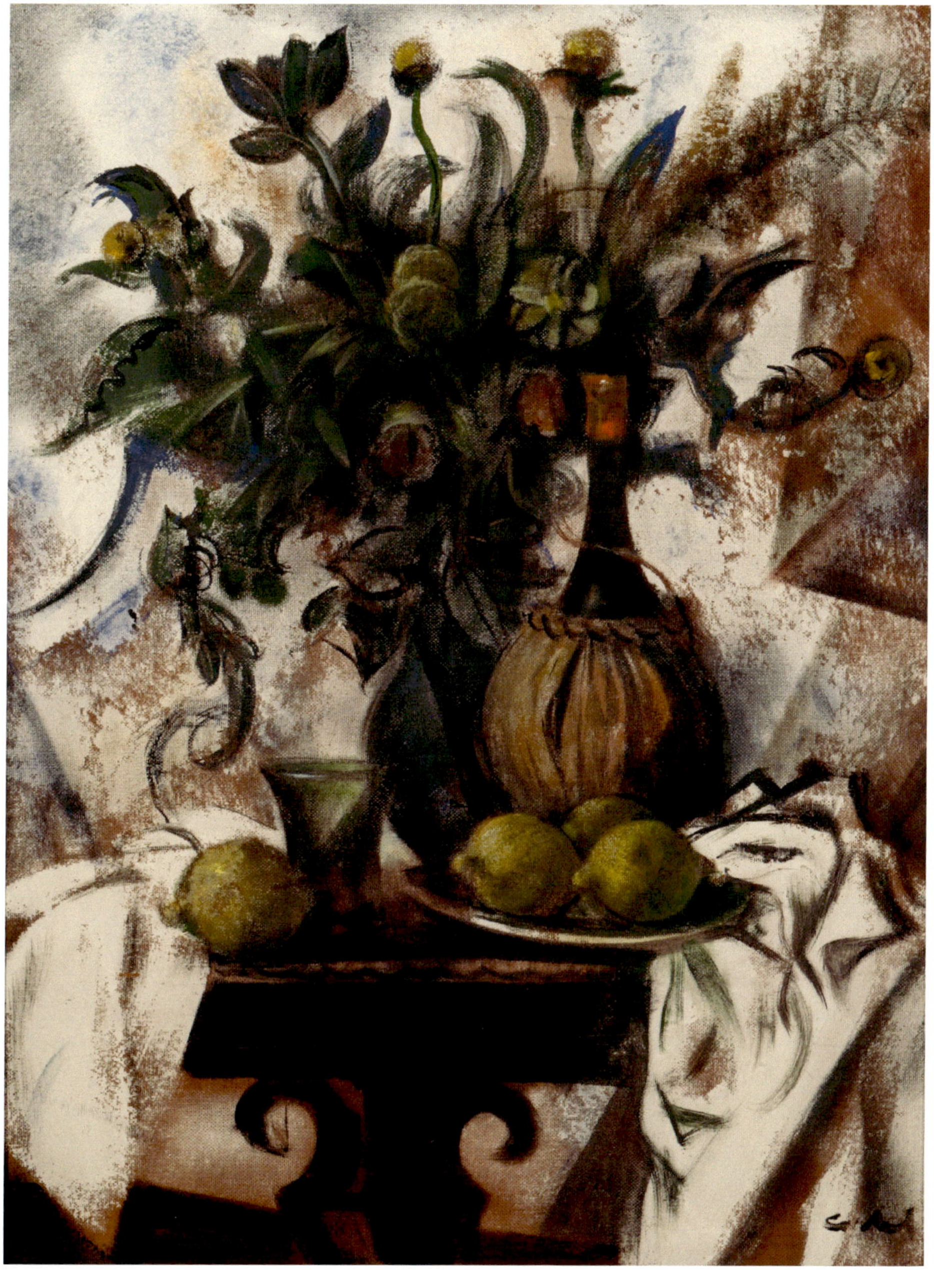

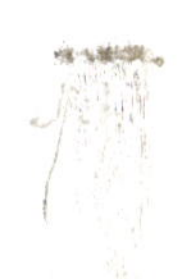

MYLNIKOV Andrei Andreevich | *Still Life with Lemons*
1986
Oil on fibreglass, 104 × 76 cm
The State Russian Museum, St Petersburg

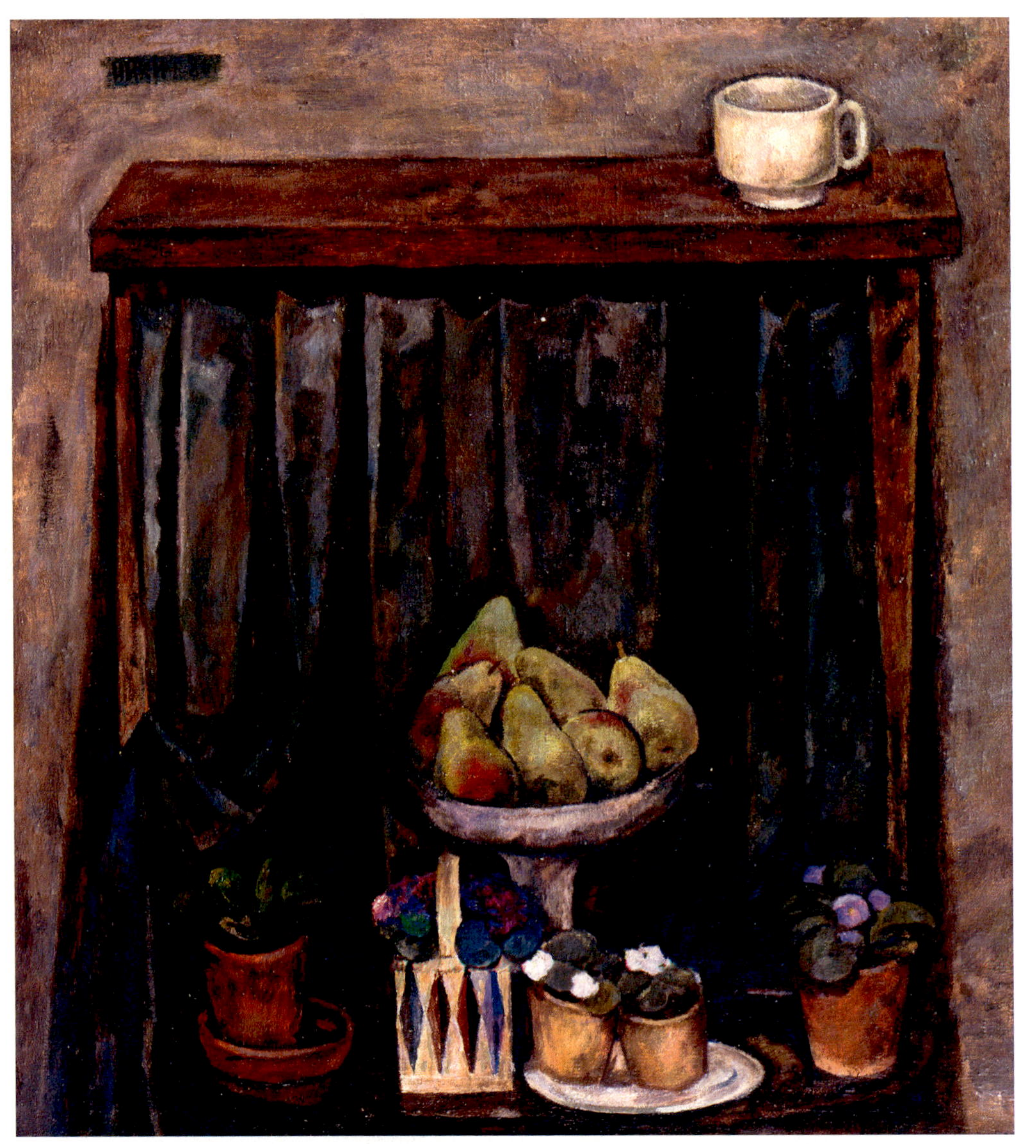

NIKITCH Anatoly Yurievich | *Still Life with Pears and Violets*
1986
Oil on canvas, 90 × 80 cm
Private collection

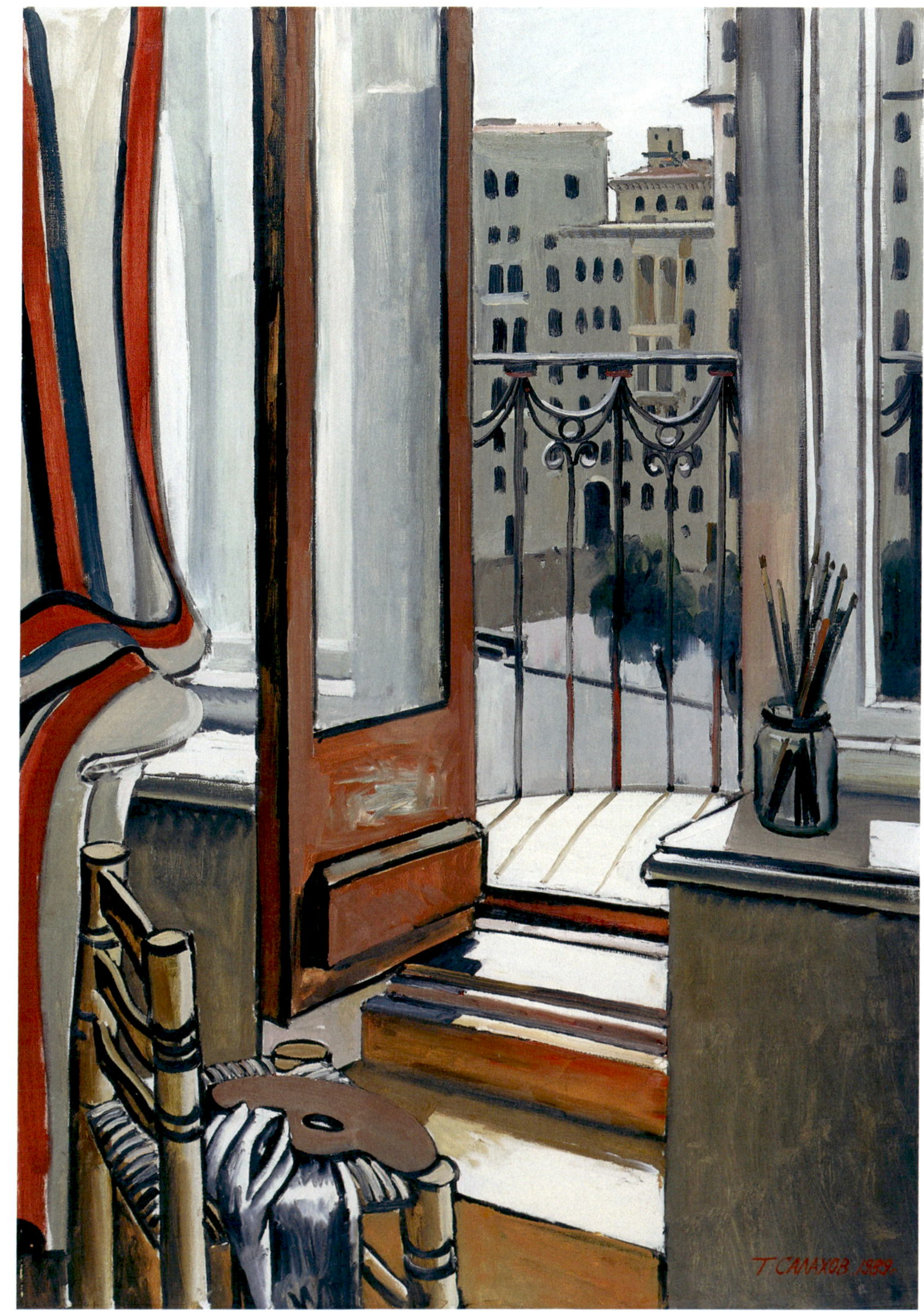

SALAHOV Tair Teymur oglu | *A View from a Window*
1989
Oil on canvas, 160 × 110 cm
Private collection

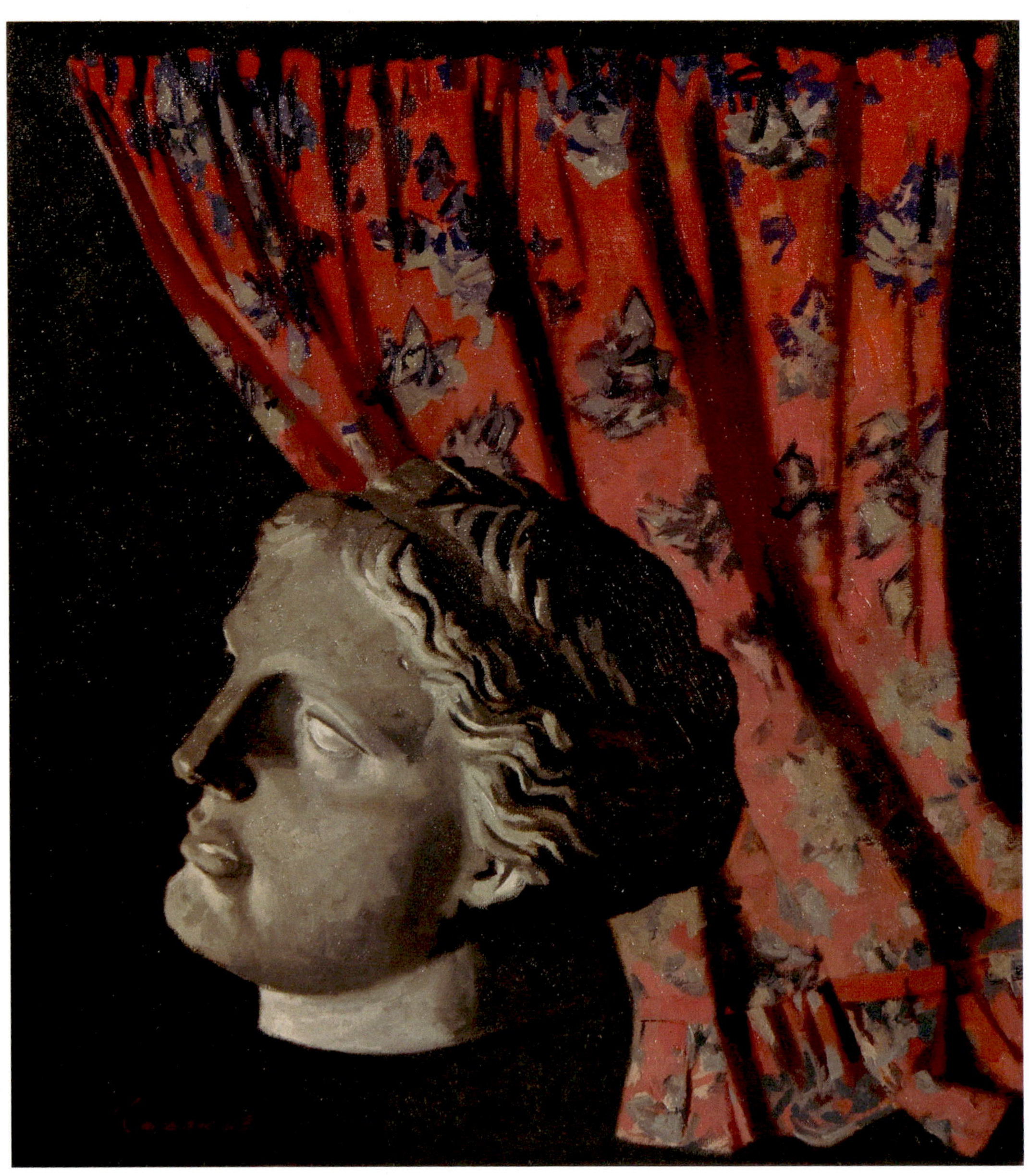

KORZHEV Geli Mikhailovich | *Venus's Head*
1990
Oil on canvas, 80 × 70 cm
Private collection

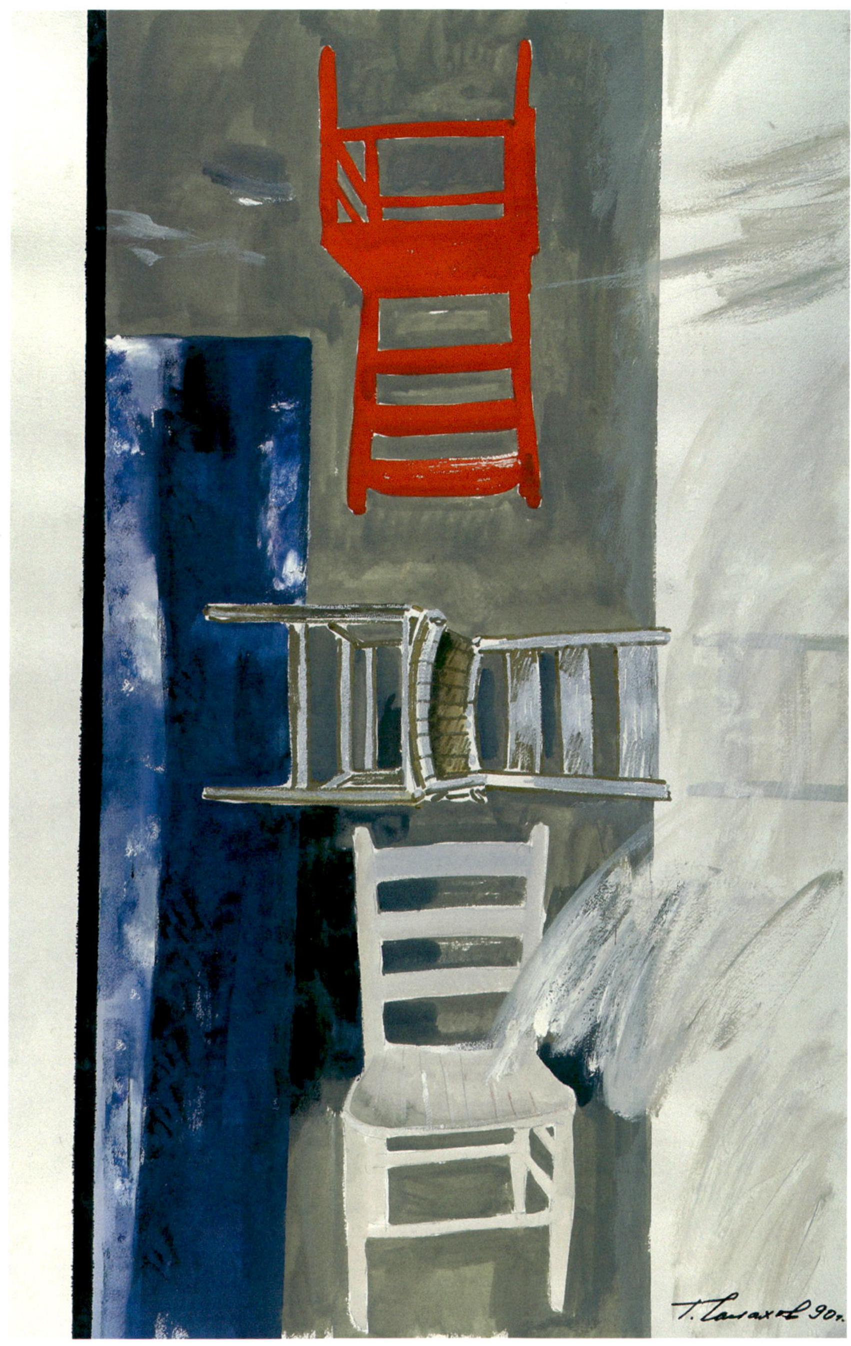

SALAHOV Tair Teymur oglu | *Rosenberger's Studio*
1990
Oil on canvas, 103 × 65 cm
Private collection

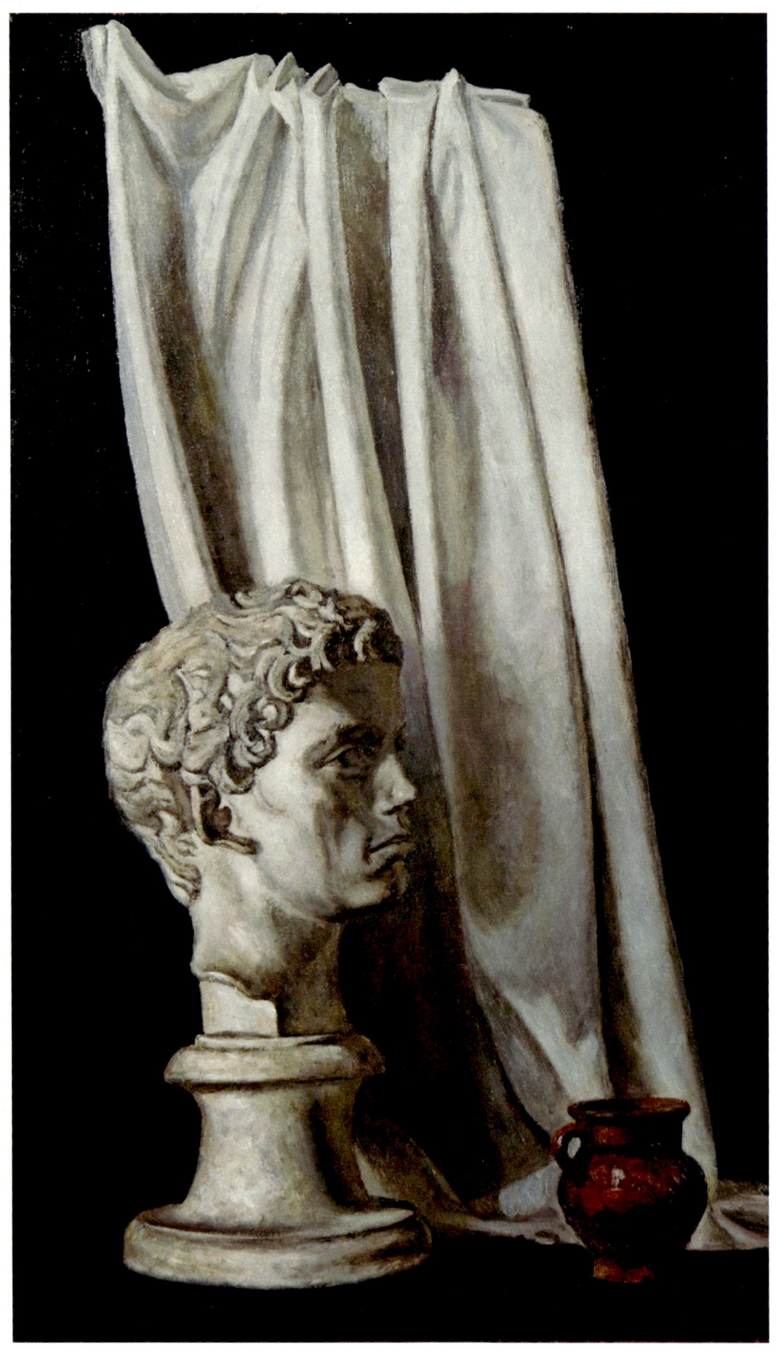

KORZHEV Geli Mikhailovich | *Still Life with Antique Bust and Jug*
c.1990
Oil on canvas, 102 × 58 cm
Private collection

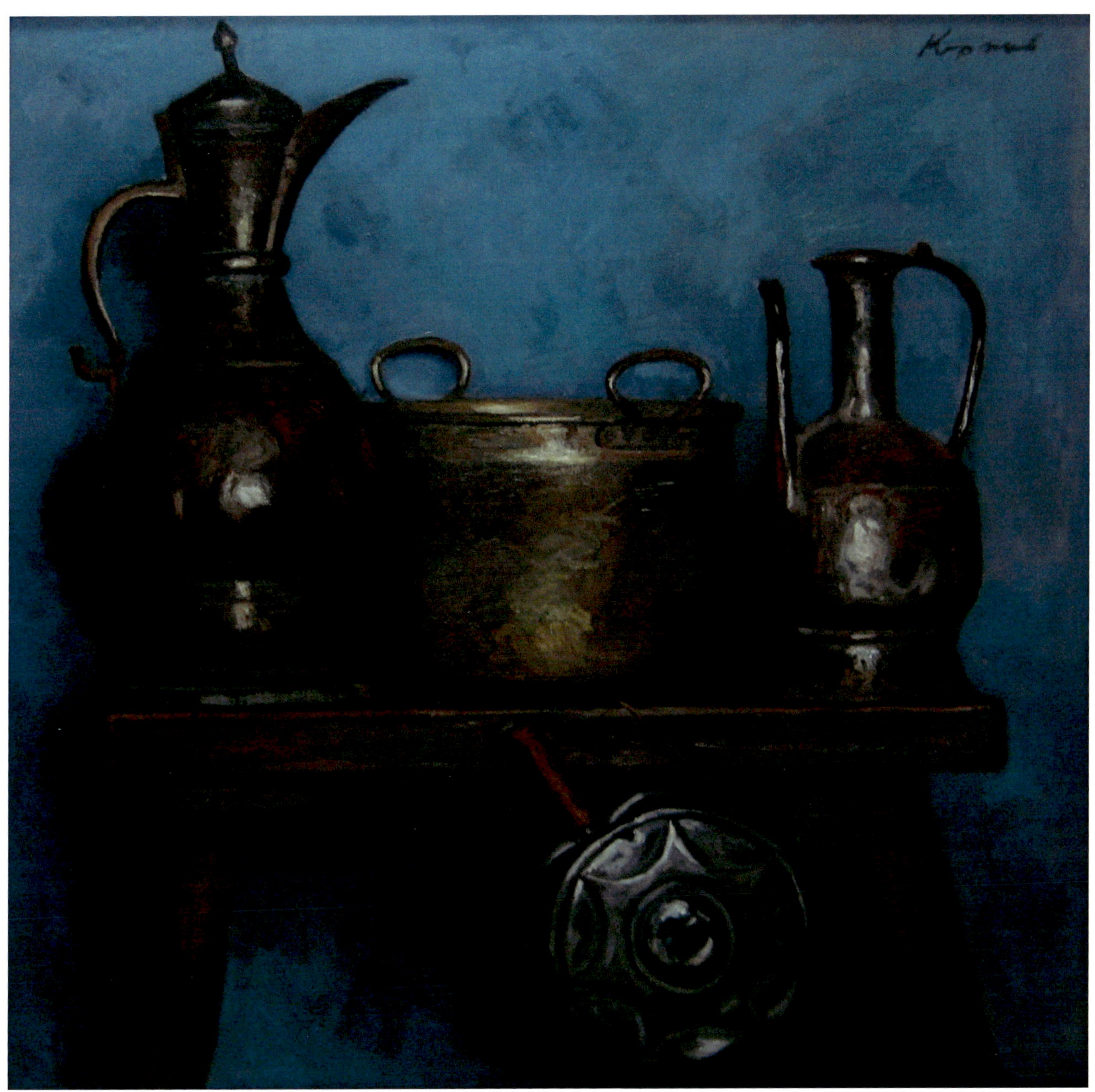

KORZHEV Geli Mikhailovich | *Still Life with Metal Jugs, Cauldron and Drinking Flask*
*c.*1990
Oil on canvas, 100 × 100 cm
Private collection

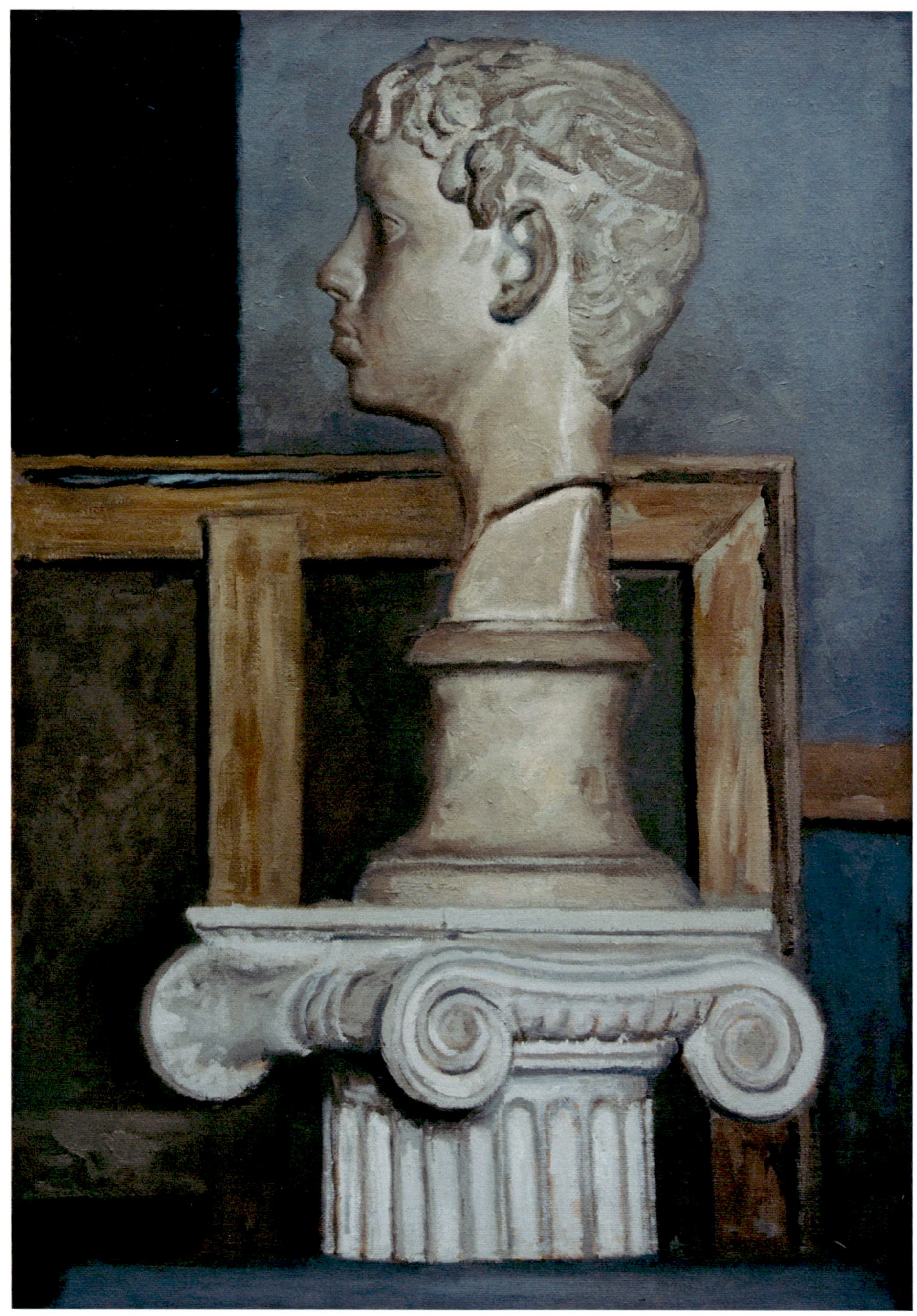

KORZHEV Geli Mikhailovich │ *Still Life with Antique Bust*
1990s
Oil on canvas, 99 × 69.3 cm
Private collection

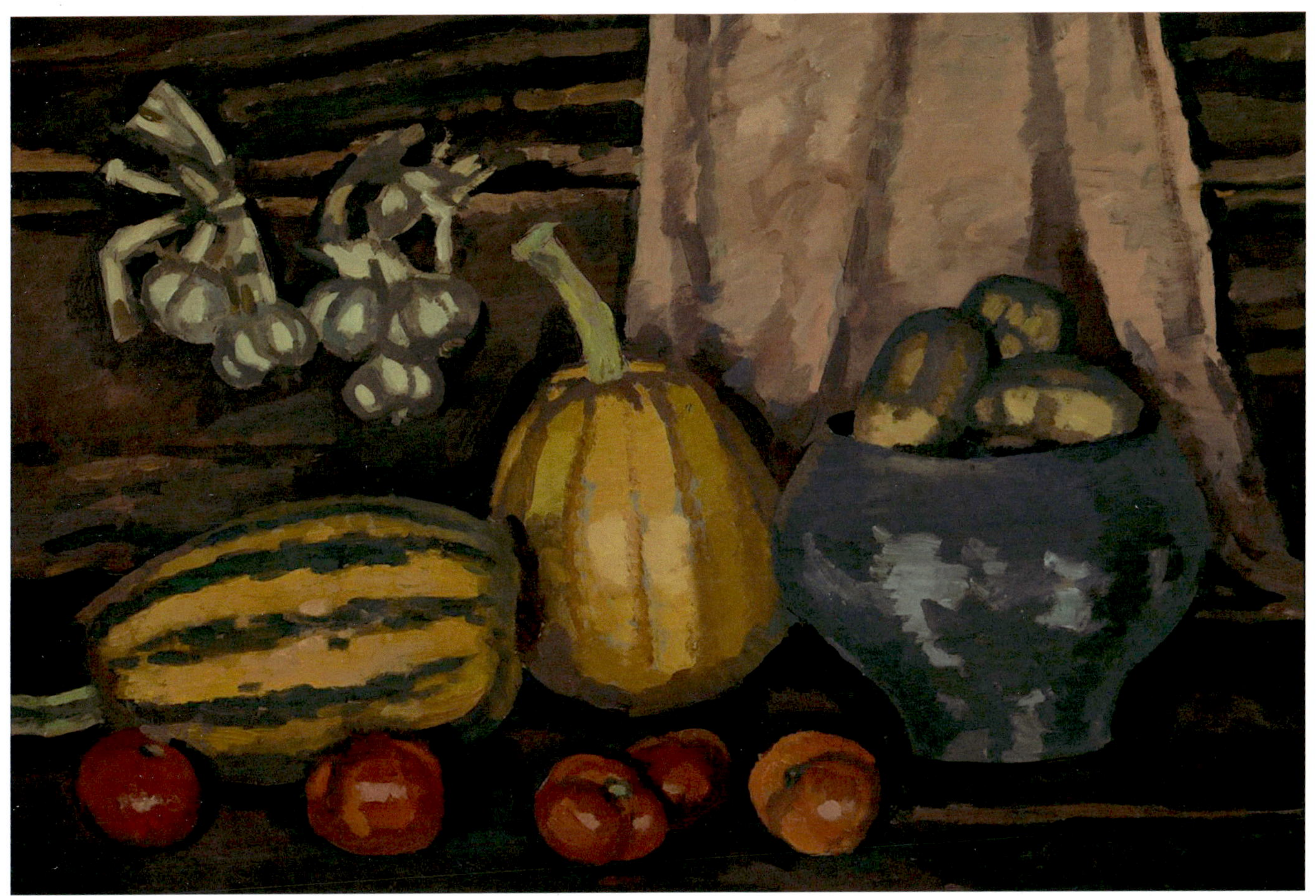

IVANOV Victor Ivanovich | *Still Life with Potatoes and Squash*
1990s
Oil on canvas, 54 × 79 cm
Private collection

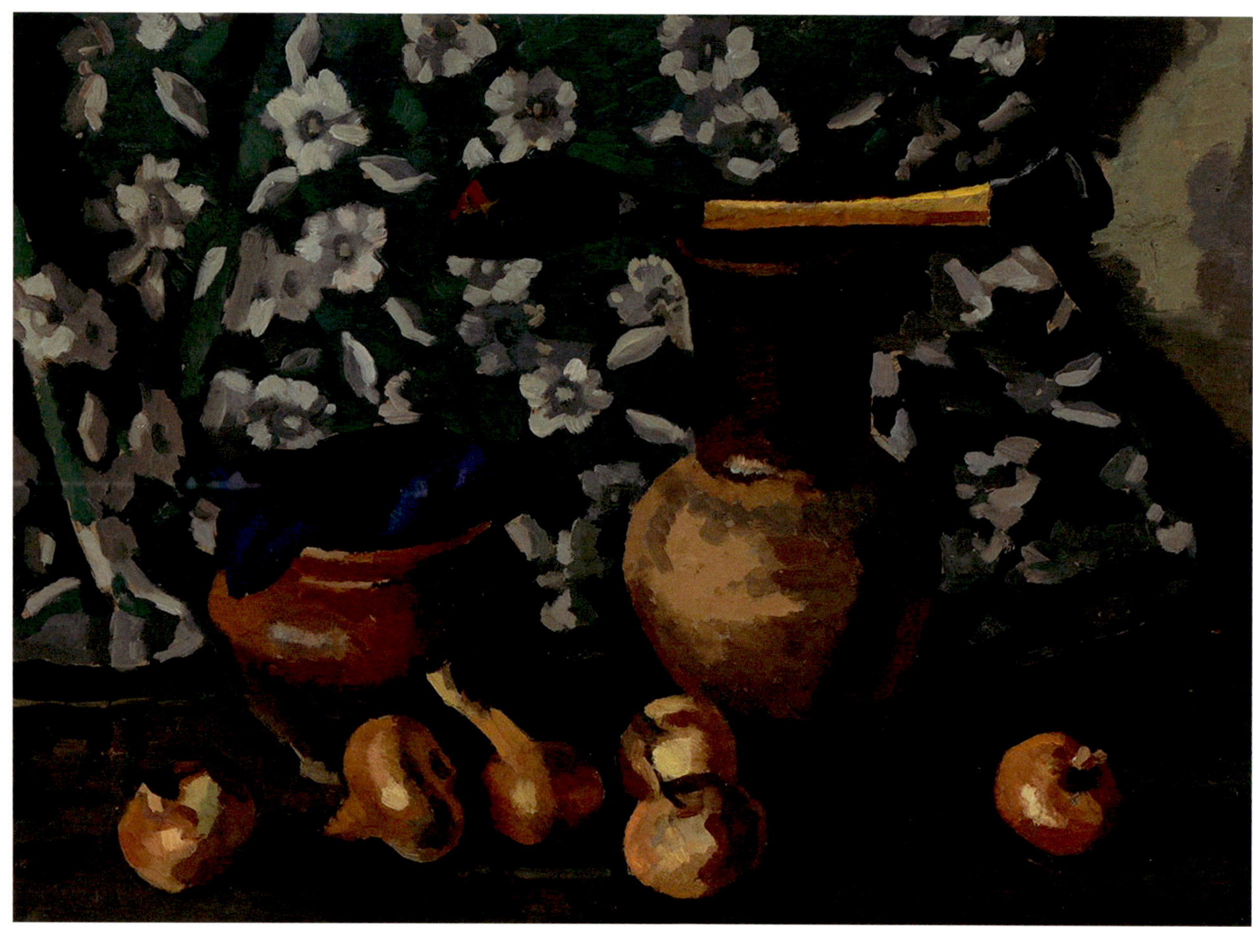

IVANOV Victor Ivanovich | *Still Life with Onions*
1990s
Oil on canvas, 54 × 75 cm
Private collection

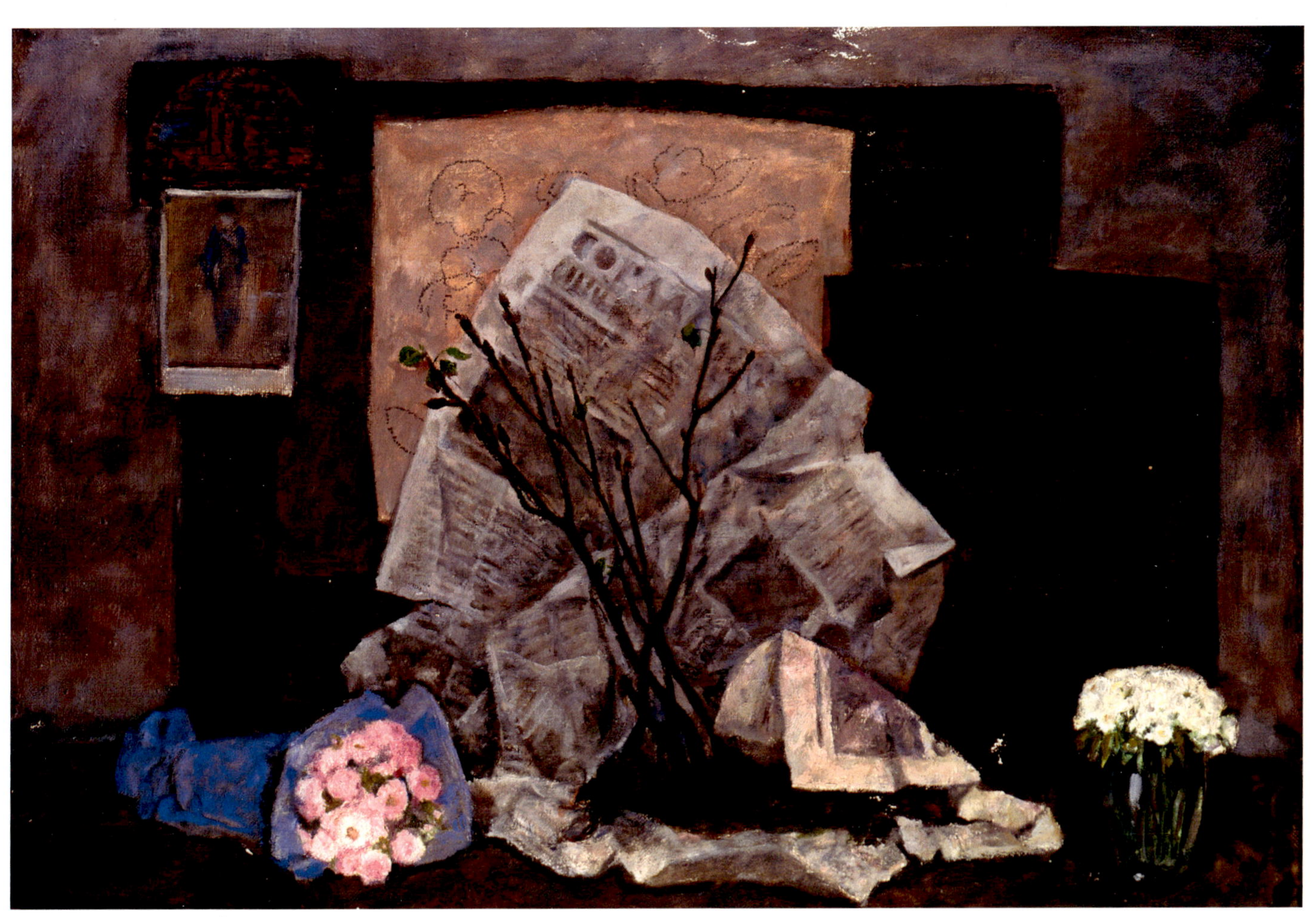

NIKITCH Anatoly Yurievich | *Still Life with Branches*
1991
Oil on canvas, 67.5 × 96.5 cm
Private collection

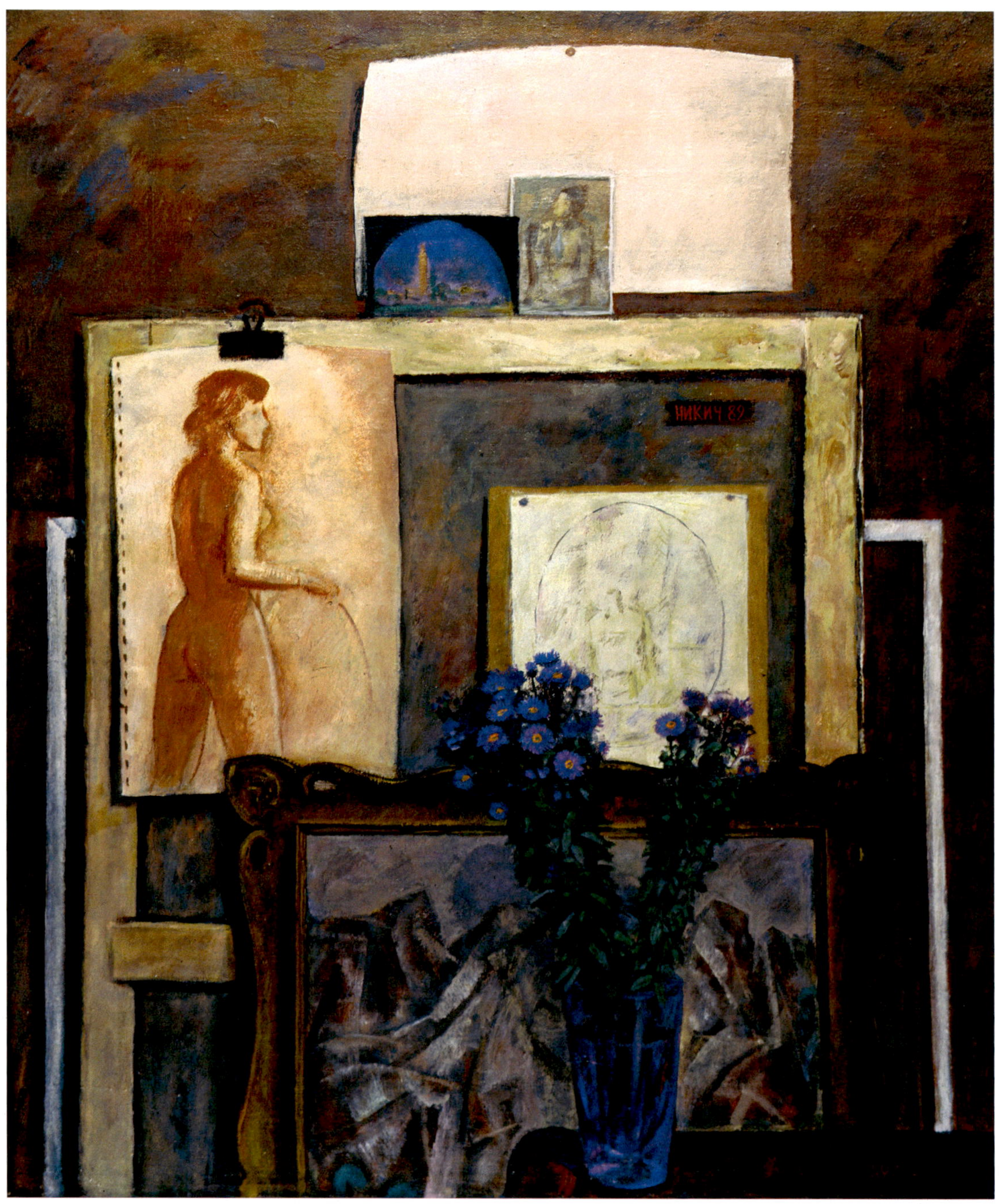

NIKITCH Anatoly Yurievich | *Still Life, Artist's Studio*
1992
Oil on canvas, 128 × 110 cm
Private collection

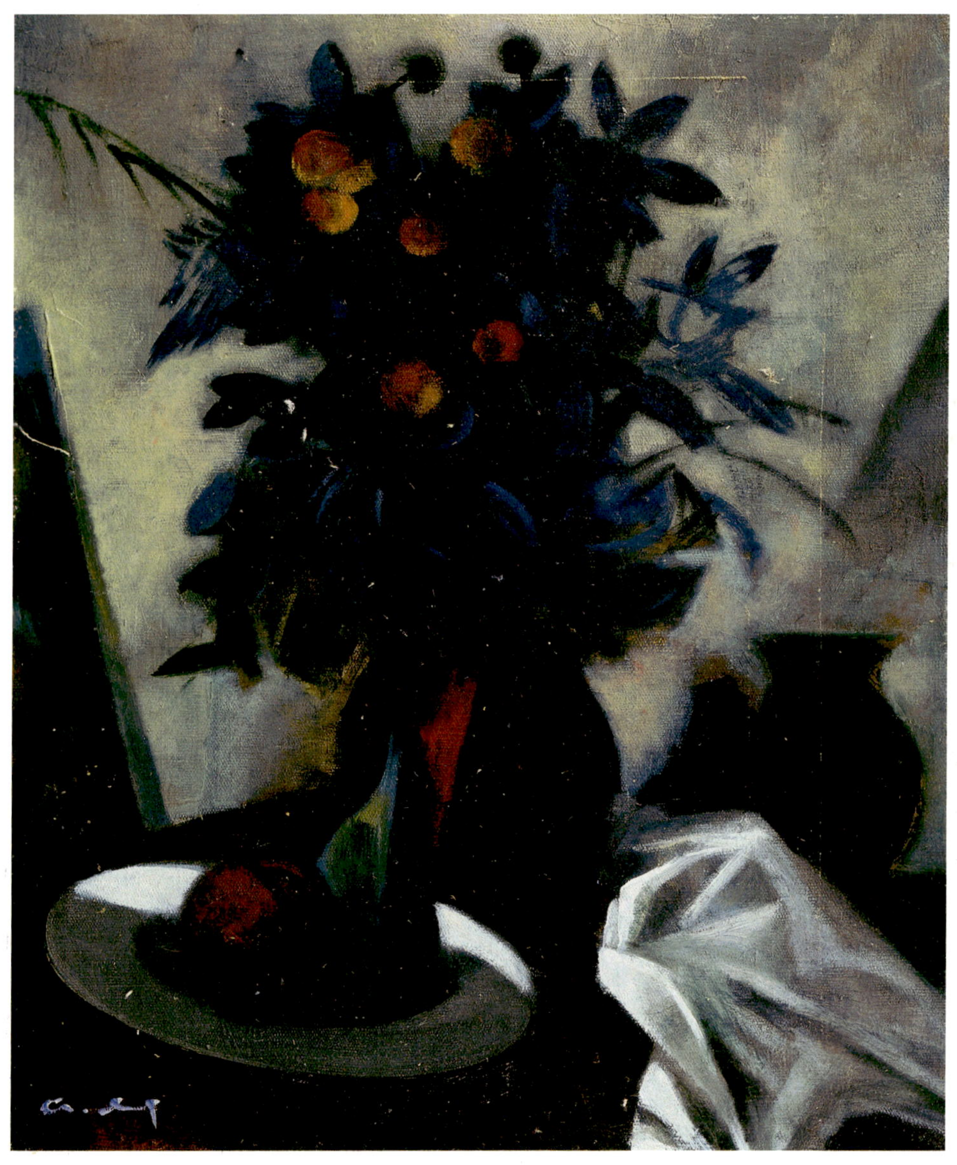

MYLNIKOV Andrei Andreevich | *Vase of Flowers, Still Life*
1992
Oil on canvas, 55 × 45 cm
Private collection

EREMEEV Oleg Arkadievich | *Flowers*
1993
Oil on canvas, 86 × 49.5 cm
Private collection

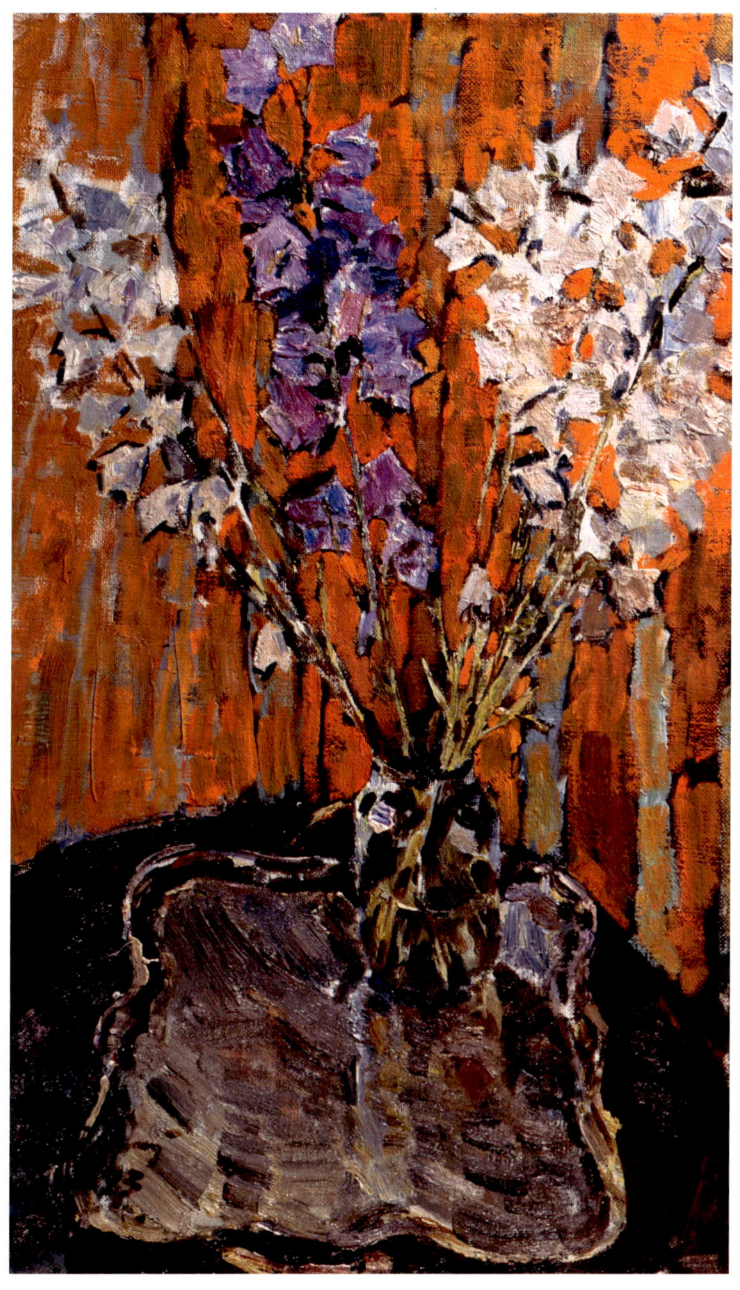

EREMEEV Oleg Arkadievich | *Flowers on a Silver Tray*
1993
Oil on canvas, 85.5 × 50 cm
Private collection

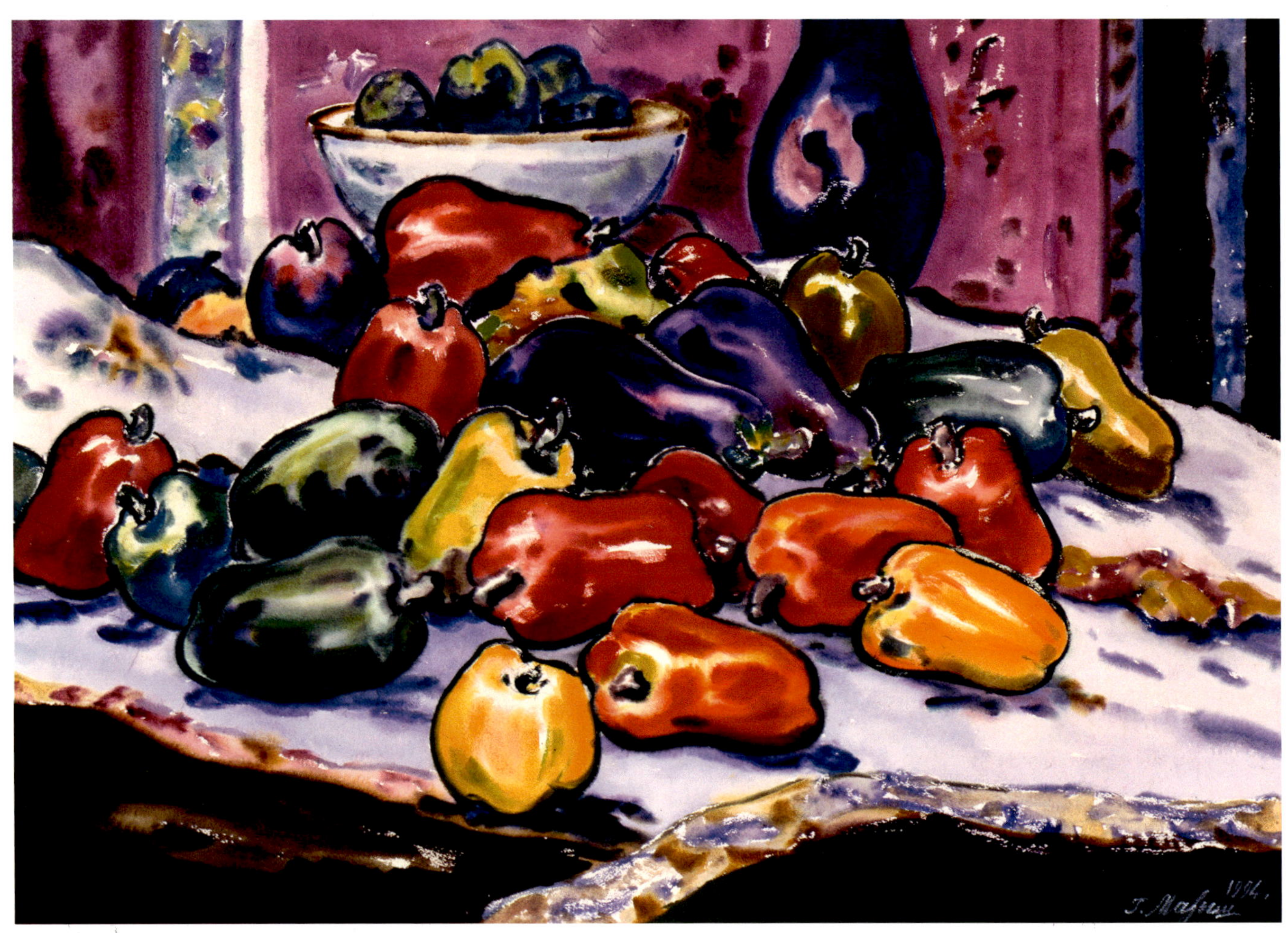

MALYSH Gavriil Kondratyevich | *Green Peppers and Eggplants*
1994
Oil on canvas, 57 × 77 cm
Private collection

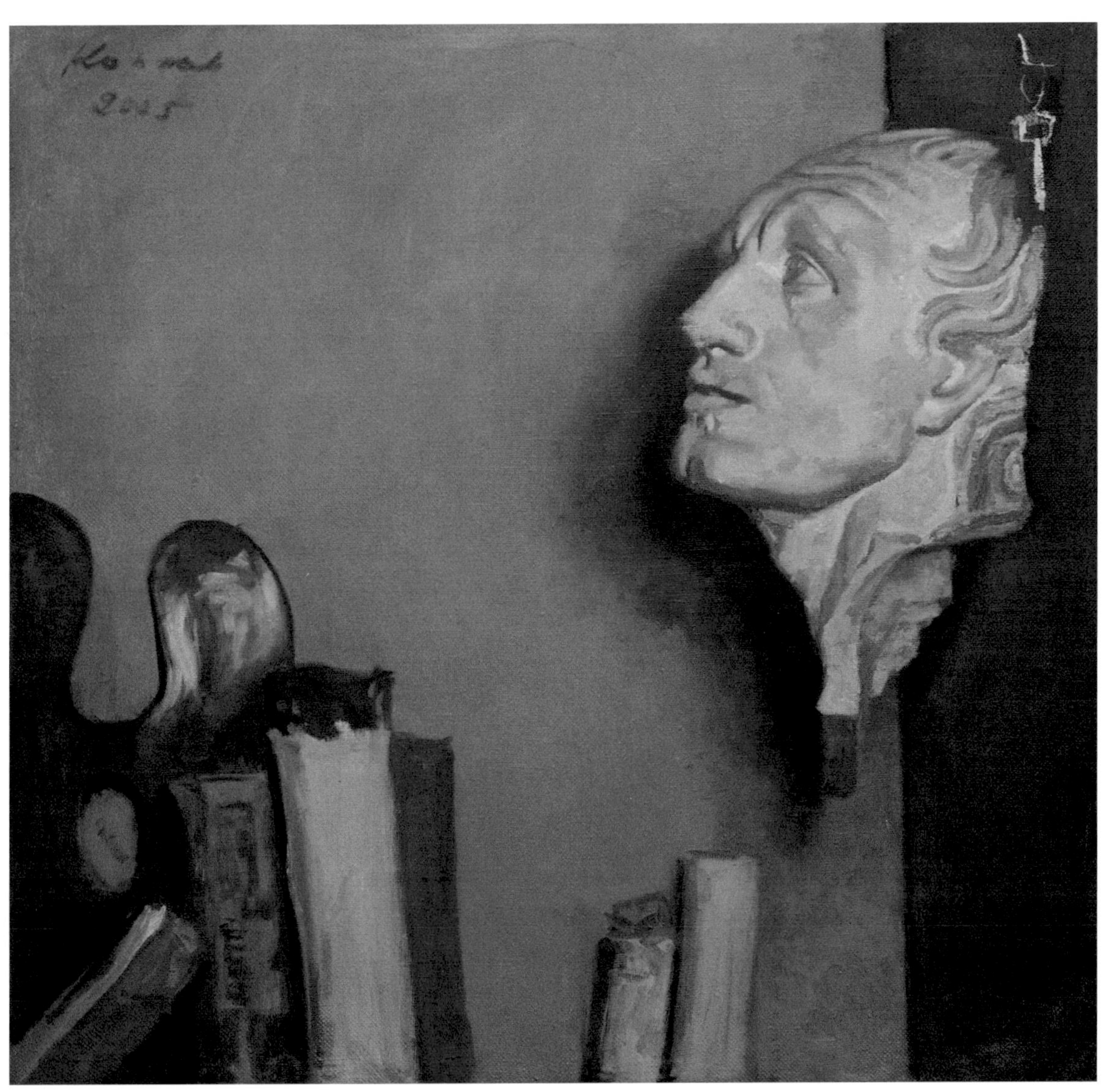

KORZHEV Geli Mikhailovich | *Artist's Studio*
| 2000s
| Oil on canvas, 68.5 × 69.5 cm
| Private collection

BIOGRAPHIES

ALTMAN Nathan Isaevich
(1889, Vinnytsya – 1970, Leningrad)

Russian and Soviet avant-garde painter, sculptor and stage designer. Studied painting and sculpture at the Art College in Odessa in painting department under K. Kostandi and G. Ladyzhensky, and in sculpture department under L. Iorini and I. Marmone. Member of the World of Art group (1913, 1915, 1916), the Union of Youth artistic group (1913–14), the Last Futurist Exhibition of Paintings 0,10 group (1915–16) and the Jack of Diamonds group (1916). Honoured Artist of the RSFSR (1968).

BOGAEVSKAYA Olga Borisovna
(1914, Petrograd – 2000, St Petersburg)

Russian and Soviet artist, painter and graphic artist. Member of the St Petersburg Union of Artists (Leningrad branch of the Union of Artists of the RSFSR until 1992). Studied at the Art and Industry College in a studio of D. Zagoskin (1931–32) and at Leningrad Institute of Painting, Sculpture and Architecture, where she was a student of S. Priselkov, G. Pavlovsky, D. Bernshtein, and A. Osmerkin (1933–40).

CHERNYSHEV Nikolai Mikhailovich
(1885, Nikolski, Tambov Region – 1973, Moscow)

Russian artist and art historian, author. Studied at the Moscow School of Painting, Sculpture and Architecture in Moscow in studious of V. Serov, A. Arkhipov, K. Korovin (1901–11); in Paris at the Academy of R. Julien (1910), at the Higher Art School at the Academy of Arts in St Petersburg under V. Mate and D. Kiplika (1911–15). Member of the Union of Artists (1919), World of Art (1921), one of the founders of the Makovets Association (1922–26), a member of the OMX (1928–29). Corresponding Member of the Academy of Natural Sciences (1927–30), professor at the Department of Monumental Painting in Moscow VKhUTEIN (until 1930). Taught at the Moscow State Institute named after V. I. Surikov (1930s–40s) People's Artist of the RSFSR (1970).

CHUPYATOV Leonid Terentievich
(1890, St Petersburg – 1941, Leningrad)

Russian and Soviet artist and avant-garde exponent. Member of the following associations: World of Art (1916–18), Zhar-tsvet (1924), Communities of Artists (1925–29) and the Union of Contemporary Artists of Ukraine (1928). Worked in the scientific research division of the Higher Art and Technical Studios (1921–25).

DEINEKA Aleksandr Aleksandrovich
(1899, Kursk – 1969, Moscow)

Soviet painter, sculptor of monuments and graphic artist. Studied at the Kursk Art Studio, the Kharkov Art Institute (1915–18) and the VKhUTEMAS (1921–25) under Favorsky and Nivinsky. Head of the Russian Telegraph/News Agency in Kursk (1919–20). Meritorious Artist of the RSFSR (1945), Full Member of the Academy of Arts (1947, vice-president 1962–66), People's Artist of the USSR (1963), winner of the Lenin Prize (1964), Hero of Socialist Labour (1969). Taught at VKhUTEIN (1928–30), the Moscow Printing Industry Institute (1930–34), the Moscow Institute of Fine Arts (1934–39), the Moscow Institute of Applied and Decorative Art (director, 1945–52), the Moscow Architectural Institute (1953–57) and the Moscow State Art Institute (1957–64). Professor from 1940.

ELKONIN Victor Borisovich
(1910, Malaya Pereshchepina, Poltava Region – 1994, Moscow)

Soviet painter and graphic artist. Studied in the studio of M. Leblanc and at VKhUTEIN under K. Istomina, L. Bruni, P.Kuznetsov, V. Favorsky (1927–30). Member of the Four Arts society of artists (1930) and the Moscow Union of Artists (1933). Meritorious Artist of the Russian Federation, Four-time winner of the First Prize of the Moscow Union of Artists (1973, 1974, 1977, 1981); Laureate of the USSR Council of Ministers Prize. Member of the society Four Arts (1930). Member of the Moscow Union of Artists (1933). Head of the of monumental painting studio (1948).

EREMEEV Oleg Arkadievich
(1922, Petrograd – 2016, St Petersburg)

Soviet Russian painter. Studied at the Institute of Painting, Sculpture and Architecture named after I. Repin under B. Ioganson (1951–57). Member of the Academy of Arts (2001, Corresponding Member 1997). People's Artist of Russia (1994). Member of the Union of Artists of the USSR (1960). Taught at the Institute of Painting, Sculpture and Architecture named after I. Repin (since 1950s, head of the institute 1990 2001).

FALK Robert Rafailovich
(1886, Moscow – 1958, Moscow)

Russian, Soviet avant-garde painter. Studied in the private art studios run by K. Yuon, Dudin and by I. Mashkov (1904–05), and in the Moscow College of Painting, Sculpture and Architecture (1905–09) under K. Korovin and V. Serov supervision among others. Founder of Jack of Diamonds (1910–16); Member of Jewish Culture League association (1921). Taught at the VKhUTEMAS (1918–28, dean of the painting faculty), occasionally at the Vitebsk Art College (from 1921). Lived and worked in Paris (1928–37).

GAVRILOV Vladimir Nikolaevich
(1923, Moscow – 1970, Moscow)

Soviet painter, graphic artist. Studied at Moscow Secondary School of Art (1939–51) and at Surikov Moscow State Art Institute (1945–51) under S. Gerasimov, V. Pochitalov and V. Yefanov. Meritorious Artist of the RSFSR (1968), winner of the Repin State Prize of the RSFSR (posthumously, 1971). Taught at Moscow State Art Institute (1968–70).

GERASIMOV Aleksandr Mikhaylovich
(1881, Kozlov, Tambovskaya Region – 1963, Moscow)

Russian and Soviet painter. Studied at the Moscow School of Painting, Sculpture and Architecture (1903–15) under A. Arkhipov, V. Serov, K. Korovin and others. Meritorious Artist of the RSFSR (1936), People's Artist of the USSR (1944). Four-time Stalin Prize winner (1941, 1943, 1945, 1947). Full member of the USSR Academy of Arts (from 1947, president until 1957), doctor of art studies (1951). Member of the Artists' Union of the USSR (chairman of its organising committee, 1939–54). Participated in the Association of Artists of Revolutionary Russia (until 1932). Taught and headed the creative studio of painting at the USSR Academy of Arts (1949–60).

GERASIMOV Sergey Vasilyevich
(1885, Mozhaisk, Moscow Region – 1964, Moscow)

Russian, Soviet painter. Studied at the Moscow Higher College of Industrial and Applied Arts (1901–07) under K. Korovin and the Moscow School of Painting, Sculpture and Architecture (1907–13) under K. Korovin and A. Arkhipov. Member of Makovets and Society of Moscow Artists; Member of the Association of Revolutionary Russian Artists; Member of the Artists' Union of the USSR from 1932 (first secretary of the board, 1958–64). Meritorious Artist of the RSFSR (1937), Full Member of the Academy of Arts (1947), People's Artist of the USSR (1958), doctor of art studies (1956). Gold medal at 1958 World Expo in Brussels; winner of the Lenin Prize (1966, posthumously). Taught at Moscow State Art Institute named after V. I. Surikov from 1936–50 (professor from 1946, director 1946–48).

GLEBOVA Tatyana Nikolaevna
(1900, St Petersburg – 1985, Petrodvorets)

Russian painter and graphic and stage design artist. Studied art at the private studio of A. I. Savinov in Leningrad (1924–26). Joined the group of Masters of Analytic Art (MAI) led by P. Filonov (1926). Together with Sterling, established the association of like-minded artists Staropetergofskaya School (1963–66).

GRABAR Igor Emmanuilovich
(1871, Budapest – 1960, Moscow)

Russian and Soviet painter, restorer and art historian. Studied law and philology at the St Petersburg University (1889–93), at Chistiakov's private art studio, at the Imperial Academy of Arts (1894–96) under I. Repin, at Ažbe's studio in Munich (1896–99) and the Académie Julian in Paris. Full member of the Imperial Academy of Arts (1913). Member of the board of trustees (1913–18) and then director (1918–25) of the Tretyakov Gallery. Meritorious Artist of the RSFSR (1928), doctor of art studies (1940). Full member of the Academy of Sciences of the USSR (1943), Head of the USSR Academy of Sciences Research Institute for the History of Art (1944–60). Member of the Soviet Academy of Arts (1947). People's Artist of the USSR (1956). Taught at Moscow State University (1920–46) and at the Moscow State Art Institute named after V. I. Surikov (1937–43), professor. Part-creator of a multi-volume History of Russian Art (1910–15).

IVANOV Victor Ivanovich
(1924, Moscow)

Soviet painter. Studied at Moscow Secondary School of Art (1939–44) and at the Surikov Moscow State Art Institute (1944–50) under A. Gritsai, Y. Kugach, V. Pochitalov and A. Yakovlev. Member of the Union of Soviet Artists (1951); Honoured Artist of the RSFSR (1968); USSR State Prize winner (1968); People's Artist of the RSFSR (1976); Member of the Soviet Academy of Arts (1988; Associate member 1978); People's Artist of the USSR (1990); State Prize laureate of the Russian Federation (1996) and the State Prize of Russia (1996). Full member of the Peter the Great Academy of Sciences and Arts. Honorary citizen of the Spassky district of Riazan region. Taught at Moscow Secondary School of Art (1950–52).

KONCHALOVSKY Petr Petrovich
(1876, Slavyansk – 1956, Moscow)

Russian and Soviet painter. Studied at the Académie Julian in Paris (1897–98) and at the St Petersburg Academy of Arts (1898–1907) under Savinsky and Kovalevsky. One of the founders of the Jack of Diamonds association; served as its Chair (1911). Member of the Union of Youth (1911), World of Art (1911–22, intermittently) and Genesis associations (1926–27). Member of the Association of Revolutionary Russian Artists; Winner of the Stalin Prize, first order (1943); People's Artist of the RSFSR (1946); Full member of the Soviet Academy of Arts (1947).

KONDRATIEV Pavel Mikhailovich
(1902, Saratov – 1985, Leningrad)

Painter, graphic artist. Studied at the State Free Artistic Workshops (1921–25), at VKhUTEIN under A. Karev, A. Savinov, M. Matyushin. Member of the group Masters of Analytical Art (1925–29); Member

of the Staropetergofskaya School, created by V. Sterligov (1963–65).

KORZHEV Geli Mikhailovich
(1925, Moscow – 2012, Moscow)

Soviet and Russian painter, exponent of the Severe Style. Studied at Moscow Secondary School of Art (1939–44) and at the Moscow State Art Institute named after V. I. Surikov (1944–50) under S. Gerasimov. Meritorious Artist of the RSFSR (1963). Member of the Soviet Academy of Arts (1970; Associate member 1962). First secretary to the Union of Artists of the RSFSR (1968–75); People's Artist of the RSFSR (1972). People's Artist of the USSR (1979). USSR State Prize laureate (1987) and State Prize laureate of the RSFSR, named after Repin (1966). Taught at the Moscow Higher College of Industrial and Applied Arts (now the Stroganov Academy) (1951–58 and 1964–68), professor (1966). Head of the creative studio of painting of the USSR Academy of Arts (1968–76).

KOTOV Pyotr Ivanovich
(1889, Vladimirovka, Astrakhan Region – 1953, Moscow)

Soviet painter. Studied at the Kazan Art School of N. Feshin (1903–09), then at the Academy of Fine Arts in the studio of F. A. Roubaud. Member of the Association of Revolutionary Russian Artists (1923–28). Meritorious Artist of the RSFSR (1946). Winner of the Stalin Prize, second order (1948). Full member of the Soviet Academy of Arts (1949). Taught at the Higher State Art Studios in Astrahan (1937–41), All Russia State Institute of Cinematography (1944–48), Moscow Art Institute named after V. I. Surikov (1949–50). Since 1940, Professor.

KUPRIN Aleksandr Vasilievich
(1880, Borisoglebsk, Voronezh Region – 1960, Moscow)

Russian and Soviet painter. Studied in the Free School of Painting and Drawing at the Society of Art Lovers in Voronezh, then at L. E. Dmitriev-Kavkazsky's studio in St Petersburg, studios of K. Yuon and I. Dudin in Moscow, the Moscow School of Painting, Sculpture and Architecture. In 1909, A. V. Kuprin participated in the salon 'Golden Fleece', Member of the Jack of Diamonds (since 1910). Member of the artistic association Moscow painters (1925). Taught at VKhUTEMAS (since 1918). Head of Nizhny Novgorod and Sormovo art workshops (1920). Taught drawing and painting at the Moscow Textile Institute (1928, professor in the department of painting, 1929). Associate member of the Soviet Academy of Arts (1954). Meritorious Artist of the RSFSR (1956).

KUZNETSOV Pavel Varfolomevich
(1878, Saratov – 1968, Moscow)

Russian painter and graphic artist. Studied in Saratov at Studio od Paining and Drawing (1891–1906); Moscow School of Painting, Sculpture and Architecture under A. Arkhipov, K. Korovin and V. Serov (1897–1904); private academies in Paris (1905). Organised the *Crimson Rose* exhibition (1904) and was a founder and leader of the Blue Rose group (1907). Taught at the Stroganov Institute (1917–18; 1945–48) and at the Moscow Institute of Fine Arts (1918–37). Head of the painting section of Narkompros (1919–24). Chair of the Four Arts society of artists (1924–31). Meritorious Artist of the RSFSR (1928).

LANSERE Evgeny Evgenievich
(1875, Pavlovsk – 1946, Moscow)

Draughtsman, aquarellist, book illustrator, painter. Studied at the Imperial Society for the Encouragement of the Arts in St Petersburg (1892–96) at the private academies of Colarossi (1895–96) and Julien (1896–97) in Paris. Member of the World of Art group (1899). Winner of the Stalin Prize (1943).

LEBEDEV Vladimir Vasilyevich
(1891, St Petersburg – 1967, Leningrad)

Russian and Soviet painter and graphic artist. Studied at the St Petersburg Academy of Arts (1912–14). Member of the Union of Youth (from 1913), the Association of New Trends in Art (1922–23) and the Four Arts societies (from 1928). Was one of the founders of the propagandistic Windows of ROST in Petrograd (1920–21). Professor of the Petrograd State Arts Studios (1918–21). People's Artist of the RSFSR

(1966); Associate member of the USSR Academy of Arts (1967).

LENTULOV Aristarkh Vasilyevich
(1882, Chernaya Pyatnitsa, Penzensk Region – 1943, Moscow)

Russian and Soviet painter and set designer. Studied at the Penza Arts School named after N. Seliverstov (1898–1900 and 1905), the Kiev Art School (1900–04) and then at the D. Kardovsky's studio in St Petersburg (1906–10). Founding member of the Jack of Diamonds group (1910–16). Member of the Association of Revolutionary Russian Artists (1926–27). Founder and Chair of the Society of Moscow Artists (1928–32). Taught at the VKhUTEMAS Higher School of Arts and adjacent institutes in 1919–43.

MAKSIMOV Konstantin Mefodovich
(1913, Shatrovo, Ivanovo Region – 1993, Moscow)

Soviet painter. Studied at the Ivanovo Art College (1930–35) and Moscow State Art Institute named after V. I. Surikov in G. Ryazhsky's class (1937–42). People's Artist of the RSFSR. Twice Laureate of the State Prize (1950, 1952). At the invitation of the DPRK government, Maksimov lived and worked in China, taught oil painting, conducted a master class in Beijing (1954–57).

MALAGIS Vladimir Ilyich
(1902, Griva – 1974, Leningrad)

Soviet painter and graphic artist. Honoured Artist of the RSFSR (1971). Member of the Leningrad branch of the Union of Artists of the RSFSR. Between 1926 and 1932, was a member of the Leningrad-based Circle of artists and October associations. Between 1931 and 1933, headed the fine arts town committee of the Professional Union of Art Workers.

MALYSH Gavriil Kondratyevich
(1907, Kitaigorodka, Ekaterinoslav Region – 1998, St Petersburg)

Russian Soviet artist, painter, watercolourist. Graduated from the Odessa Art Institute where he studied under A. Gaush and T. Fraerman (1934). Member of the Leningrad Union of Artists (1955); St Petersburg Union of Artists (1992).

MASHKOV Ilya Ivanovich
(1881, Mikhailovskaya, Don Voisko Region – 1944, Moscow)

Russian and Soviet artist. Studied at the Moscow School of Painting, Sculpture and Architecture under L. Pasternak, V. Serov, K. Korovin, A. Vasnetsov, A. Arkhipov and others (1900–05 and 1907–10). One of the founders and contributors to the Jack of Diamonds (1910) and the Society of Moscow Artists (1927–29); Member of the Russian Academy of Artistic Sciences (1921); Member of the World of Art group (from 1916) and the Moscow painters association (from 1925); Member of the Association of Artists of Revolutionary Russia (1925–32). Merited Artist of the RSFSR (1928). Taught at VHUTEMAS-VHUTEIN as a professor of the painting faculty (1919–29).

MOISEENKO Evsey Evseevich
(1916, Uvarovich, Mogilevskaya Region – 1988, Leningrad)

Soviet painter and graphic artist. Studied at Institute of Painting, Sculpture and Architecture named after I. Repin under I. Brodsky, V. Yakovlev and A. Osmerkin (since 1935). People's Artist of the USSR (1970). Member of the Academy of Arts of the USSR (1973; Associate member 1962). Winner of Lenin Prize (1974); USSR State Prize laureate (1983). Hero of Socialist Labour (1986). Taught at the Institute of Painting, Sculpture and Architecture named after I. Repin (from 1958, becoming a professor in 1963).

MYLNIKOV Andrei Andreevich
(1919, Pokrovsk – 2012, St Petersburg)

Soviet and Russian painter. Studied at Institute of Painting, Sculpture and Architecture named after I. Repin under I. Grabar and V. Oreshnikov (1940–46), postgraduate degree (1948). Professor (since 1957). People's Artist of the USSR (1976). Lenin Prize winner (1984); winner of the Stalin Prize, third order (1951) and USSR State Prize laureate (1977). Member of the All-Union Communist Party (1942). Hero of Socialist Labour (1990). Member of the Soviet Academy of Arts (1966; Associate member 1962). Vice-President of the Russian Academy of Arts (1997–2012); taught at Institute of Painting, Sculpture and Architecture

named after I. Repin (head of a workshop of monumental painting).

NARIMANBEKOV Togrul Farman oglu (in Azerbaijani, Toğrul Fərman oğlu Nərimanbəyov)
(1930, Baku – 2013, Paris)

Azerbaijani artist of the twentieth century; People's Artist of Azerbaijan (1967). People's Artist of the USSR (1989). Lived and worked in Baku and Paris.

NIKITCH Anatoly Yurevich
(1918–1994)

Soviet artist. Studied at Moscow Institute of Arts under A. Osmerkin and B. Ioganson. Member of the Moscow branch of the Union of Soviet Artists (1944). Honoured Artist of the Russian Federation.

OSMERKIN Alexander Alexandrovich
(1892, Elizavetgrad – 1953, Moscow)

Russian, Soviet artist. Studied at St Petersburg Drawing School of the Society for the Encouragement of Arts under Nicholas Roerich (1910), Kiev Art College (1911) and the school of I. Mashkov (since 1913). Contributor to the Jack of Diamonds artistic group. Taught at VKhUTEMAS, the Leningrad Academy of Arts and the Moscow Art Institute named after V. I. Surikov (1918–48). In 1947, he was accused of formalism and was persecuted.

PAVLOV Semyon Andreevich
(1893, St Petersburg – 1941, Leningrad)

Soviet artist. Studied at the art school of the Society for the Encouragement of Artists (1893), School of Painting, Sculpture and Architecture named after I. Repin under D. Kardovskiy, V. Shukaev (graduated 1922). Member of the Communities of Artists; one of the founder members of the Leningrad branch of the Association of Revolutionary Russian Artists. Taught at VKhUTEIN in Leningrad (since 1929). Died during the siege of Leningrad (1941).

PETROV-VODKIN Kuzma Sergeevich
(1878, Khvalynsk, Saratov Region – 1939, Leningrad)

Russian and Soviet painter, stage designer, graphic artist and art theorist. Studied at Baron A. Stieglitz

Central School of Technical Drawing in St Petersburg, Moscow School of Painting, Sculpture and Architecture under V. Serov (1897–1905), private academies in Paris (1905–08). Member of the World of Art (since 1911); Founding member of the Free Philosophical Association (Vol'fila, 1919–24); Member of the Four Arts artistic group (since 1924). Meritorious Artist of the RSFSR (1930). Elected as first Chair of the Leningrad branch of the Union of Soviet Artists (1932). Taught at the Petrograd State Free Art Schools, VHUTEMAS, VHUTEIN, the Institute of Proletarian Fine Arts, Institute of Painting, Sculpture and Architecture of the Academy of Arts of the USSR (1918–33).

PIMENOV Yury Ivanovich
(1903, Moscow – 1977, Moscow)

Soviet painter, stage designer, set designer and graphic artist. Studied at VKhUTEMAS in the painting and polygraphy faculties of V. Favorsky and S. Malyutin (1920–25). One of the founder members of the Stankovist Society in 1925. Merited Artist of the RSFSR (1957). Member of the Soviet Academy of Arts (1962; Associate member 1954). People's Artist of the RSFSR (1962). Lenin prizewinner (1967) and two-time Stalin prizewinner, second order (1947, 1950). People's Artist of the USSR (1970).

PLASTOV Arkady Alexandrovich
(1893, Prislonikha, Simbirsk – 1972, Ulyanovsk)

Soviet artist. Studied at the Simbirsk Theological Seminary, studio of I. Mashkov, The Imperial Stroganov Central Art and Industrial School, under F. Fedorovsky (1912–14), Moscow School of Painting, Sculpture and Architecture under A. Korin, A. Vasnetsov, A. Arkhipov, L. Pasternak (department of sculpture) under S. Volnukhin. Member of the Soviet Academy of Arts (1947). People's Artist of the USSR (1962). Lenin prizewinner (1966); winner of the Stalin Prize, first order (1946). State Prize laureate of the RSFSR named after I. Repin (posthumously, 1972).

POPKOV Viktor Efimovich
(1932, Krasnodar – 1974, Krasnogorsk)

Soviet painter and graphic artist. Studied at the Art and Graphic Pedagogical School (1948–52)

and the Moscow Surikov Institute of Fine Arts (1952–58) under E. Kibrik. USSR State Prize laureate (posthumously, 1975).

PUNI Ivan Albertovich (Jean Pougny)
(1892, Kuokkala – 1956, Paris)

Russo-French avant-garde artist. Studied at the Nikolaev's Military Academy (1900–08), studied at the academy R. Julian in Paris (1910–11). Organiser and main sponsor of the scandalous futuristic exhibitions *Tram B* and *0.10* (1915). Taught at the Art Institute in Vitebsk (1919). Emigrated through Finland to Germany (1920), then to France (1924). Lived in France until his death in 1956. Chevalier of the Order of the Legion of Honour (1952).

ROZHDESTVENSKY Alexander Illarionovich
(1901, Moscow – 1998, Moscow)

Soviet painter. Studied at A. Kharlamov's art studio in Moscow (1918), at VKhUTEMAS under A. Osmerkin (since 1923). Member of the USSR Union of Artists.

SALAHOV Tair Teymur oglu (in Azerbaijani Tahir Teymur oğlu Salahov)
(1928, Baku)

Soviet, Azerbaijani and Russian painter and stage designer. Studied at The Azerbaijan Art School named after A. Azimzade, in 1957 graduated from the Moscow State Institute named after V. I. Surikov. Member of the Soviet Academy of Arts (1975; Associate member 1966). Member of the Executive Committee of the Soviet Academy of Arts since 1979; Vice-President of the Russian Academy of Arts since 1997. Meritorious Artist of the Azerbaijan Soviet Socialist Republic (1960); People's Artist of the Azerbaijan Soviet Socialist Republic (1963). People's Artist of the USSR (1973). Hero of Socialist Labour (1989). People's Artist of the Russian Federation (1996). USSR State Prize laureate (1968) and State Prize laureate of the Russian Federation (2013).

SAMOKHVALOV Alexander Nikolayevich
(1894, Bezhetsk, Tver Region – 1971, Leningrad)

Soviet painter and graphic artist. Studied at the Higher Art School of the Imperial Academy of Arts in St Petersburg (since 1914) under V. Beliaev,

G. Zaleman, K. Petrov-Vodkin and V. Shukhayev; graduated from Petrograd VKhUTEIN in 1923. Meritorious Artist of the RSFSR (1967); Member of the Leningrad branch of the Union of Artists of the Russian Soviet Federative Socialist Republic. Awarded the Gold Medal at the International Art Fair in Paris (1937). Taught in the monumental painting department at the Leningrad Higher School of Art and Industry named V. Mukhina (1948–51). Lenin Prize winner (1967).

SEREBRIAKOVA Zinaida Yevgenyevna
(1884, Neskuchnoye, Kharkiv Region – 1967, Paris)

Russian artist, Studied at the Moscow School of Painting, Sculpture and Architecture (1901–09) under Volnukhin, P. Troubetzkoy and K. Korovin. Member of the Free Aesthetics (late 1890s); from about 1910, Jack of Diamonds, The Donkey's Tail and The Target. Participant in the Parisian Salon des Indépendants (1921–31). Joined the French artistic association '1940' in 1931. Taught at I. Mashkov's studio (1908–11) and gave private painting lessons in Paris, early 1920s.

SHAMANOV Boris Ivanovich
(1931, Leningrad – 2008, St Petersburg)

Russian and Soviet painter and graphic artist. Studied at Leningrad Higher School of Art and Industry named after V. Mukhina (1949–56). Honoured Artist of the RSFSR (1989); People's Artist of the Russian Federation (1995); Member of the St Petersburg Union of Artists. Member of the artistic group Eleven. Taught at Leningrad Higher School of Art and Industry named after V. Mukhina (since 1960, professor, head of painting department since 1988).

SHEVCHENKO Aleksandr Vasilievich
(1883, Kharkiv – 1948, Moscow)

Russian and Soviet avant-garde painter and graphic artist, art theorist. Studied at the Stroganov Art and Industry College (1898–1907), at the Moscow School of Painting, Sculpture and Architecture under A. Arkhipov and K. Korovin (1908–09). Member of Zhivscul'ptarkha (1919–20), Makovets and the Society of Moscow Artists. Head of the Literary and Art Section of the Art Board in People's Commissariat for Education (1918–21). Taught at the Higher Art and Technical Studios (1918–29). Head of the Department of Painting at the Moscow Textile Institute (since 1941).

SHTERENBERG David Petrovich
(1881, Zhytomyr – 1948, Moscow)

Russian and Soviet artist and graphic artist. Lived in Paris (1907–17). Returned to USSR after the Revolution. Commissar for Artistic Matters (1917–18). In 1918 exhibited with the group Jewish Society for the Furthering of the Arts in Moscow. Head of the Department of Fine Arts (IZO) of the People's Commissariat of Enlightenment (NARKOMPROS) (1918–20). Founding member of Stankovist Society (OST) (1925–32). Taught at VKhUTEMAS (1920–30). Meritorious Artist of the USSR (1930). Criticised for formalism in 1940s.

SOKOLOV Mikhail Ksenofontovich
(1885, Yaroslavl – 1947, Moscow)

Russian painter and graphic artist. Studied at the Moscow State Stroganov Academy of Industrial and Applied Arts (1904–07). Passed military service in the Baltic fleet (1907–09). Head of the Proletkult art Studio in Moscow (1923–25). Taught at the Art College (1905), in the Yaroslavl Pedagogical College (1925–35), the Institute of advanced training of painters and decorators in Moscow (1936–38). Since 1938 member of the Union of artists. In March 1938, arrested. Sentenced to seven years in labour camp. Rehabilitated in 1943 and died of illness acquired at the camp in 1947.

STOZHAROV Vladimir Fedorovich
(1926, Moscow – 1973, Moscow)

Russian and Soviet painter. Studied at Moscow Secondary School of Art (1939–45) and at the Surikov Moscow State Art Institute (1945–51) under Mochalsky and Pochitalov. Meritorious Artist of the RSFSR (1965). Silver medal of the Academy of Arts (1967) State Prize laureate of the RSFSR named after I. Repin (1968). Corresponding Member of the USSR Academy of Arts (1973).

TATLIN Vladimir Yevgraphovich
(1885, Moscow – 1953, Moscow)

Russian and Soviet constructivist architect and painter, graphic artist, designer and master of the theatre. Studied at the Moscow School of Painting, Sculpture and Architecture (1902, expelled 1903), at the Penza Art School (1905–10). In the 1910s participated in exhibitions of World of Art, Union of Youth, Jack of Diamonds and Donkey's Tail. Taught at Kiev Art Institute (1925–27), VKhUTEMAS in Moscow (1927–30). Meritorious Artist of the RSFSR (1931).

TETERIN Victor Kuzmich
(1922, Bakharevo, Tver Region – 1991, St Petersburg)

Russian and Soviet painter and graphic artist. Studied at Leningrad Secondary Art School (part All-Russian Academy of Art) under P. Naumov, M. Natarevich, and O. Bogaevskaya; at the Leningrad Institute of Painting, Sculpture and Architecture named after Ilya Repin under A. Osmerkin, G. Pavlovsky and G. Savinov (1944–49). Member of the Leningrad branch of the Union of Artists of the RSFSR (1953). Contributed to the artistic group Eleven.

TYRSA Nikolai Andreevich
(1887, Aralikh, Erivan Region – 1942, Vologda)

Russian and Soviet painter and graphic artist. Studied at the architecture faculty of the Imperial Academy of Arts in St Petersburg (1905–09), at E. Zvantseva's School of Painting and Drawing, under L. Bakst and M. Dobuzhinsky (1906–10); at the V. Matai studio (1910–11). Participated in the exhibitions of the group World of Art (since 1915). Taught at the Baron A. Stieglitz Central School of Technical Drawing (until 1922). Commissioner of the First State Free Art Studios (later VKhUTEMAS) (1918–22). Taught at the VKhUTEIN (1923–36), at the Civil Engineering Institute (1924–42). One of the founding members of Leningrad Union of Artists of RSFSR (1932).

UDALTSOVA Nadezhda Andreevna
(1886, Oryol – 1961, Moscow)

Russian avant-garde artist. Studied at the art school of K. Yuon and I. Dudin (1905–07), at the at Académie de La Palette (1912–13). Member of Jack of Dimonds group (1914). Member of the Institute for Artistic Culture (1920–21). Taught at VKhUTEMAS (1920–34). Was publicly criticised for formalism (1932–33). After her husband A. Drevin's arrest and execution in 1938, she was repressed until rehabilitation in 1945.

INDEX OF ARTISTS